A SERIES OF CONDUCT BOOKS

THOEMMES

FEMALE REPLIES TO SWETNAM THE WOMAN-HATER

With a new Introduction by
Charles Butler

THOEMMES PRESS

© Thoemmes Press 1995

Published in 1995 by
Thoemmes Press
11 Great George Street
Bristol BS1 5RR
England

ISBN 1 85506 379 4

This is a reprint of the 1615–20 Editions
© Introduction by Charles Butler 1995

Publisher's Note

These reprints are taken from original copies of each book. In many cases the condition of those originals is not perfect, the paper, often handmade, having suffered over time and the copy from such things as inconsistent printing pressures resulting in faint text, show-through from one side of a leaf to the other, the filling in of some characters, and the break up of type. The publisher has gone to great lengths to ensure the quality of these reprints but points out that certain characteristics of the original copies will, of necessity, be apparent in reprints thereof.

INTRODUCTION

In 1615, at Thomas Archer's bookshop near the Royal Exchange in London, a misogynistic pamphlet was published entitled *The Araignment of Lewde, idle, froward, and vnconstant women.* It proved an immediate and enduring commercial success, with three more editions appearing by 1617, and a further eighteen by 1733. In 1641 there was even a Dutch translation, which itself ran into five further editions.[1] Insofar as the *Araignment* was merely pandering to anti-female sentiment in an age when belief in the inferiority of women was encouraged by both church and state, its success, though depressing, need cause no surprise. In another sense, however, it needs explanation. The *Araignment* is in no sense a distinguished piece of literature, and even considered purely as polemic it appears to have serious defects. Its arguments are disorganized and at times contradictory, and few if any are original. Attacks on women (and defences of them) had been an established pamphlet genre for decades by the time the *Araignment* made its appearance, and the *Araignment* owes its predecessors an immense (if unacknowledged) debt, for ideas and for whole sentences. What does distinguish the *Araignment* is the comprehensiveness of its attack on

---

[1] For a full publishing history, see Francisca Wilhelmina van Heertum, ed., *A critical edition of Joseph Swetnam's 'The Araignment of Lewd, Idle, Froward, and Unconstant Women' (1615),* (Nijmegen: The Cicero Press, 1989), pp. 92–123.

women, combined with an unprecedented level of vituperation. The tone of previous contributions had often been 'academic' or tongue-in-cheek, using the praise or dispraise of women largely as a peg on which to display the author's rhetorical ingenuity and linguistic verve, or as an opportunity to regale the reader with a series of ribald stories about cuckolded husbands and cucked scolds.[2] Occasionally the same author would even write on both sides of the question: pamphlets attacking women, like Edward Gosynhill's *The Schoolhouse of Women* (c. 1541), might give rise to others written in their praise – perhaps, as in the case of Gosynhill's *Mulierum Paean* (c. 1542), with an implication that they were written in atonement for the original offence (while attempting to double the author's sales).[3] The *Araignment*, despite some hints that it is not to be taken entirely seriously, is distinguished by the indiscriminateness of its attack. While others may adopt a tone of ironic sophistication, or jocular rib-nudging, this author lacks sufficient control over his own style to indicate when and if he is assuming a pose.

The author of the *Araignment*, who had sheltered behind the pseudonym of Thomas Tel-Troth, was soon known to be Joseph Swetnam, a Bristol fencing-master. Swetnam and his pamphlet did not go unanswered. In 1617 three direct replies appeared, all of them under female names: Rachel Speght's *A Movzell for Melastomus*, Ester Sowernam's *Ester hath hang'd*

---

[2] Cornelius Agrippa, John Lyly and Thomas Nashe would fit the first description, Edward Gosynhill the second.

[3] This tactic goes back at least as far as Chaucer's *The Legend of Good Women*, supposedly written in atonement for *Troilus and Criseyde*. Ballad writers often followed the same route for commercial reasons.

Introduction   vii

Haman, and Constantia Munda's *The Worming of a mad Dogge*. Finally a play, *Swetnam the Woman-hater, Arraigned by Women*, was published anonymously in 1620, having been performed at the Red Bull playhouse, probably the previous year. In this play Swetnam appears in person as the misogynistic antihero. He uses arguments culled from his *Araignment* in order to procure the death of the princess Leonida, only to be exposed as a fool and a coward. Having suffered ritual humiliation at the hands of women, he leaves the stage wearing a muzzle.

The fact that Swetnam's pamphlet provoked so many replies gives an indication of the publicity it received. All the respondents claim as a prime motive for venturing into print the desire to stem the popularity of such a dangerous book.

> ...if it should haue had free passage without any answere at all...the vulgar ignorant might haue beleeued his Diabolicall infamies to be infallible truths, not to be infringed.
>
> (*Mouzell*, sig. A3v)

> ...seeing his books so commonly bought vp, which argueth a generall applause; we are therfore enforced to make answere in defence of our selues, who are by such an author so extreamely wronged in publike view.
>
> (*Ester*, p. 32 [sig. E4v])

>   could the straine
> Of that your barren-idle-donghill braine,
> As from a Chymick Limbeck so distill
> Your poyson'd drops of hemlocke, and so fill
> The itching eares of silly swaines, and rude
> Truth-not-discerning rusticke multitude

> With sottish lies, with bald and ribald lines
> Patcht out of English writers that combines
> Their highest reach of emulation but to please
> The giddy-headed vulgar: whose disease
> Like to a swelling dropsie, thirsts to drinke
> And swill the puddles of this nasty sinke.
>
> (*Worming*, sig. A2r–A2v)

These could easily be exaggerations, a way of building up one's opponent so as to make one's victory the more remarkable. But they find confirmation in *Swetnam the Woman-hater*, where the exiled Swetnam (alias Misogynos) glories in the memory of his literary sensation:

> *Mis*: How my Bookes tooke effect! how greedily
> The credulous people swallowed downe my hookes
> How rife debate sprang betwixt man and wife!
> The little Infant that could hardly speake,
> Would call his Mother Whore. O, it was rare!
>
> (*Woman-hater*, sig. A4v)

The fact that Swetnam should have a play named after him at all suggests the extent of his fame. Nor is he brought on stage merely to play the part of a stock misogynist. *Swetnam the Woman-hater* makes explicit reference to the controversy and assumes in its audience a fairly detailed knowledge of the contents of the *Araignment*. While it would be possible to watch and enjoy the play without having read the *Araignment* or the replies, there are many private jokes which allude to particular arguments or phrases used by Swetnam and his antagonists.

The popular success of the *Araignment* may derive partly from the sure instinct with which Swetnam was

Introduction   ix

able to reflect and appeal to the fears and prejudices of his audience, the ever-growing urban middle-class of London. His own characterization of this audience is given in the superscription to his preface, addressed to 'neither the wisest Clarke, nor the starkest Foole, but vnto the ordinary sort of giddy headed young men' (*Araignment*, sig. A3v). Male, semi-educated, either batchelors or young men newly-embarked on marriage: these seem to be the implicit readership of the *Araignment*. Their concerns are reflected in the emphases Swetnam chooses to give to the various parts of his work. Predictably, women are condemned for sexual promiscuity, but even more prominent are the stereotypes of the nagging, and especially the spendthrift, wife. Chapter one of the *Araignment* begins:

> Moses describeth a woman thus: At the first beginning (saith he) a woman was made to be a helper vnto man, and so they are indeede, for she helpeth to spend & consume that which man painefully getteth.
>
> (*Araignment*, p. 1 [sig. B1r])

In a text intended for an educated or wealthy audience, we might expect economic matters to have received less immediate prominence. Passages such as this (and there are many of them in the *Araignment*) seem to be aimed at a readership in social transition, not yet confident of its own financial security, and ambivalent about acquiring the more costly symbols of status. Swetnam was actually willing to tailor his sources so as to avoid sentiments likely to offend citizen sensibilities. At one point in the *Araignment* he purloins a passage from an Italian courtesy book, *The Civile Conversation of M. Steeven Guazzo*, in which different types of unfortunate marriage are considered in turn. As Francisca van

x   Introduction

Heertum has noted, the original discussion includes amongst the alliances to be avoided those in which one partner is 'nobly minded' and the other 'basely given'.[4] In Swetnam's version this advice, so disheartening to the dynastic hopes of the bourgeoisie, is carefully omitted. Given his inability to maintain any consistency of style or argument, Swetnam's capacity to keep the tastes of his readers so clearly in view is remarkable. His task may have been facilitated by the fact that he was of a similar background himself. The facts of Swetnam's life remain obscure, but there is plenty of evidence to suggest that he was neither highly-educated nor very wealthy. His profession as a fencing master was a socially precarious one, veering uneasily between gentlemanly pretensions and the suspicion of vagabondage; and the fact that he appears to have died in debt suggests he was not particularly successful at it.[5] As to education, in his only other extant work, a fencng manual called *The School of the Noble and Worthy Science of Defence* (1617), he states (not without a certain swagger) that he is 'no Scholler, nor have no learning; but only a little experience, which God and nature bestowed upon me'.[6] This is confirmed by his use of sources. The *Araignment* relies very heavily (amidst a welter of proverbial wisdom) on classical stories gleaned from wit book compilations, grammar school texts such as Valerius Maximus, and other such 'schooleboyes bookes' as Constantia Munda contemptuously terms them (*Worming*, p. 21 [sig. D4r]).

---

[4] *The Civile Conversation of M. Steeven Guazzo* (London: 1581), III.5. Quoted by van Heertum, p. 40.

[5] van Heertum, p. 21.

[6] Joseph Swetnam, *The School of the Noble and Worthy Science of Defence* (London: 1617), sig. A4r. Quoted by van Heertum, p. 33.

Introduction xi

The replies to Swetnam are considerably more learned; and indeed, one of their main rhetorical tactics is to mock Swetnam for his ignorance. Against Swetnam's rag-tag muster of proverbs and anecdotes they pitch a series of arguments concerned with logic, grammar, accurate use of sources, and the formal requirements of debate. This does not mean that the replies lack passion, or a talent to amuse and (especially in Munda's case) abuse; but it does suggest that they have a different, better educated, and inevitably narrower readership in mind. This is reflected in their publishing history. Throughout the seventeenth and eighteenth centuries, while the *Araignment* was going through its long series of reprints, the three replies were ignored. Only in 1807, when the *Araignment* was printed for the first time as a document primarily of historical interest, did the editor think to include one of the replies, Sowernam's *Ester hath hang'd Haman*.

There are other explanations for this neglect – nor need we rush to accuse seventeenth-century publishers and readers of anti-feminist bias. Being cast in the form of replies, the works of Speght, Sowernam and Munda inevitably have a secondary character which would be less marketable once the controversy provoked by the *Araignment* had passed. Moreover, their less populist style denied them the kind of afterlife that Swetnam's pamphlet enjoyed in later years, where it was sold primarily as a lighthearted entertainment.[7] Even so, it is a remarkable fact that – with the exception of that 1807 edition of Sowernam's work – the three replies

---

[7] See particularly the 1704 edition, where the original *Araignment* has sprouted 'A Second Part: containing Merry Dialogues, Witty Poems, and Jovial Songs'.

had to wait until the 1980s to be republished.[8] The play *Swetnam the Woman-hater* fared no better until 1880, when A B Grosart brought out a limited edition of 62 copies. Since then there has been a Tudor Facsimile edition (1914), and a critical edition dating from 1969.[9]

All these texts have benefited from the critical interest in Early Modern women's writing which has been a feature of the last decade. Ironically, it is Swetnam himself who has had to wait longest to find a modern publisher. After the antiquarian edition of 1807 the *Araignment* was out of print until 1989, when Francisca van Heertum produced a critical edition for her doctoral thesis at the University of Nijmegen.[10] In various forms and places, then, the texts of the Swetnam controversy have gradually emerged. It is only now, however, that all five have been collected into a single volume.

As I have indicated, little is known of the life of Joseph Swetnam.[11] Even the date of his birth is a matter for conjecture. He begins the *Araignment* by claiming that he has 'beene a Traveller this thirty and odde yeares' (*Araignment*, sig. A2r), which if true would suggest a writer at least in his mid-forties. He was still travelling when he died abroad in 1621,

---

[8] This is a modern spelling edition, *The Women's Sharp Revenge: Five Women's Pamphlets from the Renaissance*, ed. Simon Shepherd (London: Fourth Estate, 1985). Extracts from Sowernam and Munda also appeared in *Half Humankind: Contexts and Texts of the Controversy about Women in England, 1540–1640*, ed., Katherine Usher Henderson and Barbara F. McManus (Urbana and Chicago: University of Illinois Press, 1985).

[9] *Swetnam the Woman-hater. The Controversy and the Play*, ed. C. Crandall (West Lafayette, Indiana: 1969).

[10] van Heertum, as above. Extracts from Swetnam appear in *Half Humankind*.

[11] The few biographical facts are presented by van Heertum, pp. 20–36.

Introduction xiii

perhaps in his mid-fifties. From hints in the *School of Defence* it appears that he spent at least some of his time in active service, perhaps combining the profession of fencing master with that of soldier. A connection with Bristol seems certain: a legal document of 1626 refers to his having lived in the city;[12] the writer of *Swetnam the Woman-hater* has him setting up a fencing school there before coming to London (*Woman-hater*, sig. K1v); while the reference in the *Araignment* to the venality of 'the knauish porters in *Bristow* (*Araignment*, p. 30 [E3v]) sounds very much as if it is born out of experience. The existence of a legitimate daughter indicates that he must at one time have been married, but we know neither the name of his wife nor the duration of the relationship, still less whether she was one of the 'some women, I mean more then one' who Swetnam blames for having spurred him to write the *Araignment* (*Araignment*, sig. A2r).

From these biographical scraps it is hard to build a plausible picture of the circumstances surrounding Swetnam's brief adventure as a pamphleteer. It is not known, for example, whether the *Araignment* was written on Swetnam's own initiative, or at the behest of the publisher, Thomas Archer. Swetnam depicts himself as composing it 'in the ruffe of [his] fury' (*Araignment*, sig. A2r), but this is a conventional positition, which he could have adopted, say, from Lyly's *Euphues* (to which the opening of the *Araignment* is heavily indebted).[13] If Swetnam was hoping to pursue a career as a satirical or polemical writer, the reception of the *Araignment* would appear to have changed his mind. Possibly he did not welcome his instant notoriety. At any rate, his

---

[12] van Heertum p. 20.

[13] As Ester Sowernam first noticed (*Ester*, p. 32 [sig. E4v]).

promise of an imminent and even more inflammatory sequel, compared with which the *Araignment* would be 'but…a bul-rush' (*Araignment*, sig. A4r), was destined to remain unkept. The claim in *Swetnam the Woman-hater* that he fled England because 'two or three good wenches, in meere spight,/Laid their heads together, and rail'd him out of th'land' (*Woman-hater*, sig. K1v) may not be reliable as historical evidence, but this does not mean there is no truth behind it.

The Araignment of Women defies easy summary. The difficulties encountered by Rachel Speght when she came to rebut it are still pertinent:

> …I am not altogether ignorant of that Analogie which ought to be vsed in a literate Responsarie: but the Beare-bayting of Women, vnto which I haue framed my Apologeticall answere, beeing altogether without Concordance, and a promiscuous mingle mangle, it would admit no such order to be obserued in the answering thereof, as a regular Responsarie requireth.
> (*Mouzell*, sig. F1r)

The disorganization of Swetnam's argument lays him open to reproofs such as Speght's; but just as often it is quite effective in camouflaging his own inconsistency of thought. To tease out his contradictions one must be prepared to follow his sentences through many a tangled syntactic thicket, and by the time one emerges it is easy to miss the fact that he has subtly changed the subject. In these circumstances it may be more useful to identify some of Swetnam's habitual rhetorical tactics, and to indicate the ways in which they were countered by his respondents. (I reserve the play, which draws on all four of the earlier texts, for separate consideration.)

Long passages of the *Araignment* consist of lists of proverbs and 'observations', often drawn from natural

Introduction xv

history, which are then used to 'prove' an assertion about the nature of women. This is a typical example:

> ...a woman which is faire in showe is foule in condition, she is like vnto a glow-worme which is bright in the hedge and black in the hand; in the greenest grasse lyeth hid the greatest Serpents; painted pottes commonly holde deadly poyson: and in the clearest water the vgliest Tode, and the fairest woman hath some filthines in hir.
> (*Araignment*, pp. 12–13 [sig. C2v–C3r])

And so on. Swetnam's use of this type of argument has its immediate origins in the style known as euphuism, after Lyly's dazzling *tour de force*. The euphuistic style, with its balanced periods, its use of alliteration and assonance, and (particularly relevant here) its reliance on obscure and often inaccurate botanical and zoological parallels, enjoyed a brief but intense vogue in the Elizabethan court of the early 1580s. However, its incredible prolixity, combined perhaps with the ease with which it lent itself to parody, meant that by the time Swetnam was writing it was woefully outmoded. The logical force of argument from simile is minimal, as Sir Philip Sidney had observed more than thirty years before in his criticisms of the euphuistic fad:

> ...the force of a similitude not being to prove anything to a contrary disputer, but only to explain to a willing hearer; when that is done, the rest is a most tedious prattling, rather over-swaying the memory from the purpose whereto they were applied, than any whit informing the judgement.[14]

---

[14] Sir Philip Sidney, *An Apology for Poetry*, ed. George Shepherd (London and Edinburgh: Thomas Nelson and Sons, 1965), p. 139.

Sidney's point is valid, but he does not acknowledge that the appeal of this kind of argument is subliminal rather than logical. It assumes a certain view of the world in which patterns recur with regularity. These, it seems to suggest, are the lines along which nature works: if a principle holds true here, and here, and here, is it not likely that it will hold true in this other place also? Even Constantia Munda accepts the commonplace analogy between macrocosm and microcosm, when she calls 'Woman the second edition of the Epitome of the whole world' (*Worming*, p. 2 [sig. B2v]). If this basic correspondence holds, then Swetnam's parade of comparisons may gain much of the evidential power it would otherwise lack, and the (otherwise otiose) piling up of proverb lore and euphuistic comparison may serve to increase that power. When Munda attacks Swetnam's use of similes and proverbs it is only partly on grounds of its rhetorical superfluity:

> Lord! how you haue cudgeld your braines in gleaning multitudes of similes as twere in the field of many writers, and thrasht them together in the floure of your owne deuizor; and all to make a poore confused misceline, whereas thine owne barren soyled soyle is not able to yeeld the least congruity of speech.
> (*Worming*, p. 21 [sig. D4r])

Munda certainly sees Swetnam as having wasted his efforts in collecting together so many similes, but this is because he is too inept to fashion his heterogeneous sources into a unified argument. It is not the use of similes as such which attracts her scorn. More fundamental to Munda's criticisms here are Swetnam's dependence on other authors, and his failure to use his sources consistently. His heavy dependence on proverbial wisdom contrasts sadly with the classical learning which Munda so evidently has at her fingertips, and in singling out this aspect of Swetnam's style Munda is implicitly casting Swetnam as one of the 'giddy-headed vulgar' for whom he writes.

Another of Swetnam's favourite ploys is the illustrative example. The *Araignment* is full of stories of infamous women. Some are the anonymous subjects of jokes or anecdotes, others are figures from history or mythology. Eve, Helen of Troy, Judith, Hosea's wife, Clytemnestra, Delilah and Jezebel all come in for censure, as do numerous real or mythical courtesans and scolds. These and others are held up as warnings to men to abjure the female sex as a whole. In fact, Swetnam's choices are sometimes unfortunate. Judith may have killed Holofernes, but in doing so she saved Jerusalem from capture and became a heroine of Israel.[15] Clytemnestra may have killed her husband Agamemnon, but his sacrifice of their daughter was hardly the 'small iniury' (*Araignment*, p. 10 [sig. C1v]) Swetnam glancingly refers to. If David was tempted from the path of virtue by the sight of Bathsheba bathing, this is hardly to be laid at her door, nor was Hercules' wife aware of the fatal properties of the shirt of Nessus, as Swetnam implies. As for Hosea's wife, Speght gleefully points out that she was not a real person at all, but an allegorical personification of Israel (*Mouzell*, p. 32 [sig. F4v]). Mistakes like this abound, and often Swetnam's antagonists cite them as evidence of his ignorance. More directly, all three focus on the inadequacy of lists of the infamous as arguments against women in general. It would be just as easy, Speght replies, to produce a list (and a much longer one) of infamous men:

---

[15] As Sowernam points out (*Ester*, p. 46 [sig. G3v]); see *Araignment*, p. 23 [sig. Dr4].

xviii *Introduction*

> I may as well say *Barrabas* was a murtherer, *Ioab* killed *Abner* and *Amasa*, and *Pharaoh Necho* slew *Iosiah*.... The forme of argumentation is your owne, the which if you dislike, blame your selfe for proposing such a patterne, and blush at your owne folly....
>
> (*Mouzell*, p. 33 [sig. G1r])

Sowernam takes a complementary approach by providing a list of good women (*Ester*, pp. 19–21 [sigs. D2r–D3r]), culminating in that trump card of irreproachable feminine virtue, Queen Elizabeth: 'not onely the glory of our Sexe, but a patterne for the best men to imitate, of whom I will say no more, but that while she liued, she was the mirrour of the world, so then knowne to be, and so still remembred, and euer will be' (*Ester*, p. 21 [sig. D3r]). For Sowernam it is Swetnam's extension of his case from particular examples of bad women to encompass the whole sex that is unforgiveable. If Swetnam had kept his promise to write against lewd, idle, froward and inconstant women, while commending the virtues of others, she would have been so far from objecting to his project that she would 'haue commended so good a labour' (*Ester*, p. 1 [sig. B1r]). Instead, the pamphlet includes all women within its condemnation:

> Now let the Christian Reader please to consider how dishonestly this Authour dealeth, who vndertaking a particular, prosecuteth and persecuteth a generall, vnder the cloake and colour of lewd, idle, and froward women, to rage and raile against all women in generall.
>
> (*Ester*, p. 4 [sig. B2v])

This charge is repeatedly made by Sowernam, and forms the main item on the formal indictment of Joseph Swetnam which forms the centrepiece of her reply (*Ester*, p. 29 [sig. E3r]). Like Speght, Sowernam does not confine herself to defending individual women, but challenges Swetnam's fundamental strategy of letting the few stand for the many. If 'the fairest woman hath some filthines in hir', what becomes of Swetnam's promise on his title page to include 'a Commendation of wise, vertuous and honest women'? How can he praise a creature which does not exist? The contradiction is blithely ignored by Swetnam himself. The *Araignment* does indeed include a commendation, which finds its place in the *Araignment* under a chapter with the grudging title:

> This third Chapter sheweth a remedy against loue, also many reasons not to be to hasty in choise of a Wife. But if no remedy but thou wilt marry, then howe to choose a wife, with a Commendations of the good, vertuous, and honest women.
> (*Araignment*, p. 33 [sig. F1r])

The relevant parts of this chapter (which make up about ten per cent of the *Araignment*) show Swetnam in a very concerned light, bemoaning the pangs of childbirth, deploring wife-beating, admonishing husbands to 'satisfie the honest desires' of their wives (*Araignment*, p. 53 [sig. H3r]), to seek their comfort and to share their secrets with them. That much of this advice flatly contradicts other parts of the *Araignment* seems not to matter: it was left to Rachel Speght to point out Swetnam's inconsistencies here.[16] In writing his Commendation, Swetnam of course was

---

[16] See *Mouzell*, pp. 35–6 [sigs. G2r–G2v].

xx *Introduction*

simply borrowing ideas and phrases once again, not this time from Lyly, Nashe or the other anti-women satirists who provide his normal source material, but from courtesy books such as Stephen Guazzo's *Civile Conversation*, in which the attitude to women was considerably more friendly, and the view of marriage tended towards, if not equality, then at least mutual respect.

Whether or not Swetnam was deliberately attempting to provoke a controversy by writing the *Araignment*, he clearly foresaw that his work might give offence. Accordingly, in his introductory Epistle he takes the opportunity to 'get his retaliation in first' by imposing silence on potential critics. He does this using the time-honoured tactic of suggesting that only those guilty of the faults described in the *Araignment* could possibly object to it, and that any objection is therefore tantamount to an admission of guilt. This is another ploy he could have found in *Euphues*. In the 'cooling Carde for Philautus and all fond louers' Euphues writes:

> And yet *Philautus*, I would not that al women should take pepper in the nose, in that I have disclosed the legerdermaines of a fewe, for well I know none will winch except she bee gawlded, neither any be offended vnlesse she be guiltie.[17]

The thought duly makes its reappearance in Swetnam, in more garrulous form:

> I know I shall be bitten by many because I touch many, but before I goe any further let me whisper one worde in your eares, and that is this, whatsoeuer you

[17] John Lyly, *Euphues. The Anatomy of Wit*, 1579. *Euphues and His England, 1580*, ed. Edward Arber (London: Alex, Murray & Son, 1869), pp. 118–9.

Introduction xxi

> thinke priuately I wish you to conceale it with silence, least in starting up to finde fault you proue your selues guilty of these monstrous accusations which are heere following against some women: and those which spurne if they feele themselues touched, proue themselues starke fooles in bewraying their galled backs to the world, for this booke toucheth no sort of women, but such as when they heare it will goe about to reproue it.
>
> <div align="right">(<i>Araignment</i>, sig. A2v)</div>

This kind of double-bind is familiar to twentieth-century readers from certain brands of psychoanalysis, in which the denial of an assertion 'proves' its truth. Speght, typically dogged in her pursuit of solecisms, draws out the logical invalidity of Swetnam's conclusion: 'you might as well haue said, that because burnt folks dread the fire, therfore none feare fire but those that are burnt' (*Mouzell*, sig. B2v–B3r). All of Swetnam's critics are forced to take up this challenge in various ways, for it strikes at the heart of their right to make any reply at all. They are well aware that in making their entrance into public print they are taking a step which may seem to put them beyond the bounds of modesty at a time when silence was seen as one of the chief feminine virtues.[18]

But the full insidiousness of the admonition to silence becomes apparent only when it is combined with an elision of the original distinction between 'good' and 'bad' women. This elision duly occurs just a few lines later in Swetnam's Epistle:

> If I be too earnest beare with me a little, for my meaning is not to speake much of those that are good,

---

[18] See *Ester*, p. 1 [sig. B1r], *Worming*, p. 14 [sig. C4v].

and I shall speake too little of those that are naught, but yet I will not altogether condemne the bad, but hoping to better the good by the naughty examples of the badd; For there is no woman so good but hath one idle part or other in her which may be amended, for the clearest River that is hath some durt in the bottome....
(Araignment, sig. A2v)

The suggestion, still somewhat tentative here, that the category of 'good' women may not actually exist, is elaborated in various places in the *Araignment*. For example, Swetnam contends that a man who marries an unquiet woman might as well 'ride a trotting horse to the deuil', whereas a quiet woman will seem 'but an ambling horse to hell' (*Araignment*, p. 35 [sig. F2r]). All women, in other words, lead to an infernal destination in the end. Elsewhere he anticipates the humour of modern car window stickers with his suggestion that women 'haue two faultes, that is, they can neither say well nor yet doe well' (*Araignment*, p. 28 [sig. E2v]). Thus what Swetnam seems to offer with one hand – the prospect that by keeping silent women may escape his condemnation – is effectively withdrawn with the other. No wonder Munda gives vent to her anger:

you surmized, that inueighing against poore illiterate women, we might fret and bite the lip at you, wee might repine to see our selues baited and tost in a blanket, but neuer durst in open view of the vulgar either disclose your blasphemous and derogatiue slanders, or maintaine the vntainted puritie of our glorious sex; nay, you'l put gagges in our mouthes, and coniure vs all to silence; you will first abuse vs, then bind vs to the peace....
(*Worming*, p. 14 [sig. C4v])

Introduction xxiii

In the event, of course, Swetnam's conjuration was to prove ineffective.

The most remarkable fact about the three direct replies to Swetnam's *Araignment* is also the most obvious one: all the authors write under female names. Before 1617 most of the contributors to the 'woman debate', attackers and defenders alike, had been male.[19] With the replies from Speght, Sowernam and Munda, we find women asserting their own point of view, in defiance of the prejudice (played on by Swetnam) against any public utterances by women except of a strictly devotional character. Unlike male defenders of women, such as Daniel Tuvil, whose *Asylum Veneris; or, A Sanctuary for Ladies* (1616) may be intended partly as a rebuttal of Swetnam's arguments, they are not in a position to adopt the familiar role of chivalric defender of female honour. Instead they have to carve out a rhetorical position from which they can speak, without falling into the false opposition that Swetnam prepares for them, in which to be anything other than silent is to be a scold.

All this presupposes, of course, that the authors of the three replies *are* women. They claim to be so, but given that two of them write under obvious pseudonyms, some doubt must remain as to their true sex. Could it be that a male author, wishing to join in the controversy started by Swetnam, found it convenient to assume a female persona? It would not be a unique case. In 1640 John Taylor's *A Juniper Lecture*, published the previous year, was answered by a pamphlet entitled *The Women's Sharp Revenge*. This appeared under the clearly-pseudonymous names of two women, Mary

---

[19] A notable exception is *Jane Anger her Protection for Women* (London, 1589).

Tattlewell and Joan Hit-Him-Home; but it is almost certain that Taylor himself was the author.[20] The name Sowernam, in particular, with its aggressive inversion of Swetnam's own surname (sour versus sweet), has something of the burlesque feel of a Tattlewell or a Hit-Him-Home; and Joane Sharp, the supposed writer of the summarizing poem appended to *Ester hath hang'd Haman*, may also have assumed a surname to match her tone.

In the cases of Sowernam and Munda critics have been thrown back on the rather thin evidence provided by the pamphlets themselves. Kathleen Henderson and Barbara McManus, for example, find evidence of female authorship in their tone of 'outrage', in their evident awareness of the daring required for women to speak out in print, and in their occasional antipathy to the male sex, which they find unlikely in a male author, even writing under a pseudonym.[21] To Simon Shepherd, however, Munda's familiarity with the Roman satirists seems implausible: 'Juvenal is an unlikely author in a woman's education'.[22] Sowernam describes herself as being in London for the legal terms – a natural comment for a student at the Inns of Court, but a curious one for a woman? Then there is Sowernam's enigmatic description of herself on her title page as 'neither Maide, Wife nor Widdowe, yet really all, and therefore experienced to defend all'. This paradoxical phrase has been variously interpreted.[23] In

---

[20] See Shepherd, *Women's Sharp Revenge*, p. 160.

[21] Henderson and McManus, pp. 22–3.

[22] Shepherd, p. 126. Sowernam too implies familiarity with Juvenal (*Ester*, p. 32 [sig. E4v]), so if Shepherd is correct this counts against her female identity also.

[23] See Megan Mathchinske, 'Legislating "Middle-Class" Morality in the Marriage Market: Ester Sowernam's *Ester hath hang'd Haman*', *English Literary Renaissance* 24 (Winter 1994) pp. 154–5.

the passage from Swetnam to which it most immediately alludes (*Araignment*, p. 27 [sig. E2r]) it is a periphrastic description of a fallen women, but it seems unlikely that Sowernam, who writes from a markedly Christian perspective, would have wished this inference to be made. Perhaps, then, there is a riddling implication here that the writer is not female at all. And yet this interpretation brings its own problems. How could a male writer claim to be 'really' a wife, a widow and a maid? As it stands, the phrase might just as well imply that 'Ester Sowernam' is the corporate name of a committee of female authors of varying marital status. In short, the description remains as puzzling as it was apparently meant to be.

In the absence of further evidence, it seems reasonable to accept that Sowernam and Munda are, as they claim to be, women. The advantages of anonymity for female authors venturing into public controversy are clear enough; nor, in their references to each other, do Speght, Sowernam and Munda ever cast doubt on each other's female identity. Considering that they were to some extent rivals and that not all these references are by any means friendly, this is something we might have expected had one or more of them been known to be writing under false pretences.

In the case of Rachel Speght – the one respondent who did not choose to write under a pseudonym – we can speak with real confidence of a female author. Rachel Speght was the daughter of James Speght, the Rector of St Mary Magdelen, Milk Street in the City of London. It seems that he was one of the new breed of Puritan clerics who considered it appropriate for women be educated. In Rachel Speght he had a precocious scholar: at the time *A Mouzell for Melastomus* was published she was still in her teens. The dedicatory poem by 'Favovr B' calls her

> A Virgin young, and of such tender age
> As for encounter may be deemd too weake,
> Shee hauing not as yet seene twenty yeares,
> Though in her carriage older she appears.
> (*Mouzell*, sig. B4v)

From her account in a later work, *Mortalites Memorandum* (1621), it appears that Speght too suffered from accusations that she was not the author of her own work:

> I know that these populous times affoord plentie of forward Writers, and criticall Readers; My selfe hath made the number of the one too many by one; and hauing bin toucht with the censures of the other, by occasion of my *mouzeling Melastomus*, I am now, as by a strong motiue induced (for my rights sake) to produce and divulge this offspring of my indeuour, to proue them further futurely who haue formerly depriued me of my due, imposing my abortiue vpon the father of me, but not it.
> (*Mortalites Memorandum*, sig. A2r)

Speght's work is a powerful and effective piece of polemical writing. Nevertheless, her performance has suffered a bad press over the years, beginning with Ester Sowernam's tart comment that she would have refrained from writing had Speght's work lived up to expectations: 'I did obserue, that whereas the Maide doth many times excuse her tendernesse of yeares, I found it to be true in the slendernesse of her answer' (*Ester*, sig. A2v). Henderson and McManus, who omit Speght from their collection *Half Humankind*, find that

Introduction xxvii

her defences of women are hobbled by 'her especially religious orientation'[24] (though it is doubtful whether Speght would have found this an unwelcome description). Certainly the passage with which they illustrate this claim does not show Speght at her most resourceful or 'feminist'. In explaining why Eve rather than Adam was tempted by the serpent, she suggests it was because women are more easily corrupted: 'where the hedge is lowest, most easie it is to get ouer' (*Mouzell*, p. 4 [sig. C2v]) – unwelcome words for those who wish to find in Speght a feminist thinker *avant la lettre*. A line later, however, in a sentence not quoted by Henderson and McManus, we find a clever inversion of the idea that woman is the 'weaker vessell'. Temptation works on them more easily, 'Like as a Cristall glasse sooner receiues a cracke then a strong stone pot' (*Mouzell*, p. 4 [sig. C2v]). In comparing women to fine crystal and men to stone pots, Speght anticipates one of Sowernam's own main arguments, that women are more refined beings than men. Sowernam will go on to draw out this thread: women are Paradisian creatures (*Ester*, sig. A4r), the final (and therefore the crowning) work of God's creation, made not from inert mud but from the living flesh of Adam.

One of Speght's major contributions to the controversy, adopted and elaborated not only by Sowernam and Munda but also in the play *Swetnam the Womanhater*, is her characterization of Swetnam as a dog-like monster needing to be muzzled. The initial hint for this comes from Swetnam's own invitation, in his introductory Epistle, to 'the Bear-bayting of women' (*Araignment*, sig. A3v). Speght comments:

---

[24] Henderson and McManus, p. 17.

> In that you haue termed your virulent foame, *the Beare-bayting of Women*, you haue plainely displayed your owne dispostion to be Cynicall, in that there appeares no other Dogge or Bull, to bayte them, but yourselfe.
>
> (*Mouzell*, sig. B2r)

Swetnam's unfortunate choice of imagery is compounded a few lines later when he makes an inappropriately heroic (and inaccurate) comparison between himself and Hercules in his combat with '*Cerberus* the two headed Dog' (*Araignment*, sig. A4r).[25] In combining these images, Speght may also have had in mind the Blatant Beast of Edmund Spenser's *The Faerie Qveene* (1596). In Spenser's poem the Beast is associated with slander of a particularly indiscriminate kind. It is a many-tongued, venomous-toothed, barking monster, whose capture and binding form the central quest of Spenser's book of Courtesy. The poetic account of the Swetnam controversy which Speght incorporated into *Mortalites Memorandum* seems to evoke the image in particularly Spenserian terms. Like Artegall in Book V Canto xii of *The Faerie Qveene*, Speght comes across her monster as she returns from a successful allegorical quest (in her case, for education):

> But by the way I saw a full fed Beast,
> Which roared like some monster, or a Deuill,
> And on Eues sex he foamed filthie froth
> As if that he had the falling euill;

---

[25] Munda typically homes in on this mistake, suggesting that Swetnam may have 'snapt off' the missing head himself, and hence acquired Cerberus's dog-like character (*Worming*, p. 25 [sig. E2r]). Cerberus regained his third head only in the 1622 edition of the *Araignment*.

To whom I went to free them from mishaps,
And with a *Mouzel* sought to bind his chops.
                    (*Mortalites Memorandum*, sig. B4r)

If I am right in suspecting Spenser's Beast to be an influence on Speght's characterization of Swetnam, it serves to emphasize not only the slanderous nature of the charges he brings, but also the unconsidered randomness of his attack, and even his penchant for biting women (most of the Blatant Beast's victims are female). In any case, after Speght the image becomes the central one of the whole debate. The title of Munda's pamphlet, and the punishment of muzzling accorded Swetnam in *Swetnam the Woman-hater*, the innumerable references to Swetnam's 'dogged' or 'cynical' nature, even to his composition of 'dogrill' verse (*Worming*, p. 23 [sig. E1r]), all derive from this conceit. By turning Swetnam into an animal, Speght is able to invest him with the same lack of reason, the same instinctive unruliness, that Swetnam himself attributes to women. The muzzle of Melastomus becomes a fit counterpart to the scolds' bridle.

If Speght puts Swetnam in a muzzle, Ester Sowernam's *Ester hath hang'd Haman* brings him to trial. Although Swetnam called his pamphlet *The Araignment of Women*, he was using the legal word in a loose sense, and there is nothing in his work that equates to Sowernam's formal 'Arraignment of Joseph Swetnam' (*Ester*, p. 27 [sig. E2v]), with its full complement of allegorical jurors, witnesses and judges. The jury is made up of the seven deadly sins, eked out with Swetnam's own five senses. The two judges (both female) are Reason and Experience. Conscience is a prosecution witness. This elaborate device provides

xxx *Introduction*

Sowernam with an opportunity to summarize the case against Swetnam in an entertaining way, but its dramatic potential was not lost on the writer of *Swetnam the Woman-hater*, who went on to make a courtroom debate about the relative vices of men and women the play's centrepiece.

Sowernam has a keen nose for the double standards which operate in Swetnam's text. Swetnam, predictably, sees women's beauty as a snare for men, and accuses women who wear glamourous clothing of attempting to provoke male lust. But if this is the case, argues Sowernam, does it not reflect badly on the men who are so easily seduced?

> Your meaning is, in the disgrace of women to exalt men: but is this any commendation to men, that they haue been and are ouer-reacht by women?
> (*Ester*, p. 35 [sig. F2r])

Moreover, men are quite capable of vanity about their own appearance, yet...

> Women are so farre off from being in any sort prouoked to loue vpon the view of mens apparell, and setting forth themselues, that no one thing can more draw them from loue, then their vanitie in apparell.
> (*Ester*, p. 38 [sig. F3v])

Women are constantly solicited by men to leave the path of virtue, with poems, gifts and words; whereas 'a beautifull or personable man, he may sit long enough before a woman will solicite him' (*Ester*, p. 25, [sig. E1r]). Yet it is the man whose lapse is more likely to be pardoned. As so often in relations between the sexes, the scales are unequally weighted. If a man gets an unmarried woman pregnant, she is 'vterly vndone by it', while in him it is counted 'but as a trick of youth'. When a man is drunk, that is 'a signe of goodfellowship'; in a woman it is 'abhorred' (*Ester*, p. 24 [sig. D4v]). The analysis is sharp, and Sowernam's marginal comment takes advantage to win a tactical victory: 'Womens faults more markable because they are the better', she concludes.

Nevertheless, it is at this point that Sowernam's limits, from the point of view of modern feminism, become apparent. Instead of calling for a change in this unjust state of affairs, Sowernam finds it quite acceptable. The requirement of stricter morality from women is simply the corollary of their finer natures:

> for where God hath put hatred betwixt the woman and the serpent, it is a foule shame in a woman to carry fauour with the deuill, to stayne her womanhoode with any of his damnable qualities....
> (*Ester*, pp. 24–5 [sigs. D4v–E1r])

Although at times Sowernam comes very close to saying that women are superior to men, this does not mean she wants to see their superiority reflected in the hierarchy of the domestic household, or society at large. Men should still command, because God has ordained obedience as women's particular virtue, and the traditional arrangements give them gratifyingly frequent opportunities to practice it:

> She is commanded to obey her husband; the cause is, the more to encrease her glorie. Obedience is better then Sacrifice: for nothing is more acceptable before God then to obey: women are much bound to God, to haue so acceptable a vertue enjoyned them for their pennance.
> (*Ester*, pp. 9–10 [sigs. C1r–C1v])

This conclusion, so disquieting to a modern reader, prompts us to ask how far the apparently feminist sentiments of Speght, Munda and Sowernam are actually compatible with the modern senses of that term. As always in reading historical texts, we must beware of ventriloquizing these women's voices in our enthusiasm to make them speak directly to our own concerns. As Diane Purkiss warns:

> ...[these pamphlets] excite the desire to recognize the present in the past, to name what we can term our *own* history. But because what is at stake in these texts seems at first glance so familiar and understandable, it is possible that their estranging or culturally autonomous aspects may not be fully noticed; moreover, because they can so readily be situated in the context of gender politics, they are never fully situated in the political and discursive specificities of the early modern period.[26]

Both Speght and Sowernam, as we have seen, reply to Swetnam's lists of 'bad' women by showing that there have been just as many bad men; that there have been good women; that one cannot infer from a particular to a general. (Munda is in a slightly different category since she does not actually offer to defend women, so much as to abuse Swetnam.) But as Simon Shepherd has noted, they do not go so far as to question the definition of what makes a woman 'bad' in the first place. The chaste and pious women they hold up as glorious examples of their sex are those 'acceptable to a male world, acceptable because they have carried out

---

[26] Diane Purkiss, 'Material Girls: The Seventeenth-Century Woman Debate', in Clare Brant and Diane Purkiss, eds., *Women Texts and Histories, 1575–1670* (London and New York: Routledge, 1992), p. 70.

proficiently the tasks allotted to them by a patriarchal society'.[27] A more radical critique would take Sowernam's analysis of the double standard further, and offer an alternative explanation of the forces that perpetuate it. But this is something that neither Sowernam nor the others are willing to do. They attack Swetnam's misogyny, but misogyny and patriarchy are not the same thing. In fact, as Purkiss has argued, misogyny of Swetnam's indiscriminate type can be incompatible with the hierarchical concerns of patriarchy in that it denies women the well-defined (if subordinate) position of helpmate which patriarchy has traditionally assigned them.[28]

In the end, writers such as Sowernam and Speght are not attempting to undermine the traditional structure of their society, so much as to defend a dignified place for women within it.

> The Red Bull
> Is mostly full
> Of drovers, carriers, carters;
> But honest wenches
> Will shun the benches,
> And not there show their garters.[29]

The Red Bull, whose contemporary reputation is sufficiently witnessed in this Jacobean verse, seems an unlikely setting for a 'proto-feminist' play. An inn yard at the end of St John Street in Smithfield, this playhouse catered for popular, and, it seems, decidedly downmarket taste. Yet it was here, rather than before

---

[27] Shepherd, p. 10.

[28] Purkiss, p. 73.

[29] From an anonymous manuscript quoted by A. B. Grosart in his edition of *Swetnam the Woman-Hater* (Manchester: 1880), p. xxiv.

the sophisticated audience of a hall playhouse such as Blackfriars, that around 1619 the Queen's Players performed *Swetnam the Woman-hater*, a play that 'sides' unequivocally with the female respondents to Swetnam, and casts Swetnam himself as a dangerous buffoon.

The main plot of the play does not greatly concern Swetnam. It derives from a work attributed (it seems wrongly) to Juan de Flores, *The History of Aurelio and Isabella*. Atticus, the King of Sicily, is in despair. Of his two sons, one has died and the other, Lorenzo, has been missing since the battle of Lepanto eighteen months before. To make matters worse, his daughter Leonida refuses to choose a husband. In fact, she is in love with the prince of Naples, Lisandro – but their alliance is impossible because their fathers have quarrelled. The king's evil counsellor, Nicanor, who wishes to marry Leonida and assume the throne himself, discovers their love, and persuades Atticus to bring them to trial. Since Sicilian law dictates that only one person may be punished, the trial becomes a debate about who is primarily responsible for the affair, the man or the woman. Swetnam upholds the male cause, while Leonida is ably defended by a visiting Amazon, Atlanta (actually the missing Lorenzo, who has returned to Sicily in disguise). The judges side with Swetnam, and Leonida is condemned to death. However, Atlanta manages to fake Leonida's execution, and when Lisandro, not being privy to the deception, attempts to kill himself, Atlanta is at hand to cure his wound with a medicine 'Of knowne experience, in effecting cures/Almost impossible' (*Woman-hater*, sig. H1r). Meanwhile Atticus is stricken with remorse, having been convinced (too late, as he thinks) of the innocence of his daughter. At last Atlanta reveals her true identity

Introduction xxxv

as Lorenzo, Leonida and Lisandro are restored, their union is blessed by the penitent king, and Nicanor is forgiven.

Here is a standard Jacobean tragicomic plot, replete with coincidences, disguises, masques, miracle cures and sentimental speeches. Swetnam's formal role in all this is to provide comic relief in the subplot. Having been chased out of England by women after the publication of the *Araignment*, he has set up a fencing school in Sicily, and taken the somewhat transparent alias of Misogynos. His continuing hatred of women is given full vent, and much of what he says draws on material in the *Araignment*, while the ripostes of other characters demonstrate that they have been poring over copies of Speght, Munda and Sowernam.[30] His cowardice and incompetence as a fencer are quickly exposed by Atlanta, and in his verbal battles too Swetnam consistently comes off a poor second best. It is only in the trial of Leonida and Lisandro that Swetnam secures victory, but this, as Atlanta suggests, may be because the court is entirely composed of men:

You are all men, and in this weightie businesse,
Graue Women should haue sate as Iudges with you.
(*Woman-hater*, sig. F3r)

Atlanta's complaint is particularly significant. The debate which precedes it has used many of the arguments from the pamphlet controversy (lists of bad men set against lists of bad women, and the rest); but here Atlanta chooses to step back from the 'frame' that the trial provides, and question the competence of the court to decide the issue. In calling male rule into

---

[30] See *Woman-hater* sig. B2r, as one example amongst many, for Swetnam's jest about riding different kinds of horse to the devil, along with Speght's reply (*Mouzell*, p. 34 [sig. G1v]) about going by foot.

doubt, if only briefly and in one of its aspects, she thus goes beyond the pamphlets of Speght, Sowernam and Munda, and in this sense the play achieves a radicalism to which the female writers themselves never aspire. (Interestingly, the complaint about gender bias is anticipated in Sowernam's own arraignment of Swetnam, but in reverse. She foresees that he will consider the court unfairly constituted 'seeing the Iudgesses, the Iurie, the Accuser, and all others, most of them of the foeminine gender' (*Ester*, p. 3 [sig. E4r]). In due course the main female characters in *Swetnam the Woman-hater* do indeed form a makeshift court to try their hapless enemy.)

If the play does compromise it is in the character of Lorenzo/Atlanta. From the first, the Amazon disguise seems conspicuously exotic. Disguised princes are a staple of Renaissance drama, but one can imagine many more convincing and convenient identities than this for a prince wishing to travel incognito in sixteenth-century Sicily.[31] The explanation, of course, is that it allows Lorenzo to undertake the defence of women, *as* a woman, while retaining a male authority that can eventually be revealed to the astonished court as Atticus reasserts his (albeit chastened) rule. Even here, then, on a stage occupied entirely by male players, performing a play written (presumably) by a man, feminist critique is not something that can be safely entrusted to 'female' hands.

I have written that Swetnam is conceived of primarily as a comic character. This is true. But for a play in which the formal villain, Nicanor, is swiftly forgiven without any punishment, *Swetnam the Woman-hater*

---

[31] Given his disappearance at the battle of Lepanto, the nominal date of the play should be about 1572–73, despite its references to Swetnam's publication.

treats its eponymous anti-hero rather roughly. Swetnam is beaten by women, publicly humiliated, whipped into exile, and finally appears to deliver the Epilogue, 'muzzled, hal'd in by Women' (*Woman-hater*, sig. L1v), and, at least temporarily, repentant. Compare this with Francis Beaumont's *The Woman Hater* (1607). Here, the punishment of the misogynist Gondarino for seeking the death of Oriana is no more than to be kissed by some ladies of the court (admittedly he does not appear to enjoy it, and tries to dissuade them: 'I am given much to belching' [V.v.167]). The writer of *Swetnam the Woman-hater*, who may well have had the earlier play in mind,[32] was clearly not prepared to let Swetnam's casually malicious misogyny off so lightly – 'as but a trick of youth', perhaps. Swetnam, like other writers before him, had tried at various points to disclaim serious intent; 'I wrote this booke with my hand, but not with my heart' (*Araignment*, sig. A3r), he asserts in his introductory Epistle. Like the injunction to silence, the effect of such declarations is to forestall criticism. Who would wish it to be known that they are unable to take a joke? When we read that women's hearts 'are blacke, swelling with mischiefe, not much vnlike vnto old trees, whose outward leaues are faire and greene and yet the body rotten' (*Araignment*, p. 31 [sig. E4r]) it may be hard to see just where the humour lies, but no matter: we have Joseph Swetnam's assurance that he does not really mean it. Yet the effects of such 'jokes' can be deadly

---

[32] There are numerous similarities apart from the obvious one of the title, but it is impossible to be certain of influence given the numerous shared conventions associated with stage misogyny. See Linda Woodbridge, *Women and the English Renaissance: Literature and the Nature of Womankind, 1540–1620* (Brighton: The Harvester Press, 1984), pp. 275–99.

serious, and in *Swetnam the Woman-hater* it is the comic misogynist, not the villainous machiavel, who is stigmatized by Leonida's grieving mother as:

> *Aur.* That bloudie, cruell, and inhumane wretch,
> That slanderous Dectractor of our Sex:
> That *Misogynos*, that blaspemous Slaue
> (*Woman-hater*, sig. H2r)

We do not know whether Swetnam ever saw *Swetnam the Woman-hater*. Perhaps he had already left England by the time it was performed, as the play itself implies. In fact there is no evidence that Swetnam was even aware of the controversy his little book caused. Would he have been pleased, or appalled, to find himself so famous, and so abused? Again, we cannot know. Of the five people that wrote these texts, two are pseudonymous, one anonymous; while of Rachel Speght and Swetnam himself we have only the most rudimentary biographical knowledge. None is a 'great' writer. None can seriously have expected that their quarto pamphlets would be being read almost four hundred years later. Yet the wit, verve and forensic skills with which they conducted their debate remain impressive, and the debate itself has unique value in delineating the nature of feminism – and of misogyny – in early seventeenth-century England. Constantia Munda wrote that 'feminine modesty hath confin'd our rarest and ripest wits to silence' (p. 5 [sig. B4r]). If so, we can be grateful to Swetnam at least for providing the provocation that prompted Munda and the rest to break that silence.

Charles Butler,
Bristol, 1995

SELECT BIBLIOGRAPHY

PRIMARY TEXTS

Anonymous. *Swetnam, the Woman-hater, Arraigned by Women. A new Comedie, Acted at the Red Bull, by the late Queenes Seruants.* London, 1620.

Beaumont, Francis and Fletcher, John. *The Works of Beaumont and Fletcher.* London: George Routledge and Sons, 1866.

Lyly, John. *Euphues. The Anatony of Wit, 1579, Euphues and His England, 1580*, ed. Edward Arber. London: Alex, Murray & Son, 1868.

Munda, Constantia. *The Worming of a mad Dogge: Or, A Soppe for Cerberus the Iaylor of Hell. No Confutation But a Sharpe Redargution of the Bayter of Women.* London, 1617.

Speght, Rachel. *A Mouzell For Melastomvs, The cynicall Bayter of, and foule mouthed Barker against Evahs Sex. Or an Apologeticall Answere to that Irreligious and Illiterate Pamphlet made by Io. Sw. and by him Intituled, The Arraignment of Women.* London, 1617.

Speght, Rachel. *Mortalites Memorandum with a Dream Prefixed, imaginarie in manner, reall in matter.* London, 1621.

Sowernam, Ester. *Ester hath hang'd Haman: or An Answere to a lewd Pamphlet, entituled, The Arraignment of Women. With the arraignment of lewd, idle, froward, and vnconstant men, and Hvsbands.* London, 1617.

Swetnam, Joseph, *The Araignment of Lewde, idle, froward, and vnconstant women; Or the vanitie of them, choose you whether. With a Commendacion of wise, vertuous and honest Women. Pleasant for married Men, profitable for young men, and hurtfull to none.* London, 1615.

SECONDARY TEXTS

Brant, Clare, and Purkiss, Diane, eds. *Women, Texts and Histories, 1575–1760.* London and New York: Routledge, 1992.

van Heertum, Francisca Wilhelmina. *A Critical Edition of Joseph Swetnam's The Araignment of Lewd, Idle, Froward, and Unconstant Women (1615)* Nijmegen: The Cicero Press, 1989.

Henderson, Katherine U., and McManus, Barbara F., eds. *Half Humankind: Contexts and Texts of the Controversy about Women in England, 1540–1640.* Urbana and Chicago: University of Illinois Press, 1985.

Matchinske, Megan. 'Legislating "Middle-Class" Morality in the Marriage Market: Ester Sowernam's *Ester hath hang'd Haman*', *English Literary Renaissance* 24, Winter 1994, 154–83.

Purkiss, Diane. 'Material Girls: The Seventeenth-Century Woman Debate', in Clare Brant and Diane Purkiss, eds. *Women, Texts and Histories*, pp. 69–101.

Shepherd, Simon, *Amazons and Warrior Women: Varieties of Feminism in Seventeenth-Century Drama*. Brighton: Harvester Press, 1981.

Shepherd, Simon, ed,. *The Women's Sharp Revenge: Five Women's Pamphlets from the Renaissance*. London: Fourth Estate, 1985.

Stone, Lawrence. *The Family, Sex and Marriage in England 1500–1800*. Harmondsworth: Penguin, 1979; first published Weidenfeld & Nicolson, 1977.

Woodbridge, Linda. *Women and the English Renaissance: Literature and the Nature of Womankind, 1540–1620*. Brighton: Harvester Press, 1984.

Contents

The Araignment of Lewde, idle, froward,
and unconstant Women (1615)
Joseph Swetnam   74pp

A Mouzell for Melastomus (1617)
Rachel Speght   52pp

Ester hath hang'd Haman (1617)
Ester Sowernam   60pp

The Worming of a mad Dogge (1617)
Constantia Munda   42pp

Swetnam the Woman-hater, Arraigned
by Women (1620)
Anonymous   86pp

THE
ARAIGNMENT

Of Lewde, idle, froward, and vnconstant women: Or the vanitie of them, choose you whether.

With a Commendacion of wise, vertuous and and honest Women.

Pleasant for married Men, profitable for young Men, and hurtfull to none.

LONDON
Printed by *Edw: Allde* for *Thomas Archer*, and are to be solde at his shop in Popes-head Pallace nere the Royall Exchange.
1615.

Neither to the best nor yet to the worst, but to the common sort of Women.

MVsing with my selfe being idle, and hauing little ease to passe the time withall, and I being in a great chollor against some women, I meane more then one; And so in the ruffe of my fury, taking my pen in hand to begile the time withral, indeed I might haue imployed my selfe to better vse then in such an idle busines, and better it were to pocket vp a pelting iniury then to intangle my selfe with such vermine, for this I knowe that because women are women, therefore many of them will doe that in an hower, which they many times will repent all their whole life time after, yet for any iniury which I haue receued of thē, the more I consider of it, the lesse I esteeme of the same: Yet perhaps some may say vnto me that I haue sought for honey, caught the Bee by the taile, or that I haue been bit or stung with some of these wasps, otherwise I could neuer haue beene expert in bewraying their quallities, for the Mother would neuer haue sought her Daughter in the Ouen but that she was there first herselfe; Indeede I must confesse I haue beene a Traueller this thirty and odde yeares, and many trauaillers liue in disdaine of women, the reason is, for that their affections are so poysoned with the hainous euills of vnconstant women which they happen to be acquainted with in their trauails: for it doth so cloy their stomacks that they censure hardly of women euer afterwardes: wronged men will not be tongue-tyed: Therefore if you doe ill you must not thinke to heare well,

for

The Epistle

for although the world be bad, yet it is not come to that passe that men should beare with all the bad conditions that is in some women.

 I know I shall be bitten by many beeause I touch many, but before I goe any further let me whisper one worde in your eares, and that is this, whatsoeuer you thinke priuately I wish you to conceale it with silence, least in starting vp to finde fault you proue your selues guilty of these monstrous accusations which are heere following against some women: and those which spurne if they feele themselues touched, proue themselues starke fooles in bewraying their galled backs to the world, for this booke toucheth no sort of women, but such as when they heare it will goe about to reproue it, for although in some part of this booke I tripp at your heeles, yet I will stay you by the hand so that you shall not fall further then you are willing, although I deale with you after the manner of a shrowe which cannot otherwise ease her curst heart but by her vnhappy tongue: If I be too earnest beare with me a little, for my meaning is not to speake much of those that are good, and I shall speake too little of those that are naught, but yet I will not altogether condemne the bad, but hoping to better the good by the naughty examples of the badd; For there is no woman so good but hath one idle part or other in her which may bee amended, for the clearest Riuer that is hath some durt in the bottome, Iewels are all precious but yet they are not all of one price, nor all of one vertue: golde is not all of one picture, no more are women all of one disposition: women are all necessary euills and yet not all giuen to wickednesse, and yet many so bad, that in my conceit if I should speake the worst that I know by some women, I should make their eares glowe that heares me, and my tongue would blister to report it, but it is a great discredit for a man to be accounted for a scolde, for scolding is the manner of Shrowes, therefore I had rather answer them with silence which finde fault, then striue to win the Cucking-stoole frō them. Now me thinks I heare some curious Dames giue their rash iudgements and say, that I hauing no witt, descant vpon women which haue more wit then men, to answer you againe. If I belie you iudge me vnkinde,

but

To the Reader.

but if I speake the trueth I shall be the better beleeued another time; and if I had wrote neuer so well it is vnpossible to please all, & if neuer so ill yet I shall please some. Let it be well or ill I look for no praise for my labour, I am weined from my mothers teat, and therefore neuer more to be fed with her papp, wherefore say what you will for I will follow my owne vaine in vnfolding euery pleat, and shewing euery wrinkle of a womans disposition, and yet I will not wade so farre ouer the shooes but that I may returne dry, nor so farr in but that I may easily escape out, and yet for all that I must confesse my selfe to be in a fault, and that I haue offended you beyond satisfaction, for it is hard to giue a sufficient recompence for a flaunder, and yet hereafter if by no meanes I cannot obtaine your fauour to be one of your Pulpet men, yet you cannot deny me to be one of your Parish, & therfore if you please but to place me in the body of the Church hereafter, you shall finde my deuotion so great towardes you, as hee that kneeleth at the chancell doore: for I wrote this booke with my hand, but not with my heart.

Indeed when I first began to write this booke, my witts were gone a wooll-gathering, in so much that in a manner forgetting my selfe, and so in the rough of my fury, I vowed for euer to be an open enemy vnto women, but when my fury was a little past, I began to consider the blasphemy of this infamous booke against your sectes; I then tooke my pen and cut him in twenty peeces, and had it not beene for hurting my selfe, I would haue cut my owne fingers which held my pen: and furthermore for a peannance I doe craue that my selfe may be a Iudge against my selfe, but yet assure your selues of all euills I will choose the least, wherefore I choose rather to beare a faggot, then burne by the faggot: you may perceiue the winde is changed into another dore, and that I begin to be sea-ficke and yet not past halfe a mile on the salte water, and that my mouth hath vttered that in my fury, which my heart neuer thought, and therefore *I* confesse that my tongue hath gone beyond my wittes, for *I* doe surmise that the sauce which *I* haue made is too sharpe for your dyet, and the flowers which *I* haue gatherd are too strong for your noses; But if *I* had brought

little

The Epistle

little Dogges from *Island*, or fine glasses from *Venice*, then I am sure that you would either haue woo'd me to haue them, or wished to see them. But I will heere conclude this first Epistle, praying you with patience to heare the rest, for if I offend you at the first, I will make you amends at the last, and so I leaue you to him, whose seate is in Heauen and whose foot-stoole is the Earth.

Yours in the way of Honesty,

Thomas Tel-troth.

Read it if you please and like as you list, neither to the wisest Clarke, nor yet to the starkest Foole, but vnto the ordinary sort of giddy headed young-men I send this greeting.

YF thou mean to see the Bear-bayting of wome, then trudge to this beare-garden apace and get in betimes, and viewe euery roome where thou maist best sit, for thy owne pleasure, profite, and heartes ease, and beare with my rudenesse if I chance to offend thee: But before I doe open this trunke full of torments against women, I thinke it were not amisse to resemble those which in olde time did sacrifices to *Hercules*, for they vsed continually first to whip all their Dogges out of their Citty, and I thinke it were not amisse to driue all the women out of my hearing, for doubt least this little sparke kindle into such a flame, and raise so many stinging Hornets humming about my eares, that all the witt I haue will not quench the one nor quiet the other: for *I* feare me that I haue set downe more then they will like of, and yet a great deale lesse then they deserue, and for better proofe I referr my selfe to the iudgement of men, which haue more experience then my selfe, for *I* esteeme little of the mallice of women, for men will be perswaded with reason, but women must be answered with silence, for *I* know women will barke more at me, then

Cerberus

To the Reader.

Cerberus the two headed Dog did at *Hercules* when he came into Hell to fetch out the faire *Proserpina*, and yet *I* charge them now but with a bul-rush in respect of a second booke which is almost ready: I doe now but fret them with a false fire, but my next charge shall be with weapons, and my larum with powder and shot, for then we will goe vpon these venemous Addars, Serpents and Snakes, and tread and trample them vnder our feet, for *I* haue known many men stung with some of these Scorpions, and therefore *I* warne all men to beware the Scorpion; *I* knowe women will bite the lippe at me and censure hardly of me, but *I* feare not the curst Cowe for shee commonly hath short hornes, let them censure of me what they will for *I* meane not to make them my Iudges, and if they shoote their spite at me they may hitt themselues, and so *I* will smile at them as at the foolish flye which burneth herselfe in the candle; And so friend Reader if thou hast any discretion at all, thou maiest take a happy example by these most lasciuious and crafty, whoorish, theeuish, and knauish women, which were the cause of this my idle time spending, and yet *I* haue no warrant to make thee beleeue this which *I* write to be true, but yet the simple Bee gathereth hony where the vemenous Spider doth her poyson; And so *I* will hinder thee no longer from that which ensueth, but heer *I* will conclude least thou hast cause to say, that my Epistles are longer then my booke, a Booke *I* hope *I* may call it without any offence, for the Collyer calls his horse a Horse, and the Kings great Steed is but a Horse.

If thou Read but the beginning of a booke thou canst giue no iudgement of that which ensueth; Therefore *I* say as the Frier, who in the midst of his Sermon said often that the best was behinde: And so if thou reade it all ouer thou shalt not be deluded for the best is behinde, *I* thinke *I* haue shott so neere the white that some will account me for a good Archer: and so praying thee to looke to thy footing that thou run not ouer thy shooes, and so be past recouery before my second booke come.

Thy friend nameles,
To keepe my selfe blameles.

CHAP. 1.

This first Chapter sheweth to what vse Women were made, it also sheweth that most of them degenerate from the vse they were framed vnto, by leading a proud lasie and idle life, to the great hinderance of their poore Husbands.

Moses describeth a woman thus: At the first beginning (saith he) a woman was made to be a helper vnto man, and so they are indeede, for she helpeth to spend & consume that which man painefully getteth. He also saith that they were made of the ribbe of a man, and that their froward nature sheweth; for a ribbe is a crooked thing good for nothing else, and women are crooked by nature, for small occasion will cause them to be angry.

Againe, in a manner she was no sooner made but straight way her minde ws set vpon mischiefe, for by her aspiring minde and wanton will she quickly procured mans fall, and therefore euer since they are & haue been a woe vnto man, and follow the line of their first leader.

For I pray you let vs consider the times past with the time present, first, that of *Dauid* and *Salomon*, if they had occasion so many hundreth yeares agoe to exclaime so

B   bitterly

bitterly againſt women, for the one of them ſaid, that it was better to be a doore keeper, and better dwell in a den amongſt Lyons then to be in the houſe with a froward and wicked woman: and the other ſaid, that the climing vp of a ſandy hill to an aged man was nothing ſo wearisome as to be troubled with a froward woman: and further he ſaith, that the mallice of a beaſt is not like the mallice of a wicked woman, nor that there is nothing more dangerous then a woman in her fury.

The Lyon being bitten with hunger, the Beare being robbed of her young ones, the Viper being trode on, all theſe are nothing ſo terrible as the fury of a woman. A Bucke may be incloſed in a Parke, a bridle rules a horſe, a Woolfe may be tyed, a Tyger may be tamed, but a froward woman will neuer be tamed, no ſpur will make hir goe, nor no bridle will holde hir backe, for if a woman holde an opinion no man can draw hir from it, tell hir of hir fault ſhe will not beleeue that ſhe is in any fault, giue hir good counſell but ſhe will not take it, if you doe but looke after another woman then ſhe will be iealous, the more thou loueſt hir the more ſhe will diſdaine thee, and if thou threaten hir then ſhe will be angry, flatter hir and then ſhe will be proude, and if thou forbeare hir it maketh hir bould, and if thou chaſten hir then ſhe will turne to a Serpent; at a worde a woman will neuer forget an iniury, nor giue thanks for a good turne: what wiſe man then will exchange golde for droſſe, pleaſure for paine, a quiet life for wrangling braules, from the which the married men are neuer free.

Salomon ſaieth that women are like vnto wine, for that they will make men drunke with their deuiſes.

Againe

Againe in their loue a woman is compared to a pomming-stone, for which way soeuer you turne a pomming stone it is full of holes; euen so are womens heartes, for if loue steale in at one hole it steppeth out at another.

They are also compared vnto a painted ship, which seemeth faire outwardly & yet nothing but ballace within hir, or as the Idolls in *Spaine* which are brauely gilt outwardly and yet nothing but lead within them, or like vnto the Sea which at sometimes is so calme that a cock-bote may safely endure hir might, but anon againe without rage she is so grown that it ouerwhelmeth the tallest ship that is.

A froward woman is compared to the winde, and a still woman vnto the Sunne, for the sunne and the winde met a traueiller vpon the way and they laide a wager, which of them should get his cloake from him first; then first the winde began boistrously to blow, but the more the winde blow'd the more the traueller wrapped and gathered his cloake about him, now when the winde had done what he could and was neuer the neerer; then began the Sunne gently to shine vpon him and he threw off not onely his cloake but also his hat and Ierkin, this morall sheweth that a woman with high wordes can get nothing at the handes of hir husband, neuer by froward meanes, but by gentle and faire meanes she may get his heart bloud to doe hir good.

As women are compared vnto many thinges, euen so many and many more troubles commeth galloping after the heeles of a woman, that young men before hand doe not thinke of, for the world is not made all of otemell, nor all is not gold that glistereth, nor the way to Heauen

B 2   is not

is not strewed with rushes, no more is the cradle of ease in a womans lapp: If thou wert a Seruant or in bondage before, yet when thou doest marry, thy toile is neuer the neerer ended, for euen then and not before thou doest change thy golden time for a drop of hony, which presently afterwards turneth to be as bitter as wormwood.

  Yet there are many young men which cudgell their witts and beare theire braines and spend all their time in the loue of women, and if they get a smile or but a fauor at their loues hand, they straight way are so rauished with ioy, yea so much that they thinke they haue gotten God by the hand, but within a while after they will finde that they haue but the Deuill by the foote. A man may generally speake of women that for the most part thou shalt finde them dissembling in their deeds and in all their actions subtill and dangerous for men to deale withall, for their faces are luers, their beauties are baytes, their lookes are netts, and their wordes charmes, and all to bring men to ruine.

  There is an old saying goeth thus, that he which hath a faire wife and a white horse shall neuer be without troubles, for a woman that hath a fair face it is euer macthed with a cruell heart, and hir heauenly lookes with hellish thoughtes, their modest countenance with mercilesse mindes, for women can both smooth and sooth: they are so cunning in the art of flattery as if they had been bound prentise to the trade, they haue *Sirens* songs to allure thee, & *Xerxses* cunning to inchaunt thee, they beare two tongues in one mouth like *Iudas*, and two heartes in one brest like *Magus*, the one full of smiles and the other full of frownes, and all to deceiue the simple and plaine meaning

ning men, they can with *Satyer* out of one mouth blow both hot and colde.

And what of all this? why nothing but to tell thee that a woman is better loſt then found, better forſaken then taken. Saint *Paul* ſaieth that they which marry doe well, but he alſo ſaith that they which marry not doe better: & he no doubt was wel aduiſed what he ſpake. Then if thou be wiſe keepe thy head out of the halter and take heede before thou haue cauſe to curſe thy hard pennyworth, or with the Preiſt ſpeachles which knit the knot.

The Philoſophers which liued in the olde time, their opinions were ſo hard of marriage, that they neuer delighted therein, for one of them being asked why he married not? he anſwered; that it was too ſoone, and afterwards when he was olde, he was asked the ſame queſtion; and he ſaid then that it was too late: and further he ſaid, that a married man hath but two good dayes to be looked for, that was the marriage day and the day of his wifes death, for a woman will feede thee with hony and poyſon the with gall. *Diogenes* was ſo dogged that hee abhored all women, and *Auguſtus* he wiſhed that he had liued wifeles and dyed childles.

On a time one asked *Socrates*, whether he were better to marry or to liue ſingle? and he made anſwere; which ſo euer thou doeſt it will repent thee, for if thou marrieſt not, then thou wilt liue diſcontented and dye without iſſue, and ſo perhaps a ſtranger ſhall poſſeſſe thy goodes: and if thou doeſt marry thou ſhalt haue continuall vexations, hir dowrie will be often caſt in thy diſh if ſhee doe bring wealth with hir, again if ſhe cōplain, then hir kinsfolk will bend the browes & hir mother will ſpeake hir

B 3   pleaſure

pleasure by thee, and if thou marriest onely for faire lookes, yet thou maiest hap to goe without them when thou lookest for them: and if thou marriest one that is fruitfull in bearing of children, then will thy care be the more increased, for little doth the father know what shal be the end of his children, and if she be barren thou wilt lothe hir, and if honest thou wilt feare hir death, and if vnhonest thou wilt be wearie of thy life, for when thou hast hir thou must support hir in all hir bad actions, and that wil be such a perpetuall burden vnto thee, that thou hadst euen as good drawe water continually to fill a bottomles tubb,

A gentleman on a time said to his friend I can helpe you to a good marriage for your sonne, his friend made him this answer; my sonne (said hee) shall stay till he haue more wit, the Gentleman replied againe: saying, if you marrie him not before he hath wit, he will neuer marry so long as he liueth.

For a married man is like vnto one arested, and I think that many a man would flie vp into Heauen, if this arrest of marriage kept them not backe. It is said of one named *Domettes* that he buried three wiues, and yet neuer wet one handkercher no nor shed not so much as one teare: also *Vlisses* he had a Dog which loued him well and when that dog died he wept bitterly, but he neuer shed one teare when his wife dyed, wherefore if thou marriest without respect but onely for bare loue, then thou wilt afterwards with sorrow say that there is more belonges to housekeeping then fower bare legges in a bed: a man cannot liue with his handes in his bosome, nor buy meat in the market for honestie without money: where there

is

is nothing but bare walles, it is a fit house to breed beggers into the world: yet there are many which thinke when they are married that they may liue by loue, but if wealth be wanting hot loue will soon be colde, and your hot desires will be soone quenched with the smoke of pouerty. To what end then should we liue in loue, seeing it is a life more to be feared then death, for all thy monie wastes in toyes and is spent in banquetting, and all thy time in sighes and sobbs to thinke vpon thy trouble and charge which comonly commeth with a wife, for commonly women are proude without profit, and that is a good purgation for thy purse, & when thy purse is light then will thy heart be heauy.

The pride of a woman is like the dropsie, for as drinke increaseth the drouth of the one, euen so money enlargeth the pride of the other: thy purse must be alwayes open to feed their fancy, and so thy expences will be great and yet perhaps thy gettings small, thy house must be stored with costly stuffe, and yet perhaps thy Seruantes starued for lack of meat: thou must discharg the Mercers booke and pay the Haberdashers man, for hir hat must continually be of the new fashion, and hir gowne of finer wooll then the sheepe beareth any: she must likewise haue hir Iewel-box furnished especially if she be beautifull, for then commonly beauty and pride goeth together, and a beautifull woman is for the most part costly and no good huswife, and if she be a good huswife then no seruant will abide hir feirce cruelty, and if she be honest and chaste then commonly she is iealious: a Kinges crowne and a faire woman is desired of many.

But he that getteth either of them liueth in great troubles

bles and hazard of his life: he that getteth a faire woman is like vnto a Prisoner loaden with fetters of golde, for thou shalt not so oft kisse the sweete lippes of thy beautifull wife, as thou shalt be driuen to fetch bitter sighes from thy sorrowfull hart in thinking of the charge which commeth by hir, for if thou deny hir of such toyes as she standes not in neede of, and yet is desirous of them, then she will quickly shut thee out of the doores of hir fauour & deny thee hir person, and shew hir selfe as it were at a window playing vpon thee, not with small shot, but with a cruell tongue she will ring thee such a peale, that one would thinke the Deuill were come from Hell, saying, I might haue had those which would haue maintained me like a woman, where as nowe I goe like nobody: but I will be maintained if thou were't hanged: with such like words she will vex thee, blubbering forth abundance of dissembling teares. (for women doe teach their eies to weepe) for doe but crosse a woman although it be neuer so little, shee will straight way put finger in the eye and cry, then presently many a foolish man will flatter hir and intreat hir to be quiet: but that marres all, for the more she is intreated, the will power forth the more abundance of deceitfull teares, and therefore no more to be pittied then to see a Goose goe barefoote, for they haue teares at command, so haue they wordes at will, and oathes at pleasure, for they make as much account of an oath, as a Marchant doth which will forsweare himselfe for the getting of a penny. I neuer yet knew woman that would deny to swear in defence of hir own honesty & alwayes standing highly vpon it, although she be ashamed to weare it in winter for catching of colde, nor in summer

mer for heate fearing leaſt it may melt away.

 Many will ſay this which I write is true, and yet they cannot beware of the Deuill vntill they are plagued with his Dame ; the little Lambe skips and lepps till the Fox come, but then he quiuers and ſhakes: the Beare daunces at the ſtake till the Dogges be vpon his backe : and ſome men neuer feare their money vntill they come into the handes of theeues ; euen ſo ſome will neuer be warned and therefore is not to be pittied if they be harmed, what are women that makes thee ſo greedily to gape after them : Indeed, ſome their faces are fairer and beautifuller then others, ſome againe ſtand highly vppon their fine foote and hand, or elſe all women are alike: *Ione* is as good as my Lady according to the Countrey mans Prouerbe, who gaue a great ſumme of money to lye with a Lady, and going homewards hee made a grieuous mone for his money, and one being on the other ſide the hedge heard him ſay that his *Ione* at home was as good as the Lady. But whether this be true or no my ſelfe I doe not knowe, but you haue it as I heard it.

 If thou marrieſt a woman of euill report, hir diſcredit will be a ſpot in thy browe, thou canſt not goe in the ſtreet with hir without mocks, nor amongſt thy neighbours without frumps, and cōmonly the faireſt women are ſooneſt intiſed to yeeld vnto vanity : hee that hath a faire wife and a whetſtone, euery one will be whetting thereon, and a Caſtle is hard to keepe when it is aſſalted by many, and faire wōmen are commonly catched at, he that marrieth a faire womā euery one will wiſh his death to inioy hir, and if thou be neuer ſo rich, and yet but a Clowne in condition, then will thy faire wife haue hir

C   credit

credit to pleafe hir fancy, for a Diamond hath not his grace but in golde, no more hath a faire woman hir full commendations but in the ornament of hir brauery, by which meanes there are diuers women whofe beauty hath brought their husbandes into great pouerty and difcredit by their pride and whoordome, a faire wowan commonly will goe like a Peacocke, and hir husband muft goe like a Woodcocke.

That great Giant *Pamphimapho* who had Beares waiting vpon him like Dogges, and he could make tame any wilde beaft yet a wanton woman he could neuer rule nor turne to his will.

Salomon was the wifeft Prince that euer was, yet he lufted after fo many women that they made him quickly forfake his God which did alwaies guide his fteppes, fo long as he liued godly.

And was not *Dauid* the beft beloued of God and a mighty Prince, yet for the loue of women he purchafed the difpleafure of his God. *Samfon* was the ftrongeft man that euer was, for euery lock of his head was the ftrength of another man, yet by a woman he was ouercome, he reuealed his ftrength, and payed his life for that folly. Did not *Iefabell* for her wicked luft caufe her husbands blood to be giuen to doggs?

Iobs wife gaue her husband counfaile to blafpheme God and to curfe him.

Agamemnons wife for a fmall iniury that hir husband did her fhe firft committed adultery, and afterwards confented to his death.

Alfo the wife of *Hercules*, fhe gaue her husband a poyfoned fhirt, which was no fooner on his backe, but did
sticke

sticke so fast, that when he would haue plucked it off it tore the flesh with it.

If thou wilt auoyd these euills thou must with *Vlisses* binde thy selfe to the mast of the ship as he did, or else it would haue cost him his life, for otherwise the *Syrenian* women would haue intised him into the Sea if he had not so done.

It is wonderfull to see the madd feates of women, for she will be now merry then againe sad; now laugh then weepe, now sick then presently whole, all things which like not them is naught, and if it be neuer so bad if it like them it is excellent, againe it is death for a woman to be denied the thing which they demaund: and yet they will dispise thinges giuen them vnasked.

When a woman wanteth any thing, shee will flatter and speake faire, not much vnlike the flattering Butcher who gently claweth the Oxe, when he intendeth to knock him on the head; but the thing being once obtained and their desires gained, then they wi'l begin to looke bigge and answere so stately, and speake so scornfully, that one would imagine they would neuer seeke helpe nor craue comfort at thy hands any more. But a woman is compared vnto a ship, which being neuer so well riged, yet one thing or other is to be amended. euen so giue a woman all that she can demaund to day, yet she will be out of reparations to morrow and want one thing or other.

Women are called night Crowes for that commonly in the night they will make request for such toyes as commeth in their heades in the day, for women knowe their time to worke their craft, for in the night they will

worke

worke a man like wax, and drawe him like as the Adamant doth the Iron, & hauing once brought him to the bent of their bowe, then she makes request for a gowne of the new fashion stuffe: or for a petticote of the finest stamell: or for a hat of the newest fashion; hir husband being ouercome by hir flattring speach & partly he yeildeth to hir request, although it be a griefe to him for that he can hardly spare it out of his stock, yet for quietnesse sake he doth promise what she demaundeth, partly because he would sleepe quietly in his bed: againe euery married man knowes this that a woman will neuer be quiet if hir minde be set vpon a thing till she haue it.

Now if thou driue hir off with delayes, then hir forehead will be so full of frownes as if she threatned to make clubbs trump, and thou neuer a black carde in thy hand: for except a woman haue what she will, say what she list, and goe where shee please, otherwise thy house will be so full of smoke that thou canst not stay in it.

It is said that an olde Dog and a hungry flea byte sore, but in my minde a froward woman byteth more sorer; & if thou goe about to master a woman in hope to bring hir to humility, there is no way to make hir good with stripes except thou beate hir to death; for do what thou wilt, yet a froward woman in hir frantick mood will pull haule, swerue, scratch & teare all that stands in hir way.

What wilt thou that I say more oh thou poore married man, if women doe not feele the raine yet heere is a shower comming which will wet them to the skinnes, a woman which is faire in showe is foule in condition; she is like vnto a glow-worme which is bright in the hedge and black in the hand; in the greenest grasse lyeth
hid

hid the greatest Serpents: painted pottes commonly holde deadly poyson: and in the clearest water the vgliest Tode, and the fairest woman hath some filthines in hir.

All is not golde that glistereth, a smiling countinance is no certaine testimoniall of a merry heart, nor costly garments of a rich purse: men doe not commend a Iudge for that he weareth a skarlet gown but for his iust dealing; no more are women to be esteemed of by the ornament of their brauery, but for their good behauiour, yet there is no riuer so cleare but there is some durt in the bottome; But many a man in this Land we neede not goe any further for examples, but heere we may see many fooles in euery place snared in womens nets after a little familiarity and acquaintance with them, I thinke if they were numbred the number would passe infinite if it were possible, which for the loue of wantons haue lost their voyages at sea to their great hinderances, and many other haue neuer regarded the farre distance which they haue beene from their countrey and friends, vntill they had consumed their substance, and then being ashamed to returne home againe in such bad sort, I meane by weeping crosse and pennyles bench, many of them rather choose to deserue Newgate and so come to Tyburne, far contrary from the expectation of their friends and Parents, which had otherwise prouided for them if they had had grace or would haue beene ruled.

C 3   CHAP. II.

CHAP. II.

The Second Chapter sheweth the manner of such Women as liue vpon euill report: It also sheweth that the beauty of Women hath beene the bane of many a man, for it hath ouercome valiaunt and strong men, eloquent and subtill men. And in a word it hath ouercome all men, as by examples following shall appeare.

First that of *Salomon* vnto whom God gaue singular wit & wisedome, yet he loued so many women that he quiet forgot his God which alwaies did guide his steppes, so long as he liued godly and ruled Iustly, but after he had glutted him selfe with women, then hee could say, vanity of vanity all is but vanity: hee also in many places of his booke of Prouerbes Exclaimes most bitterly against lewde women calling them all that naught is, and also displayeth their properties, and yet I cannot let men goe blamelesse although women goe shamelesse; but I will touch them both, for if there were not receiuers then there would not be so many stealers: if there were not some knaues there would not be so many whoores for they both hold together to boulster each others villany, for alwaies birdes of a feather will flocke together hand in hand to boulster each others villany.

Men I say may liue without women, but women cannot liue without men: For *venus* whose beauty was excellent faire, yet when she needed mans helpe she tooke *vulcan* a clubfooted Smith. And therefore if a womans face

face glister, and hir Iesture pearce the marble wall, or if hir tongue be so smooth as oile or so soft as silke, and hir wordes so sweete as honey: or if she were a very Ape for witt, or a bagg of golde for wealth: or if hir personage haue stolne away all that nature can affoord, and if she be deckt vp in gorgeous apparell, then a thousand to one but she will loue to walke where she may get acquaintance, and acquaintance bringeth familiarity, and familiarity setteth all follies abroch, and twenty to one that if a woman loue gadding but that she will paune hir honour to please hir fantasie.

Man must be at all the cost and yet liue by the losse, a man must take all the paines and women will spend all the gaines, a man must watch and ward, fight and defẽd, till the ground, labour in the vineyard, and looke what hee getteth in seauen yeares, a woman will spread it abroad with a forke in one yeare, and yet little enough to serue hir turne but a great deale to little, to get hir good will, nay if thou giue hir neuer so much and yet if thy personage please not hir humour, then will I not giue a halfe-penny for hir honesty at the yeares end.

For then hir breast will be the harbourer of an enuious heart, & hir hart the storehouse of poysoned hatred, hir head will deuise villany, and hir handes are ready to practise that which their heart desireth; Then who can but say that women sprung from the Deuil, whose heads hands & hearts, mindes & soules are euill, for women are called the hooke of all euill, because men are taken by them as fish is taken wiht the hooke.

For women haue a thousand wayes to intise thee, and ten thousand waies to deceiue thee, and all such fooles as are suetors vnto them, some they keepe in hand with promises, and some they feede with flattery, and some they delay with dalliances, and some they please with kisses: they lay out the foldes of their hare to entangle men into their loue, betwixt their breasts is the vale of destruction, & in their beds there is hell, sorrow & repentance. Eagles eate not men till they are dead but women deuour them aliue, for a woman will pick thy pocket & empty thy purse, laugh in thy face and cutt thy throat, they are vngratefull, periured, full of fraud, flouting and deceit, vnconstant, waspish, toyish, light, sullen, proude, discurteous and cruell, and yet they were by God created, and by nature formed, and therefore by pollicy and wisedome to bee auoyded, for good thinges abused are to be refused, or else for a monthes pleasure she may hap to make thee goe stark naked, she will giue thee rost-meat but she will beate thee with the spitt, if thou hast crownes in thy purse she will be thy heartes golde vntill she leaue thee not a whit of white money, they are like summer birdes for they will abide no storme but flocke about thee in the pride of thy glory, and flye from thee in the stormes of affliction, for they aime more at thy welth then at thy person, and esteem more thy money then any mans vertuous quallities, for they esteeme of a man without money, as a horse doth of a faire stable without meate, they are like Eagles which will alwaies flie where the carrion is.

They will play the horse-leach to suck away thy wealth, but in the winter of thy misery she will flie away from thee. Not vnlike the Swallow, which in the summer harboureth her selfe vnder the eues of an house, and against winter

winter flieth away, leauing nothing but dirt behind her.

Salomon saith, he that wil suffer himselfe to be led away or take delight in such womens company, is like a foole which reioyceth when he is lead to the stockes. *Pro.* 7.

Hosea by marrying with a lewde woman of light behauiour was brought vnto Idolatry, *Hosea* 1. Saint *Paul* accounteth fornicators so odious, that we ought not to eat meate with them, he also sheweth that fornicators shall not inherite the kingdome of Heauen, 1.*Cor.* the 9. and 11. verse.

And in the same chapter Saint *Paul* excommunicateth fornicators, but vpon amendment he receaueth them againe. Whordome punished with death, *Deuteronomie* 22. 21 and *Genesis* 38. 24. *Phinihas* a priest thrust two adulterers both the man and the woman through the belly with a speare, *Numbers* 25.

God detesteth the mony or goods gotten by whoredome, *Deuteronomie* 22. 17. 18. Whores called by diuers names, and the properties of whores, *Prouerbes* 7. 6. and 2. A whore enuieth an honest woman, *Esdras* 16. and 42. Whoremongers God will iudge, *Hebrues* 13. & 42. They shall haue their portions with the wicked in the lake that burneth with fire and brimstone, *Reuelation* the 21. 8.

Onely for the sinne of whoredome God was sorry at the heart, and repented that euer he made man, *Genesis* 6. 67.

Saint *Paul* saith, to auoid fornication euery man may take a wife, *Corinthians* the 1. 6. 9.

Therefore he which hath a wife of his owne and yet goeth to another woman, is like a rich theefe which will steale when he hath no need.

D   There

There are three waies to know a whore: by her wanton lookes, by her speach, and by her gate. *Ecclesiasticus* 26. & in the same chapter he saith, that we must not giue our strength vnto harlots, for whores are the euil of all euils, and the vanity of all vanities, they weaken the strength of a man and depriue the body of his beauty, it furroweth his browes and make the eyes dimme, and a whorish woman causeth the feauer and the gout : and at a word, they are a great shortning to a mans life.

For although they seem to be so dainty as sweet meat, yet in tryall not so wholesome as sowre sauce: they haue wit, but it is all in craft; if they loue, it is vehement, but if they hate it is deadly.

Plato saith, that women are either Angells or Deuills, and that they either loue dearely or hate bitterly, for a woman hath no meane in her loue, nor mercy in her hate: no pitty in reuenge nor patience in her anger, therfore it is said, that there is nothing in the world which both pleaseth and displeaseth a man more then a woman, for a woman most delighteth a man and yet most deceaueth him, for as there is nothing more sweet vnto a man then a woman when she smileth, euen so there is nothing more odious then the angry countenaunce of a woman.

Salomon in his 20. of *Ecclesiastes* saith, that an angry woman will fome at the mouth like a Bore: if all this be true as most true it is, why shouldest thou spend one houre in the praise of women as some fooles doe, for some will brag of the beauty of such a maid, another will vaunt of the brauery of such a woman, that she goeth beyond all the women in the parish : againe, some study their fine

wits

wits how they may cunningly swooth women, and with Logicke how to reason with them, and with eloquence to perswade them, they are alwayes tempering their wits as fidlers do their strings, who wrest them so high, that many times they stretch them beyond time, tune and reason.

Againe, there are many that weary themselues with dallying, playing and sporting with women, and yet they are neuer satisfied with the vnsatiable desire of them; if with a song thou wouldest be brought asleepe, or with a dance be lead to delight, then a fayer woman is fit for thy dyet: if thy head be in her lap she will make thee beleeue that thou art hard by Gods seat, when indeed thou art iust at hell gate.

Theodora a monstrous Strumpet on a time made her bragges to *Socrates* of the great haunt of lusty gallants which came to her house, and furthermore she told him that she could get away more of his schollers from him then he could of hers from her.

No meruaile (quoth *Socrates*) for thy waies seeme pleasant & easie, and that is the way youth loues to walke in, but the way that leadeth to a vertuous life seemeth full of brambles and bryers, and to match with this there is an history that makes mention of three notable Curtizanes, whose names were *Lauia, Flora,* and *Layes*: *Lauia* and *Layes* were *homo*, common to all men, they would play at small game rather then sit out, these three Strumpets during their life time, were the beautifullest & richest of that trade in the world, and had three seuerall guifts whereby they allured their louers to seeke their fauours.

The Engine wherewith *Lauia* entrapped her louers, proceeded

proceeded from her eyes, for by her smiling countenance and wanton lookes she greatly inflamed all that beheld her. And *Flora* wan her louers by her excellent witt and eloquent tongue. And *Layes* enticed her louers by her sweete singing and pleasant fingering of instruments of musicke.

But now againe to *Lauis*. King *Demetrius* gaue but a glaunce of his eyes sodainly vpon her and was taken presently with her net and spent eleuen talents of siluer vpon her which he had prouided and appointed to pay his souldiours; and furthermore he quite forlooke his owne wife and neuer left the company of this Strumpet vntill death tooke her from him, & after she was dead he made great moane for her death, he also kissed and embraced her, and caused her to be buried vnder his windowe, that so often as he did see her graue he might bewaile her death.

Lays likewise had a King whose name was *Pirrhus* which was her chiefe friend, but yet he serued but as it were for a cloke, for he continued not very long with her in Greece, but went himselfe to the warres in Italy, but in his absence she was not onely soughtto, but obtained of many, and set downe her price that before she would do her worke she would haue her mony.

Now to *Flora*, she was a Kings daughter, her parents died when she was of the age of fifteene yeares, and she was left as rich as beautifull, she had the bridle of liberty throwne on her necke, so that she might runne whether she would, for she was left without controulment, so that sodainely she determined to trauaile & see the wars of Africa, where she made sale both of her personage and honour. King

King *Menelaus* was the first that made loue vnto her, as he was marching to the warres of Carthage, and spent more mony vpon her then in conquering his enemies.

But as she was of noble race, so it is said that she neuer gaue her selfe ouer to meane or petty company as the other two did, but she had a scroule set ouer her gate, the tennor whereof was thus, King, Prince, Emperour or Bishop: enter this place and welcome, neither was this *Flora* so greedy of gold as the other two were, for on a time one of her familier friends asked her the cause why she did not make price of her loue? she made this answere, I commit my body to none but to Princes and Noblemen, and I sweare there was neuer man gaue me so little but that I had more then I would haue asked or that I looked for, and furthermore she said, that a noble woman ought not to make price of her loue: all things are at a certaine rate except Loue, and that a woman of great beauty should be so much esteemed of as she esteemes of her selfe. She died at the age of forty yeares, and the wealth she left behinde her in Rome was valued to be so much as would haue builded new walles round about the City if there had beene no walles at all.

Was not that noble city of Troy sacked and spoyled for the faire *Hellena*, & when it had cost many mens liues and much blood was shed, and when they had got the conquest they got but a harlot: by this & that which followeth, thou shalt see the power of women how it hath beene so great, and more preuailed in bewitching mens witts and in ouercomming their sences, then all other thinges whatsoeuer. It hath not onely vanquished Kings & Keisars, but it hath also supprised castles & countries,

D 3 nay

nay what is it that a woman cannot doe, which knowes her power?

 Therefore stay not alone in the company of a woman trusting to thy owne chastity, except thou be more stronger then *Sampson*, more wiser then *Saloman*, or more holy then *Dauid*, for these and many more haue beene ouercome by the sweete intisements of women, as thou shalt read hereafter.

 It is said that the Gods themselues did change their shapes, for the loue of such women as they lusted after, *Iupiter* he transformed himselfe into a Bull, *Neptune* into a Horse, and *Mercury* into a Goate.

 Aristippus desired sweete meat for his belly, and a faire woman for his bed.

 But in my minde hee that layes his net to catch a faire woman, he may chance to fall into the sprindge which was laide for a woodcocke, therefore I doe admonish young men, and I aduise olde men, and I counsell simple men, and I warne all men, that they flie from a wicked woman as from the pestilence, or else they wil make thee flye in the end.

 Aristotle for keeping company with a queane in *Athens* was faine to runne away to saue himselfe from punishment, and yet he had dwelt there, and wrote many books for the space of thirty yeares.

 Again of *Sampson* & *Hercules* for all their great strength and conquest of Giants and monsters, yet the one yeelded his club at *Diaueras* foote, and the other reuealed his strength to *Dalyla*, and he paide his life for his folly.

 The sugred and renowned Orators *Demosthenes* and *Hortentius*, the one came from *Athens* vnto *Corinth*, to compound

compound and agree with *Layes* a common strumpet as you heard before of her, and yet he had but one nights lodging with her. And the other was so farr in loue with another bird of the same cage, the which he could not obtaine, nor yet could he conquer his affection, vntill he had quite pined himselfe away, so that in short time he had wasted himselfe to nothing.

Plato for all his great Philosophy and knowledge, yet he kept company with *Archenasse* when she was olde and forsaken of all her louers, for she had giuen herselfe to a number in her youth, yet neuertheles *Plato* so loued her, that he wrote many verses in commendation of her.

Also of *Socrates* for his grauity and wisedome is renowned throughout all the world, yet he most dearely loued *Aspasy* an olde and ouerworne strumpet.

Loue stayed King *Antiochus* in *Calcidea* a whole winter, for one maide that he fancied there, to his great hinderance.

Loue stayed King *Hannibal* in *Capua* a long season laying all other his necessary affaires aside, the which was no small hinderance to him, for in the meane while his enimies inuaded a great part of his Countrey.

Likewise *Iulius Ceasar* he continued in *Alexandria* a long season not for the loue of one, but he lusted after many, to his great infamy and disgrace.

That great Captain *Holofernes*, whose sight made many thousands to quake, yet he lost his life and was slaine by a woman.

Was not *Herods* loue so great to a woman that he caused *Iohn Baptist* to loose his head for her sake?

Wherefore to auoide the sight, many times is the best
rasor

rasor, to cut of the occasion of the euill which commeth by women; For had not *Holofernes* seene the beauty of *Iudeth*, and marked the finenes of her foote, hee had not lost his head by her: If *Herod* had not seen *Herodias* daughter daunce, he had not so rashly graunted her Saint *Iohn Baptist* head: Had not *Eua* seene the Apple and also shee was tempted with the beauty of the Serpent who as our Schoole-men doth write, that he shewed himselfe like a faire young man, but had not she seene it I say, she had not eaten therof to her owne griefe and many more. By sight, the wife of *Putyphar* was moued to lust after her seruant *Ioseph*; It is saide of *Simerrymes* of *Babilon*, that after her husbands death, she waxed so vnsatiable in carnall lust, that two men at one time could not satisfie her desire, and so by her vnsatiablenesse at length all *Persia* grew full of whoores.

And likewise of one *Venise* a strumpet in *Ciprts* it is supposed that by her fame and ill life, caused all *Cipris* at length to be full of queanes.

And of one faire *Rodap* in Ægypt who was the first noted woman in that Countrey, but at length all the whole countrey became full of Strumpets.

Is it not strange that the seede of one man, should breede such woe vnto all men.

One saide vnto his friend come let vs goe see a pretty wench, the other made this answer; I haue (said he) shaken such fetters from my heeles, and I will neuer goe where I knowe I shall repent afterwards, but yet happily some may say vnto me: if thou shouldest refuse the company or the curtesie of a woman, then she would account thee a soft spirited foole, a milk-sop, & a meacock.

But

But alas fond foole, wilt thou more regard their babble then thine owne blisse, or esteeme more their strumps, then thine owne welfare? dost thou not knowe that women alwaies striue against wisedome, although many times it be to their vtter ouerthrow? Like the Bee which is often hurt with hir owne honey, euen so women are often plagued with their owne conceit, waying downe loue with discurtesie, giuing him a weed, which presents them with flowers: as their catching in iest, and their keeping in earnest, and yet she thinks that she keepes her selfe blamelesse and in all ill vices she would goe namelesse, but if she carry it neuer so cleane, yet in the end she will be accounted but for a cunny catching quean, and yet she will sweare that she will thriue, as long as she can finde one man aliue, for she thinkes to doe all her knauery inuisible, she will haue a figg leafe to couer her shame, but when the fig leafe is dry and withered, it doth showe their nakednesse to the world, for take away their painted cloathes, and then they looke like ragged walls: take away their ruffes and they looke ruggedly, their coyfes and stomachers and they are simple to beholde: their haire vntrust and they looke wildely, and yet there are many which laies their netts to catch a pretty woman, but he which getteth such a prize gaines nothing by his aduenture, but shame to the body and danger to the soule, for the heat of the young blood of these wantons, leades many vnto destruction for this worlds pleasure. It chaunts your mindes, and infeebleth your bodyes with diseases, it also scandalleth your good names, but most of all it indangereth your soules; how can it otherwise choose, when lust and vncleanesse continually

E keepes

keepes them company, gluttony and sloth serueth them at the table, pride and vaine glory apparelleth them, but these seruants will wax weary of their seruice, and in the end they shall haue no other seruantes to attend them, but onely shame, griefe and repentance; but then, oh then (you will say) when it is too late; Oh would to God that we had beene more carefu'l of true glorious modesty, and lesse cunning to keepe wantons company: Oh therefore remember and thinke beforehand, that euery sweete hath his sower; then buy not with a drop of honey a gallan of gall, doe not thinke that this worlds pleasure will passe away with a trifle and that no sooner done but presently forgotten; No, no, answer your selues that the punishment remaineth eternally, and therefore better it were, to be an addle egg then an euill bird. For we are not borne for our selues to liue in pleasure, but to take paines and to labour for the good of our Countrey, yet so delightfull is our present sweetnes, that we neuer remember the following sower, for youth are to to easie woone and ouercome with the worlds vanities: Oh too soone (I say) is youth in the blossomes deuoured with the caterpillars of foule lust and lasciuious desires, the black Feind of Hell by his inticing sweete sinne of lust drawes many young witts to confusion, for in time it drawes the hart blood of your goodnames, & that being once lost is neuer gotten againe.

Againe, Lust causeth you to doe such foule deedes, which makes your foreheads for euer afterwards seeme spotted with blacke shame and euerlasting infamy, by which meanes your graues after death are closed vp with times scandall. And yet women are easily wooed and
soone

soone won, got with an apple and lost with the paring, young witts are soone corrupted, womens bright beauties breedes curious thoughtes, and golden guiftes easily ouercome wantons desires, with changing modesty into pastimes of vanity, and being once delighted therein, continues in the same without repentance: you are only the peoples wonder, and misfortunes banding ball tost vp and downe the world with woe vppon woe, yea ten thousand woes will be galloping hard at your heeles and pursue you wheresoeuer you goe, for those of ill report cannot stay long in one place, but rome and wander about the world and yet euer vnfortunate, prospering in nothing, forsaken and cast out from all ciuill companies, still in feare least authority with the sword of Iustice bar them of liberty: Loe thus your liues are dispised walking like night Owles in misery, and no comfort shall be your friend but onely repentance comming to late and ouer-deare bought : A pennance and punishment, due to all such hated creatures as these are.

 Therefore beleeue all you vnmarried wantons, and in beleeuing grieue, that you haue thus vnluckily made your selues neither maidens, widowes, nor wiues, but more vile then filthy channell durt fit to be swept out of the heart and suburbes of your Countrey, oh then suffer not this worldes pleasure to take from you the good thoughtes of an honest life : But downe downe vppon your knees you earthly Serpents , and wash away your black sinne with the cristall teares of true sorrow and repentance, so that when you wander from this inticing world, you may be washed and cleansed from this foule leprosie of nature.

E 2   Loe

Loe thus in remorse of minde, my tongue hath vttered to the wantons of the world the aboundance of my heartes griefe, which I haue perceiued by the vnseemely behauiour of vnconstant both men and women, yet men for the most part are touched but with one fault, which is drinking too much, but it is said of women that they haue two faultes, that is, they can neither say well nor yet doe well.

For commonly women are the most part of the forenoone painting themselues and frizling their haires, and prying in their glasse, like Apes to pranck vp themselues in their gaudies; like Poppets, or like the Spider which weaues a fine web to hang the flie: amongst women she is accounted a slut which goeth not in her silkes, therefore if thou wilt please thy Lady thou must like and loue, sue and serue, and in spending thou must lay on load, for they must haue maintainance how soeuer they get it, by hooke or by crooke, out of *Iudas* bag or the Deuills budget, thou must spare neither lands nor liuing, mony nor gold.

For women will account thee a pinch-penny if thou be not prodigall, and a dastard if thou be not ventrous, for they account none valiant except they be desperate: if silent, a sot, if full of words, a foole, iudging all to be Clownes which be not Courtiers. If thou be cleanely in thine apparrell they will terme thee proud, if meane in apparrell a slouian, if tall, a lunges, if short, a dwarfe, for they haue ripe wittes and ready tonges, and if they get an inch they will claime an elle: she will coll thee about the necke with one hand, but the other shall be diuing into thy pocket, and if thou take her with the manner, then it

was

was but in ieſt, but many times they take in ieſt (and if they be not ſpied) keepe it in earneſt, but if thy pockets growe empty, and thy reuenues will not hold out longer to maintaine her pompe and brauery, then ſhe preſently leaues to make much of thy perſon, and will not ſticke to ſay vnto thee, that ſhe could haue beſtowed her loue on ſuch a one as would haue maintained her like a woman, ſo by theſe means they weaue the web of their own woe, and ſpinne the thred of their owne thraldome, if they lacke they will lacke at the laſt, for they will cut it out of the whole cloath ſo long as the peece will hold out.

Is not the Bee hiued for his hony, the ſheepe ſheared for his fliece, the oxe necke wrought for his maiſters profite, the fowle plucked for her feathers, the tree grafted to bring foorth fruit, and the earth laboured to bring foorth corne: but what labour or coſt thou beſtoweſt on a woman is all caſt away, for ſhe will yeelde thee no profite at all, for when thou haſt done all, and giuen them all that they can demaund, yet thou ſhalt be as well rewarded as thoſe men were whome *Eſop* hired for three halfe pence a day to heare him recite his fables. Theſe things being wiſely conſidered, then what a foole art thou to blinde thy ſelfe in their bold behauiour, and bow at their beckes, and come at their calls, and ſell thy lands to make them ſwimme in their ſilkes, and ſit in their iewells, making *Iill* a Gentlewoman, inſomuch that ſhe careth not a penny for the fineſt, nor a figge for the proudeſt, ſhe is as good as the beſt although ſhe haue no more honeſty then barely to ſerue her owne turne, ſuffring euery mans fingers as deepe in the diſh as thine are in the platter, and euery man to angle where thou caſteſt thy hooke,

E3

hooke, holding vp to all that come, not much vnlike a Barbers chaire, that so soone as one knaue is out another is in, a common hackney for euery one that will ride, a boat for euery one to rowe in: now if thy wealth doe begin to faile, then she biddeth thee farewell, & giueth thee the *adieu* in the deuills name, not much vnlike the knauish porters in *Bristow*, who will crie, a new maister a new, and hang vp the old: if the matter be so plaine then consider this, that the house where such a one keepeth her residence is more odious with slander then carrion doth infect the ayre with stinke, let them flatter how they will there is no loue in them, but from the teeth outward. I blaze their properties the plainer & giue thee the stronger reasons, because I would haue thee loath the alluring traines of such deceitfull & lasciuious women, although she make great protestations of loue, and therto bindeth her selfe with most damnable oathes, then beleeue her left of all, for there is no more hold in her oathes nor in her loue then is certainly of a faire day in Aprill although it look neuer so cleere, yet it may turne to a fowle. I haue seene a Courtizan thus pictured out?

First a faire young man blind, and in his armes a beautifull woman with one hand in his pocket, shewing her theft, and a knife in the other hand to cut his throat.

Now peraduenture thou maist say vnto that thou dost not know one woman from another without some triall, because all women are in shape alike, for the sowre crab is like the sweet pippin: true it is, so the Rauen is a bird, and the Swan is but a bird, euen so many women are in shape Angells, but in quallities Deuills, painted coffins with rotten bones: the Estridge carrieth faire feathers

but

but ranck flesh: the hearb *Molio* carrieth a flower as white as snowe, but a roote as black as inke.

Although women are beautifull, shewing pitty, yet their heartes are blacke, swelling with mischiefe, not much vnlike vnto old trees, whose outward leaues are faire and greene and yet the body rotten: if thou haunt their houses thou wilt be enamoured, and if thou doe but hearken to these *Syrens* thou wilt be inchanted, for they will allure thee with amorous glances of lust, and yet kill thee with bitter lookes of hate: they haue dymples in their cheeks to deceiue thee, & wrinckles in their browes to betray thee: they haue eies to intice, smiles to flatter, imbracements to prouoke, beckes to recall, lippes to inchant, kisses to enflame, and teares to excuse themselues.

If God had not made them only to be a plague to men, he would neuer haue called them necessary euills, and what are they better? for what do they either get or gain, saue or keepe? nay they doe rather spend and consume all that which man painefully getteth: a man must be at all the cost and yet liue by the losse.

It is very easie for him which neuer experienced himselfe in that vaine pleasure, or repenting pleasure, choose you whether, I meane the accompanying of lewde women, but such as are exercised and experimented in that kinde of drudgery: they I say haue a continuall desire, and temptation is ready at hand, therefore take heede at the first, suffer not thy selfe to be led away into lustfull folly, for it is more easie for a young man or maid to forbeare carnall act then it is for a widdow, and yet more easie for a widdow then for her that is married and hath her husband wanting, then take heede at the first, for there is nothing

nothing gotten by women but repentance.

For women are like the bay tree which is euer greene but without fruit, or like the vnprofitable thorne which beareth as trim a blossome as the apple, this is nothing but to tell thee that thou must not iudge of gold by the colour, nor of womens quallities by their faces, nor by their speaches, for they haue delicate tongues which will rauish and tickle the itching eares of giddy headed young men, so foolish, that they thinke themselues happy if they can but kisse the dasie whereon their loue doth tread, who if she frowne then he descends presently into hell, but if she smile then is he carried with winges vp into heauen, there is an old saying that when a dogge wagges his taile he loues his maister.

Some thinke that if a woman smile on them she is presently ouer head and eares in loue, one must weare her gloue, another her garter, another her coulers of delight, and another shall spend and liue vpon the spoile which she getteth from all the rest, then if thou wilt giue thy body to the Chirurgian and thy soule to the Deuill, such women are fit for thy diet. Many creatures of euery kinde resemble women in conditions, for some horse an vnskilfull rider can hardly disorder, and some againe in despight of the best rider that is will haue a iadish tricke: some Hauke although he be ill serued yet will sit quiet, and some if neuer so well serued yet will continually flie at checke: againe, some hounds by no meanes will forsake their vndertaken game, and some againe in despite of the huntsman will continually runne at randome: and some men will steale if their hands were bound behinde them, and some againe wil rather sterue then steale, euen

so

so some women will not be wonne with seauen yeares louing, and some againe will offend with an houres liberty.

Therefore if thou study a thousand yeares thou shalt finde a woman nothing else but a contrary vnto man, nay, if thou continue with her a hundreth yeares yet thou shalt finde in her new fancies and contrary sortes of behauiour, therefore if all the world were paper, and all the sea inke, and all the trees and plants wer pens, and euery man in the world were a writer, yet were they not able with all their labour and cunning to set downe all the crafty deceits of women.

Now me thinkes I heare some of you say that young wits are soone corrupted, and that womens bright beauty breedeth curious thoughts in men, also golden guifts easily ouercommeth wanton womens desires, and therby makes them become Venus darlings, quite changing customes of modesty, into passions of vanity, wherein once delighted they continue in the same without repentance or sorrow; But our alas you lasciuious Dames these leude conditions of yours, will speedily bring all your ioyes to sorrow.

CHAP. III.

This third Chapter sheweth a remedy against loue, also many reasons not to be to hasty in choise of a Wife. But if no remedy but thou wilt marry, then howe to choose a wife, with a Commendations of the good, vertuous, and honest women.

F   BE

BE not to hasty to marry, for doubt least thou marry in hast, and repent by leasure; For there are many troubles which cometh galloping at the heeles of a woman, which many young men before-hand doe not thinke of, the world is not all made of otemeale, nor all is not golde that glisters, nor a smiling countenance is no certaine testimoniall of a merry heart, nor the way to heauen is not strewed with rushes; no more is the cradle of ease in a womans lapp, if thou wer't a seruant or in bondage before, yet when thou marriest, thy toile is neuer the nere ended, but euen then & not before, thou changest thy golden life which thou didest lead before, in respect of the married, for a drop of honey which quickly turneth to be as bitter as worm-wood; And therefore farre better it were to haue two plowes going then one cradle, and better a barne filled then a bed, therefore cut of the occasion which may any way bring thee into fooles paradice. Then first and aboue all shun Idlenes, for idlenes is the beginner and maintainer of loue, therefore apply thy selfe about some affaires, or occupied about some businesse, for so long as thy minde or thy body is in labour the loue of a woman is not remembred nor lust neuer thought vpon, but if thou spend thy time idlely amongst women, thou art like vnto him which playeth with the Bee, who may sooner feele of her sting then taste of her honey, he that toucheth pitch may be defiled therewith, Roses vnaduisedly gathered prickles our fingers; Bees vngently handled stinges our faces, and yet the one is pleasant and the other is profitable, and if thou be in company of women, the Deuill himselfe hath

not

not more illusions to gett men into his net, then women haue deuises & inuentions to allure men into their loue, and if thou suffer thy selfe once to be lead into fooles paradice, (that is to say) the bed or closet wherein a woman is, (then I say) thou art like a bird snared in a lime bush, which the more she striueth the faster she is. It is vnpossible to fall amongst stones and not to be hurt, or amongst thornes and not be prickt, or amongst nettles and not be stung, a man cannot carry fire in his bosome and not burne his cloathing, no more can a man liue in loue but it is a life as wearisome as hell, and hee that marrieth a wife matcheth himselfe vnto many troubles. If thou marieft a still and a quiet woman, that will seeme to thee that thou ridest but an ambling horse to hell, but if with one that is froward and vnquiet, then thou wert as good ride a trotting horse to the deuil: herein I will not be my owne caruer, but I referre you to the iudgement of those which haue seene the troubles and felt the torments; for none are better able to iudge of womens qualities, then those which haue them; none feeles the hardnes of the Flint but he that strikes it; none knowes where the shooe pincheth but he that weares it. It is said that a man shold eat a bushel of Salte with one which he meanes to make his freind, before he put any great confidence or trust in him; And if thou be so long in choosing a freind, in my minde thou hadst need to eate two bushels of Salte with a woman before thou make her thy wife; otherwise, before thou hast eaten one bushell with her, thou shalt taste of tenne quarters of sorowe, & for euery dram of pleasure an ounce of paine, and for euery pinte of honey a gallon of gall, and for euery ynche of mirth an ell

F 2   of mone.

of mone. In the beginning a womans loue seemeth delightfull, but endeth with destruction, therefore he that trusteth to the loue of a woman shall be as sure as he that hangeth by the leafe of a tree in the later end of Summer, and yet there is great difference betwixt the standing poole and the running streame, although they are both waters.

Therefore of two euills choose the least and auoid the greatest, but my meaning is not heere to aduise thee to choose the least woman, for the little women are as vnhappy as the greatest, for though their statures be little yet their heartes are big, then speake faire to all but trust none, and say with *Diogenes*, it is too soone for a young man to marry and too late for old men. One asked a Philosopher what the life of a married man was, he answered, misery, and what is his felicity? misery, for he still lingers in hope of a further ioy, and what is his end? and he still answered, misery.

There are sixe kindes of women which thou shouldest take heede that thou match not thy selfe to any one of them, that is to say, good nor bad, faire nor foule, rich nor poore, for if thou marriest one that is good thou maist quickly spill her with too much making of her, for when prouender pricks a woman then she will growe knauish: and if bad, then thou must support her in all her bad actions, and that will be so wearisome vnto thee that thou hadst as good drawe water continually to fill a bottomlesse tub: if she be faire then thou must doe nothing else but watch her: and if she be foule and loathsom who can abide her: if she be rich then thou must forbeare her because of her wealth: and if she be poore then thou must

must maintaine her.

   For if a woman be neuer so rich in dowry, happy by her good name, beautiful of body, sober of countenance, eloquent in speach, and adorned with vertue, yet they haue one ill quallity or other which ouerthroweth all the other, like vnto that Cow which giueth great store of milke and presently striketh it down with her foote, such a cow is as much to be blamed for the losse as to be commended for the guift, or like as when men talke of such a man or such a man, he is an excellent good workeman, or he is a good Chirurgian, or a good Phisition, or he is a pretty fellowe of his hands, but if they conclude with this word, but it is pitty he hath one fault, which commonly in some men is drunkennesse, then I say, if he were endued with all the former quallities, yet they cannot gaine him so much credit to counterpoise the discredite that commeth thereby.

   It is said of men that they haue that one fault, but of women it is said that they haue two faultes, that is to say, they can neither say well nor doe well: there is a saying that goeth thus, that things farre fetcht and deare bought are of vs most dearely beloued, the like may be said of women, although many of them are not farre fetched yet they are deare bought, yea and so deare, that many a man curseth his hard penniworths and bannes his owne heart, for the pleasure of the fairest woman in the world lasteth but a honny moone, that is, while a man hath glutted his affections and reaped the first fruit, his pleasure being past sorrowe and repentance remaineth still with him.

   Therefore to make thee the stronger to striue against these

F 3

these tame Serpents thou shalt haue more strings to thy bowe then one, it is safe riding at two ankers, alwaies looke before thou leape least thy shinnes thou chance to breake, now the fire is kindled let vs burne this other fagot and so to our matter againe.

If a woman be neuer so comely thinke her a counterfeit, if neuer so straite thinke her crooked, if she be well set call her a bosse, if slender a hazell twig, if browne thinke her as blacke as a crowe, if well coloured a painted wall, if sad or shamefac'd then thinke her a clowne, if merry and pleasant then she is the liker to be a wanton. But if thou be such a foole that thou wilt spend thy time and treasure, the one in the loue of women, & the other to delight them, in my minde thou resemblest the simple Indians, who apparell themselues most richly when they goe to be burned.

But what should I say? some will not giue their bable for the Tower of London. He that hath sailed at sea hath seene the dangers, and he that is married can tell of his owne woe, but he that was neuer burnt will neuer dread the fire Some will goe to dice although they see others loose all their mony at play, and some will marry though they beg together, is it not strange that men should bee so foolish to doat on women who differ so farre in nature from men? for a man delights in armes & in hearing the ratling drums, but a woman loues to heare sweet musicke on the Lute, Cittern, or Bandora: a man reioyceth to march among the murthered carkasses, but a woman to dance on a silken carpet: a man loues to heare the threatnings of his Princes enemies, but a woman weepes when she heares of wars: a man loues to lye on the cold grasse,

but a

but a woman must be wrapped in warme mantles: a man tryumphes at warres, but a woman reioyceth more at peace.

If a man talke of any kinde of beast or fowle, presently the nature is knowne: as for example, the Lyons are all strong and hardy, the Hares are all fearefull & cowardly, the Doues are all simple, and so of all beasts and fowle the like, I meane few or none swaruing from his kinde; but women haue more contrary sorts of behauiour then there be women, and therefore impossible for a man to know all, no nor one part of womens quallities all the daies of thy life.

Some with sweete words vndermine their husbands, as *Dalila* did *Samson*, and some with bhiding and brauling are made weary of the world, as *Socrates* and others: *Socrates* when his wife did chide and braul would goe out of the house till all were quiet againe, but because he would not scold with her again it grieued her the more; for on a time she watched his going out and threwe a chamber pot out of a window on his head, ha ha quoth he I thought after all this thunder there would come raine.

There is an history maketh mention of one named *Annynious*, who inuited a friend of his to goe home with him to supper, but when he came home he found his wife chyding and brawling with her maydens, whereat his guest was very much discontented. *Annynious* turning to him, said; good Lord how impacient art thou? I haue suffred her these twenty yeares, and canst not thou abide her two houres? by which meanes he caused his wife to leaue chyding, and laughed out the matter.

There

There is no woman but either she hath a long tongue or a longing tooth, and they are two ill neighbours, if they dwell together, for the one will lighten thy purse if it be still pleased, and the other will waken thee from thy sleepe if it be not charmed. Is it not strange of what kinde of mettall a womans tongue is made of, that neither correction can chastise nor faire meanes quiet, for there is a kinde of venome in it, that neither by faire meanes nor fowle they are to be ruled: all beasts by man are made tame, but a womans tongue will neuer be tame, it is but a small thing and seldome seene, but it is often heard, to the terror and vtter confusion of many a man.

Therefore as a sharpe bit curbes a froward horse, euen so a curst woman must be roughly vsed, but if women could hold their tongues, then many times men would their hands. As the best metled blade is mixt with jron, euen so the best woman that is is not free from faults, the goodliest gardens are not free from weedes, no more is the best nor the fairest woman void of ill deedes.

He that vseth troth to tell
May blamed be though he say well.
If thou be young marry not yet,
If thou be old thou wilt haue more wit,
For young mens wiues will not be taught,
And olde mens wiues are good for naught.
When he that for a woman striueth by lawe
Shall striue like a coxcomb and proue but a dawe.
Then buy not thou with ouermuch cost
The thing which yeildes but labour lost.

Diuers beasts and fowle by nature haue more strength in one part of the body then in another, as the Eagle in
the

the beake, the Vnicorn in the horne, the Bull in the head, the Beare in his armes, the Horse in his breast, the Dog in his teeth, the Serpent in his taile, but a womans chiefe strength is in her tongue, the Serpent hath not so much venome in his taile as she hath in her tongue, and as the Serpent neuer leaueth hissing and stinging and seeking to doe mischiefe: euen so some women are neuer well except they be casting out venome with their tongues to the hurt of their husbands or of their neighbours, therefore he that will disclose his secrets to a woman is worthy to haue his haire cut with *Samson*, for if thou vnfoldest any thing of secret to a woman the more thou chargest her to keepe it close the more she will seeme as it were to be with childe till she haue reuealed it amongst her gossips, yet if one should make doubt of her secresie she would seeme angry, and say, I am no such light huswife of my tongue as they whose secretes lye at their tongues ends, which flyes abroad so soone as they open their mouthes, therefore feare not to disclose your secrets to me, for I was neuer touched with any staine of my tongue in all my life, nay she will not sticke to sweare that she will tread it vnder foote or bury it vnder a stone, yet for all this beleeue her not, for euery woman hath one especiall gossip at the least which she doth loue and affect aboue all the rest, and vnto her she runneth with all the secrets she knoweth.

There is an history maketh mention of one *Lyas* whom King *Amasis* commaunded to goe into the market and to buy the best and profitablest meat he could get, and he bought nothing but tongues, the King asked him the reaso why he bought no other meat, who made this answer,

G   I was

I was commaunded to buy the best meate, and from the tongue come many good and profitable speaches, then the King sent him againe and bad him buy the worst and vnprofitablest meat, and he likewise bought nothing but tongues, the King againe asked him the reason, from nothing (said he) commeth worse venome then from the tongue, and such tongues most women haue.

A Romaine history maketh mention of one of the chiefe gouernors of Rome that had a sonne whose name was *Papirius*, whose father tooke him with him to the Councell-house that thereby he might learne wisdome, wishing him withall to keepe their secrets: his mother was diuers times asking of the boy what they did at the Counsaile-house, and what the cause was of their often meeting; on a time young *Papirius* fearing to displease his father, and hoping to satisfie his mother told her this, mother (said he) there is hard hold amongst them about the making of a law that euery man shall haue two wiues or euery woman two husbands, and so farre as I can perceiue it is likely to be concluded vpon that euery man shall haue two wiues.

The next day when his father and he were gone to the Counsaile-house she bestirred her selfe, and got most of the chiefe women of the City together, and told them what a law was like to be made if it were not preuented, and so to the Counsaile-house they went a great flocke of them, but when they came in the Gouernours were all amazed, and asked the cause of their comming? and one of the women hauing leaue to speake said thus; wheras you are about to make a law that euery man shall haue two wiues, consider with your selues what vnquietnesse

nesse and strife thereby will arise, but (said she) it were better that one woman should haue two husbands, that if the one were on businesse abroad the other might be at home: now when the Gouernours heard this speach they meruailed wherupon it should arise; then young *Papirius* requested that he might speake, who presently resolued them the cause of the womens comming, so they greatly commended the boy and laughed the women to scorne.

Heere thou maist perceiue by a tast what wine is in the butt, if the Dragons head be full of poyson what venome then thinke you lurketh in his tayle? All this is but to tell thee of the doubts and dangers that come by marriage, yet I would not haue all men feare to lye in the grasse because a Snake lyeth there, nor all men feare to goe to Sea because some men are drowned at Sea, neither doe I warrant al men to feare to goe to their beds because many dye in their beds, then marry a Gods name, but againe and againe take heede to the choyce of thy wife.

Marry not for beauty without vertue, nor choose for riches without good conditions: *Salomon* amongst many other notable sentences fit for this purpose saith, that a faire woman without discreet manners is like a gold ring in a Swines snowte; and if thou marriest for wealth, then thy wife many times will cast it in thy dish saying, that of a begger she made thee a man: againe, if thou marriest for beauty and aboue thy calling thou must not onely beare with thy wiues folly, but with many vnhappy words, for she will say she was blinded in fancying thee, for she might haue had Captaine such a one, or this Gentleman, or that, so that thou shalt neuer neede to craue a

foule

foule word at her hands in seauen yeares, for thou shalt haue enowe without asking, besides I feare me thou wilt be better headed then wedded, for she will make thee weare an Oxe feather in thy cap, yet he which hath a faire wife will aduenture on a thousand infamies only in hope to keepe her in the state of an honest woman, but if she be ill giuen doe what thou canst, break thy heart & bend thy study neuer so much, yet all will not serue, thou maist let her goe all houres of the night she will neuer meete with a worse then her selfe, except she meete with the deuill himselfe.

 Therefore yet once more I aduise thee in the choyce of thy wife to haue a speciall regard to her quallities and conditions before thou shake hands or iumpe a match with her: Also inquire and marke the life and conuersation of her Parents, let the old prouerbe put thee in minde hereof, that an euill Bird layeth an ill Egge, the Cat will after hir kinde, an ill Tree cannot bring foorth good friute, the young Crab goeth crooked like the Damme, the young Cocke croweth as the olde, and it is a very rare matter to see children tread out of the paths of their Parents. He that commeth into a Fayre to buy a Horse will prye into euery part to see whether he be sound of winde and limb, and without cracke or flaw, and whether his breeding were in a hard soyle, or whether he be well pac'd, and likewise he will haue a care that his horse shall haue all outward markes which betoken a good horse, yet with all the cunning he hath he may be deceiued, but if he proue a iade he may put him away at the next Fayre.

But

But if in choise of thy wife thou be deceiued as many men are, thou must stand to thy worde which thou madest before the whole Parish, which was to take her for better or worse for there is no refusing, she will sticke to thee as close as a saddle to a horses backe, and if she be frowardly giuen, then she will vexe thee night and day.

Amongst the quietest coupples that are yet houshold iarres will arise, but yet such quarrells which happen in the day are often quallified with kisses in the night, but if it be not so ended, their thirst will goe foreward like the carriage which is drawne betweene two horses taile to taile, & if she cannot reuenge hir selfe with hir tongue nor with her handes, nor with conuaying thy goods, yet she will pay thee home priuately, for if thou strike with thy sword she will strike with the scabard, choose not the rapier by his ringing, nor thy wife by her singing, for if thou doest thou maist be very well deceiued in both, for thy rapier may proue a gad, and thy wife but little better.

Now if thou aske me howe thou shouldst choose thy wife, I answere that thou hast the whole world to make choise, & yet thou maist be deceiued: An ancient Father being asked by a young man howe he should choose a wife, he answered him thus? When thou seest a flock of maidens together, hudwinke thy selfe fast and runne amongst them, and looke which thou chafest, let her be thy wife, the young man tolde him that if he went blindfolded he might be deceiued: and so thou maiest (quoth the olde man) if thy eyes were open, for in the choise of thy wife, thou must not trust thy owne eyes for they will deceiue thee and be the cause of thy woe, for she may seeme good whose waste is like a wande, or she which

hath

hath a spider fingered hand, or she which on her tiptoes still doth stand, and neuer read but in a goulden booke, nor will not be caught but with a golden hooke, or such a one as can stroke a beard, or looke a head, and of euery flea make herselfe affraide, if thou hadest a spring such a wench would make him a begger if he were halfe a King, then this is no bargaine for thee. But harke a little further, the best time for a young man to marry, is at the age of twenty and fiue, and then to take a wife of the age of seauenteene yeares or there about, rather a maide then a widdow, for a widdow she is framed to the conditions of another man & can hardly be altred, so that thy paines will be double, for thou must vnlearne a widdow and make her forget and forgoe her former corrupt and disordered behauiour, the which is hardly to be done, but a young womā of tender yeares is flexable and bending, obedient and subiect to doe any thing, according to the will and pleasure of her husband.

And if thy state be good, marry neare home and at leisure, but it thy state be weake and poore, then to better thy selfe after enquiry made of her wealth & conditions, goe farre off & dispatch it quickly, for doubt least tatling speaches which commonly in these cases runns betwixt party and party and breakes it off euen then when it is come to the vp shot, but as I haue already saide, before thou put thy foote out of doores make diligent enquiry of her behauiour, for by the market-folke thou shalt heare how the market goeth, for by enquiry thou shalt heare whether she be wise, vertuous and kinde, wearing but her owne proper haire, and such garments as her friends estate will affoord, or whether she loue to keepe within

within the house, and to the seruantes haue a watchfull eie, or if she haue a care when to spend & when to spare, and be content with what God doth send, or if she can shed no kinde of vnstained teares but when iust cause of hearty sorrow is, and that in wealth and woe, in sicknesse and in health she will be all alike, such a wife will make thee happy in thy choise.

Although some happen on a deuillish and vnhappy woman yet all men doe not so, and such as happen ill it is a warning to make them wise, if they make a second choise, not that all other shall haue the like fortune, the sunne shineth vpon the good and bad, and many a man happeneth sooner on a shrew then a ship: Some thriue by dicing but not one in an hundreth therefore dicing is ill husbandry, some thriue by marriage, and yet many are vndone by marriage, for marriage is either the making or marring of many a man, and yet I will not say but amongst dust there is Pearle found, and in hard rockes Dyamonds of great value, and so amongst many women there are some good, as that gracious and glorious Queene of all women kinde the Virgin *Mary* the mother of all blisse, what wun her honour but an humble minde and her paines and loue vnto our Sauiour Christ.

Sara is commended for the earnest loue that she bare to her husband, not onely for calling him Lord, but for many other quallities: Also *Susanna* for her chastity and for creeping on her knees to please her husband, but ther are meaner Histories which makes mentiō of many others, as that of *Demetryes* how that she was content to run Lackey by her husbands side.

Likewise *Lucretia* for the loue and loyalty, that shee
bare

bare to her husband, being vnkindely abused by an vnchast lecher against her will, she presently slew herselfe in the presence of many, rather then she would offer her body againe to her husband being but one time defiled.

It is recorded of an Earle called *Guzcalles*, that vpon the Kinges displeasure was committed to prison, and his wife hauing liberty to visit him in prison, on a time she caused him to put of his apparell and to put on hers, and so by that meanes got out by the Porter and she remained in prison, and so by this meanes he escaped the angry rage of his Prince, and afterwards his wife was deliuered also.

Likewise it was no small loue that *Artymenes* bare to her husband, for after his death she built such a famous Sepulcher (and bestowed the greatest part of her wealth thereon) in so much that at this day it is called one of the seauen great wonders of the world.

Also *Plinie* makes mention of a fisher-man which dwelt neere vnto the sea side, and he fell sicke of an vncurable disease, by which meanes he indured such torment and paine, that it would haue grieued any creature to beholde him, his carefull and louing wife laboured & trauelled farre and neare to procure his health againe, but at last seeing all meanes in vaine, she brake out with him in these wordes: Death at one time or another will come, and therefore rather then you should any longer indure this miserable life, I am content that both of vs preuent death before he come, so this poore grieued man did yeild to her counsel, and they went foorth to the top of an exceeding high Rock, and there this woman bound herselfe fast to her husband, and from thence casting themselues

themselues downe, ended thiir liues together.

Now I doe not commend this death to be godly, although it shewed great loue in the woman, no doubt but the King of *Ayra* had a very kinde and louing wife as shal appeare, for when *Alexander* the great had depriued him of the greatest part of his Kingdome yet he bare it out very patiently with a valiant and manly courage, and without any showe of outward griefe at all, but when newes was brought him that his wife was dead, he then most grieuously brake into teares and wept bitterly, and withall he said : that the losse of his whole kingdome should not haue grieued him so much, as the death of his wife.

It is also recorded of *Allexander*, that at the death of his wife he made such a sorrowfull kinde of speach for her, saying : Death were kinde if he tooke nothing but that which offendeth, but he hath taken her away which neuer offended, oh death thou hast bereaued me of the better part of my life.

It is also said of *Valerius Maximus* that he on a time finding two Serpents in his bed-chamber being strangely amazed thereat, he demaunded of the South-saiers what it meaned? and they answered him : That of necessity he must kill one of them, and if he killed the male then he himselfe must first dye, and if the female then his wife should dye before him, & because he loued his wife better then himselfe, he most grieuously made choise of the male and killed him first, and shortly after he dyed leauing his wife a widdow.

Such a kinde foole to his wife was *Adam*, for hee was forbidden on paine of death not to eate of the tree of

H good

good and euill, yet for all that *Adam* notwithstanding to gratifie his wiues kindnesse, and for loue he bare her refused not to hassard his life by breach of that commaundement.

But because in all thinges there is a contrary which sheweth the difference betwixt the good and the bad, euen so both of men and women there are contrary sortes of behauiour, if in thy choise thou happen on a good wife desire not to change, for there is a prouerbe saieth, seldome commeth a better, & there is none poorer then those that haue had many wiues, thou maiest beare a good affection towards thy wife, & yet let her not know it, thou maist loue her well and yet not carry her on thy backe, a man may loue his house well and yet not ride on the ridge, loue thy wife and speake her faire although thou doe but flatter her, for women loue to be accounted beautifull, and to be mistresses of many maides, & to liue without controlement, and kinde wordes as much please a woman as any other thing whatsoeuer, and a mans chiefest desire should be first the grace of God, a quiet life and an honest wife, a good report and a friend in store, and then what neede a man to aske any more.

Saint *Paul* saith those which marry doe well, but he also saith those which marry not doe better, but yet also he saieth that it is better to marry then to burne in lust; A merry companion being asked by his friend why he did not marry, he made this answere and said; That he had beene in Bedlam two or three times, and yet he was neuer so mad to marry, and yet there is no ioy nor pleasure in the world which may be compared to marriage, so the parties are of neere equall yeares and of good qualities,

lities, then good fortune and badde is welcome to them, both their cares are equall, and their ioyes equall, come what will all is welcome & all is common betwixt them, the husband doth honour and reuerence her, and if he be rich he committeth all his goods to her keeping, and if he be poore and in aduersity, then hee beareth but the one halfe of the griefe, & furthermore she will comfort him with all the comfortable meane she can deuise, and if he will stay sollitary in his house she will keepe him company, if hee will walke into the fieldes why she will goe with him, and if he be absent from home she sigheth often and wisheth his presence, being come home he findeth content sitting smyling in euery corner of his house to giue him a kinde and a hearty welcome home, and she receiueth him with the best and greatest ioy that she can, many are the ioyes and sweet pleasures in marriage, as in o. children, being young they play, prattle, laugh, and sheweth vs many pretty toyes to moue vs to mirth and laughter, and when they are bigger growne and that age or pouerty hath afflicted the Parents, then they shew the duty of children in releeuing their olde aged parents with what they can shift for, and when their parents are deade they bring them to the earth from whence they came.

 Yet now consider on the other side, when a wrinkled and toothles woman shall take a beardles boy (a short tale to make of it) there can bee no liking nor louing betweene such contraries but continuall strife and debate, so likewise when matches are made by the Parentes, and the dowery told and paid before the young couple haue any knowledge of it, & so many times are forced against

H 2   their

their mindes, fearing the rygor and displeasure of their parents, they often promise with their mouthes that which they refuse with their hearts.

Also if a man marry a wife for faire lookes without dowrie, then their loue will soone wax colde, in somuch that they vse them not like wiues but rather like kitchinstuffe, wheras those which marry rich wiues they haue alwaies something to be in loue withall; It is a common thing now adaies, that faire women without riches finde more louers then husbands.

Choose not a wife too faire, nor too foule, nor too rich, for if she be faire euery one will be catching at her, and if she be too foule a man will haue no minde to loue her which no body likes, & if too rich thou thinkest to marry with one which thou meanest to make thy companion, thou shalt finde her a commaunding mistresse; so that riches causeth a woman to be proud, beauty makes her to be suspected, and hard fauoured maketh her to be hated. Therefore choose a wife young, well borne, and well brought vp, reasonable rich, and indifferent beautifull, and of a good witt and capacity; also in choise of a wife a man should note the honesty of the parents, for it is a liklyhood that those children which are vertuously brought vp will follow the steppes of their parents, but yet many a tree is spoiled in the hewing, there are some which haue but one only Daughter and they are so blinded with the extreame loue that they beare her, that they will not haue her hindred of her will whatsoeuer she desireth, so suffering her to liue in all wanton pleasure and delicacy, which afterwardes turneth to be the cause of many inconueniences.

Now

Now the Father before he marry his daughter is to sift throughly the quallities, behauiour, and life of his Son in lawe, for he which meeteth with a ciuil and an honest sonne in lawe getteth a good sonne, and he which meeteth with an ill one, casteth away his daughter.

The husband must prouide to satisfie the honest desires of his wife, so that neither by necessity nor superfluity be the occasion to worke her dishonour, for both want and plenty, both ease and disease makes some women oftentimes vnchaste: and againe many times the wife seeing the husband to take no care for her, making belike this reckoning that no body else will care for her or desire her: but to conclude this point, shee onely is to be accounted honest, who hauing liberty to doe amisse yet doth it not.

Again, a man should thus accoūt of his wife, as the onely treasure he enioyeth vpon earth, and he must also accoūt that there is nothing more due to the wife, then the faithfull, honest, and louing company of the husband, he ought also in signe of loue to impart his secrets and counsell vnto his wife, for many haue found much comfort and profit by taking their wiues counsell, and if thou impart any ill hap to thy wife she lighteneth thy griefe, either by comforting thee louingly, or else in bearing a part thereof patiently: Also if thou espie a fault in thy wife, thou must not rebuke her angerly or reprochfully, but onely secretly betwixt you two, alwaies remembring that thou must neither chide nor playe with thy wife before company, those that play and dally with them before company, they doe thereby set other mens teeth an edge, and make their wiues the lesse shamefaste.

H 3   It

It behooueth the married man alwaies to shew himselfe in speech and countenance both gentle and amiable, for if a woman of modest behauiour seeth any grose inciuilitie in her husband, she doth not only abhorre it but also thinketh with her selfe, that other men are more discreete and better brought vp, therefore it standeth him vpon to be ciuill and modest in his doings least he offend the chaste thoughts of his wife, to whose liking he ought to confirme himselfe in all honest and reasonable things, and to take heede of euery thing which may mislike her.

Why some men loue their louers better then their husbands, the reason is, the louer in the presence of his Lady is very curious of his behauiour, that he vseth no vnseemely gestures, whereby there may no suspition of iealousie or any acception be taken by any thing he doth: it behoueth euery woman to haue a great regard to her behauiour, and to keepe her selfe out of the fier, knowing that a woman of suspected chastity liueth but in a miserable case, for there is but small difference by being naught and being thought naught, and when she heareth other women ill spoken of, let her thinke in her minde what may be spoken of her, for when a woman hath gotten an ill name, whether it be deseruedly or without cause, yet she shall haue much adoe to recouer againe her honour and credit thereof: let a woman auoide so much as may be the company of a woman which hath an ill name, for many of them indeauour by their euill fashions and dishonest speach, to bring others to do as they do, and many of them wish in their hearts that all women were like vnto themselues: it may be said

of

of many women that the feathers are more worth then the birds, therefore it behoueth euery woman to behaue herselfe so sober and chaste in countenance and speach that no man may be so bolde as to assaile her: for commonly Castles, if they come once to parlie, are at point to yeeld, therefore if a woman by chance be set vpon let her make this anfwer, when I was a maide I was at the disposition of my parents, but now I am married I am at the pleasure of my husband, therefore you were best speake to him and to knowe his minde what I shall doe, and if her husband be out of the way, let her alwaies behaue her selfe as if he were present.

Also a woman may consider, if her husband be choloricke and hasty she must ouercome him with milde speach, and if he chide she must holde her peace, for the answer of a wise woman is silence, and she must stay to vtter her minde vntill he be appeased of his fury and at quiet, for if women many times would houlde their tongues they might be at quiet: there was a very angry cupple married together, and a friend being with them at supper asked them how they could agree together being both so froward and testy: the goodman made him this anfwere, when I am angry my wife beareth with me, and when she is angry I beare with her, for with what heart can a man so much as touch a haire of his wiues head, (I meane rigorously) for the husband ought to rebuke hir with wordes secretly, and seeke to reforme her by good counsaile, he ought to lay before her the shame of ill dooing, and the praise of well doing, if this will not serue yet he ought rather paciently to forbeare her then rigorously to beate her, for she is flesh of thy flesh,

flesh & there is no man so foolish to hurt his owne flesh, a man ought to be a comforter of his wife, but then he ought not to be a tormenter of her, for with what face can a man imbrace that body which his hands hath battered and bruised, or with what heart can a woman loue that man which can finde in his heart to beat her.

Also when a man findeth a painfull and a carefull woman, which knoweth when to spend and when to spare and to keepe the house in good order, then the husband, will not deny such a wife any necessary thing belonging to the house : But if she be a light huswife who liueth without doing of any thing, without caring for husband children or seruantes, or any other thing belonging to the house, thereby shewing although her body be in the house yet her minde is abroad, which redowneth to her shame and to her husbands great hinderance, for when the Mistres is occupied in vanity, the seruantes care lesse for her propfit but looke to their owne, for while the mistresse playeth the mayden strayeth.

But these men are to be laughed at, who hauing a wife and a sufficient wife to doe all the worke within doores which belongs for a woman to doe, yet the husband will set hennes abroad, season the pott, and dresse the meate, or any the like worke which belongeth not to the man. Such husbands many times offend their wiues greatly & they wrong themselues ; for if they were imployed abroad in matters belonging to men they would be the more desirous being come home to take their ease, then to trouble their wiues & seruantes in medling with their matters, for the rule and gouerment of the house belongeth to the wife.

And

And he that hath a wife of his owne and goeth to another woman, is like a rich theefe which will steale when he hath no neede.

Amongst all the creatures that God hath created, there is none more subiect to misery then a woman, especially those that are fruitfull to beare children, for they haue scarce a monthes rest in a whole yeare, but are continually ouercome with paine, sorrow & feare, as indeed the danger of child-bearing must needes bee a great terror to a woman which are counted but weake vessells, in respect of men, and yet it is supposed that there is no disease that a man indureth, that is one halfe so grieuous or painefull as child-bearing is to a woman ; Let it be the tooth-ache, goute or collick, nay if a man had all these at once, yet nothing comparable to a womans paine in hir trauaile with childe.

Now if thou like not my reasons to expell loue, then thou maiest try *Ouids* arte who prescribes a salue for such a sore, for hee counsels those which feeles this horrible heate, to coole their flames with hearbs which are colde of nature, as Rew and Lettis, and other hearbes too long to resite : also he saith, thou shouldest abstaine from excesse of meate and drinke, for that prouokes thy minde greatly to lust: also to hunt, to hawke, to shoot, to bowle, to run, to wrastle and some other play, for this will keep thy minde from thinking of lust: also shun slothfulnes & idlenes, for these are the onely nurces of loue, eschew malancholly or sadnes and keepe merry company, turne thy eyes from the place where bewitching spirits are, least the remembrance doe increase and rubb thy galled minde : also to eschew the place where thou didst first

I

feele

feele the fire that burneth thy minde with such vnquiet thought; Likewise saith hee, beware thou doe not twise peruse the secret flattering letters of thy supposed frendly ioy, for if thou doe not refuse the often view thereof, it will much increase thy griefe, dolour and annoy: vse no talke of her whome thou louest, nor once name her, for that will increase thy care, by thinking in thy minde that thou beholdest her face: but some are perswaded that no rules of reason can asswage this griefe, for loue is lawles and obeyes no lawe, no nor yet no counsell can perswade nor take effect or subdue the affection of his bewitched spirits. Furthermore *Ouid* prescribes other reasons to expell the heat of loue, for where loue is setled the louers are many times hindered of their purpose: Somtimes for want of friends consent, or distance of place; then & in such a case his counsell is to loue two or three, for loue being so diuided, makes the loue of one the lesse thought vpon: or else saeth hee satisfie thy lust vpon some other dame, for it wil also helpe to weare the former loue out of thy minde; Loe thus *Ouid* shot but yet he mist the marke, not for want of learning but for want of grace, for grace subdues and treads all vices vnder foote, although morral meanes doth prescribe diuerse other dicts to waste the heate of loues desire, as long absence from the place where thy liking liues, for the coales of company doth kindle and heate the heart, that with absence would be voide of harme, for absence doth quallifie that fire and coole the minde of those which many times the cōpany of wantons doth warme for he which doth not shun the place where *Venus* in her glory sits, hath no care of himselfe but suffers her to supprise his witts.

The

The Bearbaiting or the vanity of Widdowes: choose you whether.

Woe be vnto that vnfortunate man that matcheth himselfe vnto a widowe, for a widowe will be the cause of a thousand woes, yet there are many that doe wish themselues no worse matched then to a rich widowe, but thou dost not knowe what griefes thou ioynest with thy gaines, for if she be rich she will looke to gouerne, and if she be poore then art thou plagued both with beggery and bondage; againe, thy paines will be double in regard of him which marrieth with a maide, for thou must vnlearne thy widowe, and make her forget her former corrupt and disordered behauiour, the which if thou take vpon thee to doe, thou hadst euen as good vndertake to wash a Blackamore white, for commonly widowes are so froward, so waspish, and so stubborne, that thou canst not wrest them from their wills, and if thou thinke to make her good by stripes thou must beate her to death. One hauing married with a froward widowe she called him theefe & many other vnhappy names, so he tooke her and cut the tongue out of her head, but she euer afterwards would make the signe of the gallowes with her fingers to him.

It is seldome or neuer seene that a man marrieth with a widowe for her beauty nor for her personage, but only for her wealth and riches, and if she be rich & beautifull withal', then thou matchest thy selfe to a she deuill, for she will goe like a Peacocke and thou like a Woodcocke, for she will hide her money to maintaine her pride: and if thou at any time art desirous to be merry in her company,

pany, she wil say thou art merry because thou hast gotten a wife that is able to maintaine thee, where before thou wast a begger and hadst nothing: and if thou shewe thy selfe sad she will say thou art sad because thou canst not bury her thereby to inioy that which she hath: if thou make prouision to fare well in thy house she will bid thee spend that which thou broughtest thy selfe.

If thou shewe thy selfe sparing she will say thou shalt not pinch her of that which is her owne, and if thou doe any thing contrary to her minde she will say her other husband was more kinde: if thou chance to dine from home she will bid thee goe sup with thy Harlots abroad: if thou go abroad and spend any thing before thou commest home, she will say a begger I found thee and a begger thou meanest to leaue mee: if thou stay alwaies at home she will say thou art happy that hast gotten a wife that is able to maintaine thee idle: if thou carue her the best morsell on the table, though she take it yet she will take it scornefully and say, she had a husband that would let her cut where she liked her selfe.

And if thou come in wel disposed thinking to be merry, and intreating her with faire words, she will call thee dissembling hipocrit, saying, thou speakest me faire with thy tongue but thy heart is on thy minions abroad. Loe these are the franticke trickes of froward widowes, they are neither well full nor fasting, they will neither goe to Church nor stay at home, I meane in regard of their impatient mindes, for a man shall neither be quiet in her sight nor out of her sight, for if thou be in her sight she will vexe thee as before said, & out of her sight thy owne conscience will torment and trouble thy minde to think

on the

on the purgatory which perforce thou must indure when thou commest home.

  She will make Clubs trump when thou hast neuer a blacke card in thy hand, for with her cruell tongue shee will ring thee such a peale that one would thinke the deuill were come from Hell, besides this thou shalt haue a brended slut like a hell-hagge with a paire of pappes like a paire of dung-pots shall bring in thy dinner, for thy widow wil not trust thee with a wench that is hansome in thy house, now if that vpon iust occasiō thou thorwest the platters at the maides head, seeing thy meate brought in by such a slutte and so sluttishly drest, then will thy widdow take pepper in the nose and stampe and stare, and looke so sower as if she had come but euen then from eating of Crabs, saying, if thou hadst not maried with me thou wouldest haue beene glad of the worst morsell that is heere, then thou againe replying sayest, if I had not bene so mad, the deuill himselfe would not haue had thee, and then without cause thou blamest her of olde age and of iealousie and for hiding her money, and by cōuaying away of her goods which thou hast bought with the displeasure of thy friends and discredite to thy selfe, in regard of her yeares; then againe she on the other side runneth out to her neighbours, and there she thundereth out a thousand iniuries that thou dost her, saying, my Corne he sendeth to the market, and my Cattell to the fayre, and looke what he openly findeth he taketh by force, and what I hide secretly he priuily stealeth it away, and playeth away all my money at dice. Loe thus he consumeth my substance and yet hateth my person, no longer then I feede him with money can I enioy
                                              his

his company, now he hath that he sought for he giueth me nothing else but froward answeres and foule vsage, and yet God knowes of pure loue I married him with nothing, but now his ill husbandry is like to bring to ruine both me and my children, but now all this while she doth not forget to tell of her owne good huswifery, saying, I sit working all day at my needle or at my distaffe, and he like an vnthrift and a whoremonger runneth at randome, thus they are alwaies stretching their debate vpon the racke of vengeance.

 Loe heere is a life, but it is as wearisome as hell, for if you kisse in the morning being friends, yet ere noone ready to throwe the house out at the windowe. The Papists affirme that Heauen is won by Purgatory, but in my minde a man shall neuer come into a worse Purgatory then to be matched with a froward widowe: He that matcheth himselfe to a widowe and three children matcheth himselfe to foure theeues. One hauing maried with a widowe, it was his lucke to bury her, but not before he was sore vexed with her, for afterwards he lying on his death-bed his friends exhorted him to pray vnto God that his soule might rest in Heauē, & he asked them this question, whether (said he) doe you thinke my wife is gone? and they said vnto him no doubt but that your wife is gone to Heauen before you, he replied, I care not whether I goe so I goe not where my wife is, for feare I meete with her and be vexed with her as I haue beene heeretofore.

 Another hauing married with a widowe being one day at a sermon heard the Preacher say, whosoeuer will be saued let him take vp his crosse and follow me, this
mad

mad fellow after sermon was ended tooke his wife vpon his backe and came to the Preacher and said, heere is my crosse, I am ready to follow thee whether thou wilt.

Another hauing married with a widowe which shewed herselfe like a Saint abroad but a Deuill at home, a frend of her husbands told him that he had gotten him a good, still and a quiet wife, yea marry quoth the married man you see my shooe is faire and new, but yet you know not where it pincheth me.

Another merry companion hauing married with a widowe and carrying her ouer the Sea into France there sodainely arose a great storme, in so much that they were all in danger of drowning, the maister of the Ship called vnto the marriners & bad them take & throw ouer bord all the heauiest goodes in the Ship, this married man hearing him say so, hee tooke his widdow and threw her ouer-boord, and being asked the reason why he did so, he said that he neuer felt any thing in all his life that was so heauy to him as she had beene.

Another hauing married with a widdow, and within a while after they were married, she went out into the garden, and there finding her husbands shirt hang close on the hedge by her maides smocke, she went presently and hanged herselfe for a iealous conceit that she tooke, and a merry fellow asked the cause why she hanged herselfe, and being tolde that it was for iealousie: I would said he that all trees did beare such fruit.

Thou maist thinke that I haue spoken inough concerning Widdowes, but the further I runne after them the further I am from them, for they are the summe of the seauen deadly sinnes, the Feinds of Sathan and the gates

of

of Hell; Now me thinketh I heare some say vnto me that I should haue tolde them this lesson sooner, for too late cometh medicine when the patient is dead, euen so too late commeth counsaile when it is past remedy, but it is better late then neuer, for it may be a warning to make others wise.

But why do I make so long a harueft of so little corne? seeing the corne is bad my harueft shall cease, for so long as women doe ill they must not thinke to be well spoken of, if you would be well reported of or kept like the Rose when it hath lost the colour, then you should smell sweet in the bud as the Rose doth, or if you would be tasted for old wine you should be sweet at the first like a pleasant Grape, then should you be cherished for your courtesie, and comforted for your honesty, so should you be preserued like the sweete Rose, & esteemed of as pleasant wine, but to what purpose do I go about to instruct you knowing that such as counsell the deuill can neuer amend him of his euill.

And so praying those which haue already made their choyse and seene the troubles and felt the torments that is with women, to take it merrily, and to esteeme of this booke onely as the toyes of an idle head.

Nor I would not haue women murmer against me for that I haue not written more bitterly against men, for it is a very hard winter when one Woolfe eateth another, and it is also an ill bird that defileth her owne nest and a most vnkinde part it were for one
man to speake ill of
another.

FINIS.

A MOVZELL FOR MELASTOMVS,

The Cynicall Bayter of, and foule mouthed Barker against *EVAHS SEX.*

Or an Apologeticall Answere to that *Irreligious and Illiterate* Pamphlet made by *Io. Sw.* and by him Intituled, *The Arraignement of Women.*

By *Rachel Speght.*

PROVERBS 26. 5.
Answer a foole according to his foolishnesse, lest he bee wise in his owne conceit.

LONDON,
Printed by *Nicholas Okes* for *Thomas Archer*, and are to be sold at his shop in Popeshead-Pallace. 1617.

To all vertuous Ladies Honourable or Worshipfull, and to all other of Heuahs sex fearing God, and louing their iust reputation, grace and peace through Christ, to eternall glory.

IT was the similie of that wise and learned *Lactantius*, that if fire, though but with a small sparke kindled, bee not at the first quenched, it may worke great mischiefe and dammage: So likewise may the scandals and defamations of the malevolent in time proue pernitious, if they bee not nipt in the head at their first appearance. The consideration of this (right Honourable and Worshipfull Ladies) hath incited me (though yong, and the vnworthiest of thousands) to encounter with a furious enemy to our sexe, least if his vniust imputations should continue without answere, he might insult and account himselfe a victor; and by such a conceit deale, as Historiographers report the viper to doe, who in the Winter time doth vomit forth her poyson, and in the spring time sucketh the same vp againe, which becommeth twise as deadly

deadly as the former: And this our pestiferous enemy, by thinking to prouide a more deadly poyson for women, then already he hath foamed forth, may euaporate, by an addition vnto his former illeterate Pamphlet (intituled *The Arraignement of Women*) a more contagious obtrectation then he hath already done, and indeed hath threatned to doe. Secondly, if it should haue had free passage without any answere at all (seeing that *Tacere is, quasi consentire*) the vulgar ignorant might haue beleeued his Diabolicall infamies to be infallible truths, not to bee infringed; whereas now they may plainely perceiue them to bee but the scumme of Heathenish braines, or a building raised without a foundation (at least from sacred Scripture) which the winde of Gods truth must needs cast downe to the ground. A third reason why I haue aduentured to fling this stone at vaunting *Goliah* is, to comfort the mindes of all *Heuahs* sex, both rich and poore, learned and vnlearned, with this Antidote, that if the feare of God reside in their hearts, maugre all aduersaries, they are highly esteemed and accounted of in the eies of their gracious Redeemer, so that they need not feare the darts of enuy or obtrectators: For shame and disgrace (saith *Aristotle*) is the end of them that shoote such poysoned shafts. Worthy therefore of imitation is that example of *Seneca*, who when he was told that a certaine man did
exclaime

The Epistle Dedicatorie.

exclaime and raile against him, made this milde answere; Some dogs barke more vpon custome then curstnesse; and some speake euill of others, not that the defamed deserue it, but because through custome and corruption of their hearts they cannot speake well of any. This I alleage as a paradigmatical patterne for all women, noble & ignoble to follow, that they be not enflamed with choler against this our enraged aduersarie, but patiently consider of him according to the portraiture which he hath drawne of himselfe, his Writings being the very embleme of a monster.

This my briefe Apologie (Right Honourable and Worshipfull) did I enterprise, nor as thinking my selfe more fit then others to vndertake such a taske, but as one, who not perceiuing any of our Sex to enter the Lists of encountring with this our grand enemy among men, I being out of all feare, because armed with the truth, which though often blamed, yet can neuer be shamed, and the Word of Gods Spirit, together with the example of vertues Pupils for a Buckler, did no whit dread to combate with our said malevolent aduersarie. And if in so doing I shall bee censured by the iudicious to haue the victorie, and shall haue giuen content vnto the wronged, I haue both hit the marke whereat I aymed, and obtained that prize which I desired. But if *Zoilus* shall adiudge me presumptuous in Dedicating this my *Chirograph*

The Epistle Dedicatorie,

graph vnto personages of so high ranke; both because of my insufficiency in literature and tendernesse in yeares: I thus Apologize for my selfe; that seeing the *Bayter of Women* hath opened his mouth against noble as well as ignoble, against the rich as well as the poore; therefore meete it is that they should be ioynt spectators of this encounter: And withall in regard of my imperfection both in learning and age, I need so much the more to impetrate patronage from some of power to sheild mee from the biting wrongs of *Momus*, who oftentimes setteth a rankling tooth into the sides of truth. Wherefore I being of *Decius* his mind, who deemed himselfe safe vnder the shield of *Cæsar*, haue presumed to shelter my selfe vnder the wings of you (Honourable personages) against the persecuting heate of this fierie and furious Dragon; desiring that you would be pleased, not to looke so much *ad opus*, as *ad animum*: And so not doubting of the fauourable acceptance and censure of all vertuously affected, I rest

Your Honours and worships Humbly at commandement,

Rachel Speght.

A

I f Reason had but curb'd thy witlesse will,
O r feare of God restrain'd thy rauing quill,
S uch venime fowle thou would'st haue blusht to spue,
E xcept that Grace haue bidden thee adue:
P rowesse disdaines to wrastle with the weake,
H eathenish affected, care not what they speake.

S educer of the vulgar sort of men,
W as Sathan crept into thy filthie Pen,
E nflaming thee with such infernall smoake,
T hat (if thou had'st thy will) should women choake?
N efarious fiends thy sence heerein deluded,
A nd from thee all humanitie excluded.
M onster of men, worthie no other name,
  For that thou d d'st assay our Sex to shame.

     Ra. Sp.

Faults escaped in this Impression.

Page 1. lin. 12. in the Preface for *rearing* reade *roauing*.
page 4. line 17. for *Ironica* reade *Ironia*.
page 7. line 19. for *not touch* reade *not to touch*.
page 11 line 20. for *Meriam* reade *Miriam*.
page 21. line 13. for *tongs* reade *tongues*.
page 32. line 21. for *adulterous* reade *idolatrous*.
page 33. line 20. for *Arganox* reade *Organo*.

B   Not

¶ Not vnto the veriest Ideot that euer set Pen to Paper, but to the Cynicall Bayter of Women, or, metamorphosed Misogynes, Ioseph Swetnam.

From standing water, which soon putrifies, can no good fish be expected; for it produceth no other creatures but those that are venemous or noisome, as snakes, adders, and such like. Semblably, no better streame can we looke, should issue from your idle corrupt braine, then that whereto the ruffe of your fury (to vse your owne words) hath moued you to open the sluce. In which excrement of your roaring cogitations you haue vsed such irregularities touching concordance, and obserued so disordered a methode, as I doubt not to tel you, that a very Accidence Scholler would haue quite put you downe in both. You appeare heerein not vnlike that Painter, who seriously indeuouring to pour-

The Preface.

pourtray *Cupids Bowe*, forgot the String : for you beeing greedie to botch vp your mingle mangle inuectiue againſt Women, haue not therein obſerued, in many places, ſo much as as Grammer ſenſe. But the emprieſt Barrell makes the lowdeſt ſound; and ſo we wil account of you.

Many propoſitions haue you framed, which (as you thinke) make much againſt Women, but if one would make a Logicall aſſumption, the concluſion would be flat againſt your owne Sex. Your dealing wants ſo much diſcretion, that I doubt whether to beſtow ſo good a name as the Dunce vpon you : but Minority bids me keepe within my bounds; and therefore I onlie ſay vnto you, that your corrupt Heart and railing Tongue, hath made you a fit ſcribe for the Diuell.

In that you haue termed your virulent foame, *the Beare-bayting of Women*, you haue plainely diſplayed your owne diſpoſition to be Cynicall, in that there appeares no other Dogge or Bull, to bayte them, but your ſelfe. Good had it beene for you to haue put on that Muzzell, which Saint *Iames* would haue all Chriſtians to weare; *Speake not euill one of another* : and then had you not ſeemed ſo like the Serpent *Porphirus*, as now you doe; which, though full of deadly poyſon, yet being toothleſſe, hurteth none ſo much as himſelfe. For you hauing gone beyond the limits not of *Humanitie* alone, but

Iames 4. 11.

B 2 of

The Preface.

of Christianitie, haue done greater harme vnto your owne soule, then vnto women, as may plainely appeare. First, in dishonoring of God by palpable blasphemy, wresting and peruerting euerie place of Scripture, that you haue alleadged; which by the testimony of Saint *Peter*, is to the destruction of them that so doe. Secondly, it appeares by your disparaging of, and opprobrious speeches against that excellent worke of Gods hands, which in his great loue he perfected for the comfort of man. Thirdly, and lastly, by this your hodge-podge of heathenish Sentences, Similies, and Examples, you haue set forth your selfe in your right colours, vnto the view of the world: and I doubt not but the Iudicious will account of you according to your demerit: As for the Vulgar sort, which haue no more learning then you haue shewed in your Booke, it is likely they will applaud you for your paines.

1.Pet.3.16.

As for your *Bugge-beare* or aduice vnto Women, that whatsoeuer they doe thinke of your Worke, they should conceale it, lest in finding fault, they bewray their galled backes to the world; in which you allude to that Prouerbe, *Rubbe a galled horse, and he will kicke:* Vnto it I answere by way of Apologie, that though euerie galled horse, being touched, doth kicke; yet euery one that kickes, is not galled: so that you might as well haue said, that because bur. folks dread the fire, therfore none feare fire but those

that

The Preface.

that are burnt, as made that illiterate conclusion which you haue abſurdly inferred.

In your Title Leafe, you arraigne none but lewd, idle, froward and vnconſtant women, but in the Sequele (through defect of memorie as it ſeemeth) forgetting that you had made a diſtinction of good from badde, condemning all in generall, you aduiſe men to beware of, and not to match with any of theſe ſixe ſorts of women, *viz. Good* and *Badde*, *Faire* and *Foule*, *Rich* and *Poore*: But this doctrine of Diuells Saint *Paul* foreſeeing would be broached in the latter times, giues warning of.   1.Tim.4.3.

There alſo you promiſe a Commendation of wiſe, vertuous, and honeſt women, when as in the ſubſequent, the worſt words, and filthieſt Epithites that you can deuiſe, you beſtow on them in generall, excepting no ſort of Women. Heerein may you be likened vnto a man, which vpon the doore of a ſcuruie houſe ſets this Superſcription, *Heere is a very faire houſe to be let*: whereas the doore being opened, it is no better then a dogge-hole and darke dungeon.

Further, if your owne words be true, that you wrote with your hand, but not with your heart, then are you an hypocrite in Print: but it is rather to be thought that your Pen was the bewrayer of the abundance of your minde, and that this was but a little morter to dawbe vp agayne the wall, which you intended to breake downe.

The Preface.

The reuenge of your rayling Worke wee leaue to Him, who hath appropriated vengeance vnto himselfe, whose Pen-man hath included Raylers in the Catalogue of them; that shall not inherite Gods Kingdome, and your selfe vnto the mercie of that iust Iudge, who is able to saue and to destroy.

Your vndeserued friend,

RACHEL SPEGHT.

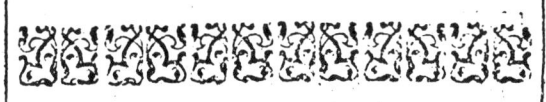

In praise of the Author and her Worke.

IF little Dauid, that for Israels sake,
  esteemed neyther life nor limbe too deare,
In that he did aduenture without dread,
  to cast at him, whom all the hoste did feare,
A stone, which brought Goliah to the ground,
Obtain'd applause with Songs and Timbrels sound.

Then let another young encombatant
  receiue applause, and thankes, as well as hee:
For with an enemie to Women kinde,
  she hath encountred, as each wight may see:
And with the fruit of her industrious toyle,
To this Goliah she hath giuen the foyle.

Admire her much I may, both for her age,
  and this her Mouzell for a blacke-mouth'd wight,
But praise her, and her worke, to that desert,
  which vnto them belongs of equall right
I cannot; onely this I say, and end,
Shee is vnto her Sex a faithfull friend.

PHILALETHES.

IF he that for his Countrie doth expose
  himselfe vnto the furie of his foe,
Doth merite praise and due respect of those,
  for whom he did that perill vndergoe:
Then let the Author of this Mouzell true
Receiue the like, of right it is her due.

For she to shield her Sex from Slaunders Dart,
  and from inuectiue obtrectation,
Hath ventured by force of Learnings Art,
  (in which she hath had education)
To combate with him, which doth shame his Sex,
By offring feeble women to perplex.

PHILOMATHES.

PRaise is a debt, which doth of due belong
  To those, that take the path of Vertues trace,
Meating their wayes and workes by Reasons rule,
  Hauing their hearts so lightned with Gods grace,
That willlingly they would not him offend,
But holily their liues beginne and end.

Of such a Pupill vnto Pietie
As is describ'd, I doe intend to speake,
A Virgin young, and of such tender age,
As for encounter may be deemd too weake,
  Shee hauing not as yet seene twenty yeares,
  Though in her carriage older she appeares.

Her wit and learning in this present Worke,
More praise doth merit, then my quill can write:
Her magnanimitie deserues applaud,
In ventring with a fierie foe to fight:
  And now in fine, what shall I further say?
  But that she beares the triumph quite away.

FAVOVR B.

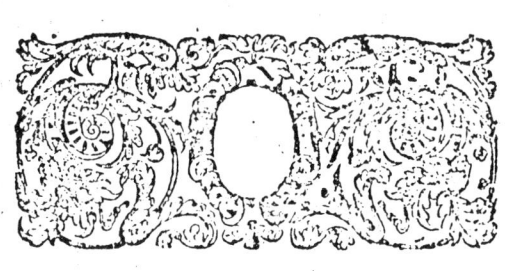

A Mouzell for *Melastomus* the
Cynicall Bayter of, and foule-
mouthed Barker against
Evahs Sex.

PROVERBS 18. 22.

He that findeth a wife, findeth a good thing, and receiueth fauour of the Lord.

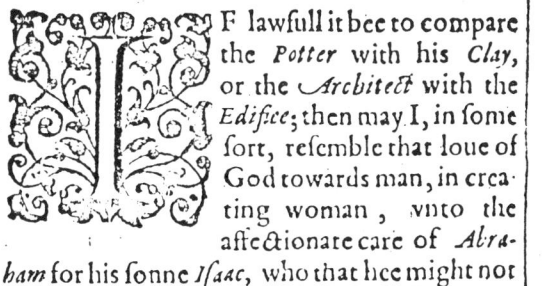

IF lawfull it bee to compare the *Potter* with his *Clay*, or the *Architect* with the *Edifice*; then may I, in some sort, resemble that loue of God towards man, in creating woman, vnto the affectionate care of *Abraham* for his sonne *Isaac*, who that hee might not take to wife one of the daughters of the *Canaanites*, did prouide him one of his owne kindred. Gen. 24. 4.

Almighty

C

Almighty God, who is rich in mercie, hauing made all things of nothing, and created man in his owne image: that is, (as the Apostle expounds it) *In wisedome, righteousnesse and true holinesse*; making him Lord ouer all: to auoide that solitarie condition that hee was then in, hauing none to commerce or conuerse withall but dumbe creatures, it seemed good vnto the Lord, that as of euery creature hee had made male and female, and man onely being alone without mate, so likewise to forme an helpe meete for him. *Adam* for this cause being cast into a heauy sleepe, God extracting a rib from his side, thereof made, or built, Woman; shewing thereby, that man was as an vnperfect building afore woman was made; and bringing her vnto *Adam*, vnited and married them together.

Thus the resplendent loue of God toward man appeared, in taking care to prouide him an helper before hee saw his owne want, and in prouiding him such an helper as should bee meete for him. Soueraignety had hee ouer all creatures, and they were all seruiceable vnto him; but yet afore woman was formed, there was not a meete helpe found for *Adam*. Mans worthinesse not meriting this great fauour at Gods hands, but his mercie onely mouing him thereunto: I may vse those words which the *Iewes* vttered when they saw Christ weepe for *Lazarus, Behold how hee loued him*: Behold, and that

Ephe.2 4.

Col.3 30.
Ephe.4.24.

Gen.2.20.

Gen.c.20.

Iohn 11.36.

that with good regard, Gods loue; yea his great loue, which from the beginning hee hath borne vnto man: which, as it appeares in all things; so next, his loue in Christ Iesus apparantly in this; that for mans sake, that hee might not be an vnite, when all other creatures were for procreation duall, hee created woman to bee a solace vnto him, to participate of his sorrowes, partake of his pleasures, and as a good yoke-fellow beare part of his burthen. Of the excellencie of this Structure, I meane of Women, whose foundation and original of creation, was Gods loue, do I intend to dilate. 1.Cor.11.9.

Of Womans Excellency, with the causes of her creation, and of the sympathie which ought to be in man and wife each toward other.

THe worke of Creation being finished, this approbation thereof was giuen by God himselfe, That *All was very good*: If All, then *woman*, who, excepting man, is the most excellent creature vnder the Canopie of heauen. But if it be obiected by any. Gen.1.31.

First, that woman, though created good, yet by giuing eare to Sathans temptations, brought death & misery vpon all her posterity. 1 Obiect.

Secondly, That *Adam was not deceiued, but that the woman was deceiued, and was in the transgression.* 2 Obiect. 1.Tim.2.14.

C 2 Thirdly,

3 Obiect. 1.Cor.7.1.	Thirdly, that Saint *Paul* saith, *It were good for a man not to touch a woman.*
4 Obiect. Eccles.7.30.	Fourthly, and lastly, that of *Salomon*, who seemes to speake against all of our sex; *I haue found one man of a thousand, but a woman among them all haue I not found*, whereof in it due place.
Obiect. answered.	To the first of these obiections I answere; that Sathan first assailed the woman, because where the hedge is lowest, most easie it is to get ouer, and she being the weaker vessell was with more facility to be seduced: Like as a Cristall glasse sooner receiues a cracke then a strong stone pot. Yet we shall finde the offence of *Adam* and *Eue* almost to paralell: For as an ambitious desire of being made like vnto God, was the
Gen.3.22.	motiue which caused her to eate, so likewise was it his; as may plainely appeare by that *Ironica*, *Behold, man is become as one of vs:* Not that hee was so indeed; but heereby his desire to attaine a greater perfection then God had giuen him, was reproued. Woman sinned, it is true, by her infidelitie in not beleeuing the Word of God, but giuing credite to Sathans faire pro-
Gen.3.4.	mises, that *shee should not die*; but so did the man too: And if *Adam* had not approoued of that deed which *Eue* had done, and beene willing to treade the steps which she had gone, hee being her Head would haue reproued her, and haue made the commandement a bit to re-straine him from breaking his Makers Iniuncti-on:

on: For if a man burne his hand in the fire, the bellowes that blowed the fire are not to be blamed, but himselfe rather, for not being carefull to auoyde the danger: Yet if the bellowes had not blowed, the fire had not burnt; no more is woman simply to bee condemned for mans transgression: for by the free will, which before his fall hee enioyed, hee might haue auoyded, and beene free from beeing burnt, or singed with that fire which was kindled by Sathan, and blowne by *Eue*. It therefore serued not his turne a whit, afterwardes to say, *The woman which thou gauest mee, gaue mee of the tree, and I did eate*: For a penalty was inflicted vpon him, as well as on the woman, the punishment of her transgression being particular to her owne sex, and to none but the female kinde: but for the sinne of man the whole earth was cursed. And he being better able, then the woman, to haue resisted temptation, because the stronger vessell, was first called to account, to shew, that to whom much is giuen, of them much is required; and that he who was the soueraigne of all creatures visible, should haue yeelded greatest obedience to God. Genesis 3.12.

Genesis 3.17.

True it is (as is already confessed) that woman first sinned, yet finde wee no mention of spirituall nakednesse till man had sinned: then it is said, *Their eyes were opened*, the eies of their mind and conscience; and then perceiued they themselues naked, that is, not onely bereft of that Genesis 3.7.

that integritie, which they originally had, but felt the rebellion & disobedience of their members in the disordered motions of their now corrupt nature, which made them for shame to couer their nakednesse: then(and not afore) is it said that they saw it, as if sinne were imperfect, and vnable to bring a depriuation of a blessing receiued, or death on all mankind, till man (in whom lay the actiue power of generation) had transgressed. The offence therefore of *Adam* and *Eue* is by Saint *Austin* thus distinguished, *the man sinned against God and himselfe, the woman against God, her selfe, and her husband:* yet in her giuing of the fruit to eate had she no malicious intent towardes him, but did therein shew a desire to make her husband partaker of that happinesse, which she thought by their eating they should both haue enioyed. This her giuing *Adam* of that sawce, wherewith Sathan had serued her, whose sowrenesse afore he had eaten, she did not perceiue, was that, which made her sinne to exceede his: wherefore, that she might not of him, who ought to honour her, be abhorred, the first promise that was made in Paradise, God makes to woman, that by her Seede should the Serpents head be broken: whereupon *Adam* calles her *Heuah, life,* that as the woman had beene an occasion of his sinne, so should woman bring foorth the Sauiour from sinne, which was in the fullnesse of time accomplished; by which was manifested,

1 Pet.3.7.

Genesis 3.15.

sted, that he is a Sauiour of beleeuing women, no lesse then of men, that so the blame of sinne may not be imputed to his creature, which is good; but to the will by which *Eue* sinned, and yet by Christs assuming the shape of man was it declared, that his mercie was equiualent to both Sexes; so that by *Herods* blessed Seed (as Saint *Paul* affirmes) it is brought to passe, that *male and female are all one in Christ Iesus*. *(Galat. 4. 4.)* *(Galat. 3. 28.)*

To the second obiection I answer, That the Apostle doth not heereby exempt man from sinne, but onely giueth to vnderstand, that the woman was the primarie transgressour; and not the man, but that man was not at all deceiued, was farre from his meaning: for he afterward expresly saith, that as *in Adam all die, so in Christ shall all be made aliue*. *(2 Obiection answered.)* *(1 Cor. 15. 22.)*

For the third obiection, *It is good for a man not touch a woman*: The Apostle makes it not a positiue prohibition, but speakes it onelie because of the *Corinths* present necessitie, who were then persecuted by the enemies of the Church, for which cause, and no other, hee saith, *Art thou loosed from a wife? seeke not a wife*: meaning whilst the time of these perturbations should continue in their heate; *but if thou art bound, seeke not to be loosed: if thou marriest, thou sinnest not*, only increasest thy care: *for the married careth for the things of this world, And I wish that you were without care, that yee might cleaue fast vnto the Lord without separation*: For *(3 Obiection answered.)* *(1 Cor. 7.)*

the

the time remaineth, that they which haue wiues be as though they had none : for the persecuters shall depriue you of them, eyther by imprisonment, banishment, or death; so that manifest it is, that the Apostle doth not heereby forbid marriage, but onely aduiseth the *Corinths* to forbeare a while, till God in mercie should curbe the fury of their aduersaries. For (as *Eusebius* writeth) *Paul* was afterward married himselfe, the which is very probable, being that interrogatluely he saith, *Haue we not power to leade about a wife, being a sister, as well as the rest of the Apostles, and as the brethren of the Lord and Cephas?*

1. Corint. 9.5.

4. Object answered.

Eccles.7.30.

. The fourth and last obiection, is that of *Salomon*, *I haue found one man among a thousand, but a woman among them all haue I not found*: for answere of which, if we looke into the storie of his life, wee shall finde therein a Commentary vpon this enigmaticall Sentence included : for it is there said, that *Salomon* had seuen hundred wiues, and three hundred concubines, which number connexed make one thousand. These women turning his heart away from being perfect with the Lord his God, sufficient cause had hee to say, that among the said thousand women found he not one vpright. Hee saith not, that among a thousand women neuer any man found one worthy of commendation, but speakes in the first person singularly, *I haue not found*, meaning in his owne experience: for this assertion is to be holden a part of the confession of

1 King.11.3.

Pagnine.

of his former follies, and no otherwise, his repentance being the intended drift of *Ecclesiastes*.

Thus hauing (by Gods assistance) remoued those stones, whereat some haue stumbled, others broken their shinnes, I will proceede toward the period of my intended taske, which is, to decipher the excellency of women: of whose Creation I will, for orders sake obserue; First, the efficient cause, which was God; Secondly, the materiall cause, or that whereof shee was made; Thirdly, the formall cause, or fashion, and proportion of her feature; Fourthly and lastly, the finall cause, the end or purpose for which she was made. To beginne with the first.

The efficient cause of womans creation, was *Iehouah* the *Eternall*; the truth of which is manifest in *Moses* his narration of the sixe dayes workes, where he saith, *God created them male and female* : And *Dauid* exhorting all *the earth to sing vnto the Lord*; meaning, by a Metonimie, *earth*, all creatures that liue on the earth, of what nation or Sex soeuer, giues this reason, *For the Lord hath made vs.* That worke then can not chuse but be good, yea very good, which is wrought by so excellent a workeman as the Lord: for he being a glorious Creator, must needes effect a worthie creature. Bitter water can not proceede from a pleasant sweete fountaine, nor bad worke from that workman which is perfectly good, & in proprietie, none but he.

Genesis 1. 28.

Psal. 100. 3.

Psal. 100. 4.
Math. 19. 17.

D Secondly,

Secondly, the materiall cause, or matter whereof woman was made, was of a refined mould, if I may so speake: for man was created of the dust of the earth, but woman was made of a part of man, after that he was a liuing soule: yet was shee not produced from *Adams* foote, to be his too low inferiour; nor from his head to be his superiour, but from his side, neare his heart, to be his equall; that where he is Lord, she may be Lady: and therefore saith God concerning man and woman iointly, *Let them rule ouer the fish of the Sea, and ouer the foules of the Heauen, and ouer euery beast that moueth vpon the earth*: By which words, he makes their authority equall, and all creatures to be in subiection vnto them both. This being rightly considered, doth teach men to make such account of their wiues, as *Adam* did of *Eue*, *This is bone of my bone, and flesh of my flesh*: As also, that they neyther doe or wish any more hurt vnto them, then vnto their owne bodies: for men ought to loue their wiues as themselues, because hee that loues his wife, loues himselfe: And neuer man hated his owne flesh (which the woman is) vnlesse a monster in nature.

Thirdly, the formall cause, fashion, and proportion of woman was excellent: For she was neyther like the beasts of the earth, foules of the ayre, fishes of the Sea, or any other inferiour creature, but Man was the onely obiect, which she did resemble. For as God gaue man

Genesis 2.7.

Genesis 1.26.

Genesis 2.23.

Ephes.5.28.

a lofty countenance, that hee might looke vp toward Heauen, so did he likewise giue vnto woman. And as the temperature of mans body is excellent, so is womans. For whereas other Creatures, by reason of their grosse humours, haue excrements for their habite, as foules, their feathers, beasts, their haire, fishes, their scales, man and woman onely, haue their skinne cleare and smoothe. And (that more is) in the Image of God were they both created; yea and to be briefe, all the parts of their bodies, both externall and internall, were correspondent and meete each for other. *Gen. 1. 26.*

Fourthly and lastly, the finall cause, or end, for which woman was made, was to glorifie God, and to be a collaterall companion for man to glorifie God, in vsing her bodie, and all the parts, powers, and faculties thereof, as instruments for his honour: As with her voice to sound foorth his prayses, like *Meriam*, and the rest of her company; with her tongue not to vtter words of strife, but to giue good councell vnto her husband, the which hee must not despise. For *Abraham* was bidden to giue eare to *Sarah* his wife. *Pilate* was willed by his wife not to haue anie hand in the condemning of CHRIST; and a sinne it was in him, that hee listned not to her: *Leah* and *Rachel* councelled *Isacob* to do according to the word of the Lord: and the Shunamite put her husband in mind of harbouring the Prophet *Elisha*: her hands shold *Exod. 15. 20.* *Genesis 21. 12* *Math. 27. 19.* *Genesis 31. 16* *2 Kings 4. 9.*

be open according to her abilitie, in contributing towards Gods seruice, and distressed seruants, like to that poore widdow, which cast two mites into the Treasurie; and as *Marie Magdalen*, *Susanna*, and *Ioanna* the wife of *Herods* Steward, with many other, which of their substance ministred vnto CHRIST. Her heart should be a receptacle for Gods Word, like *Mary* that treasured vp the sayings of CHRIST in her heart. Her feete should be swift in going to seeke the Lord in his Sanctuarie, as *Marie Magdalen* made haste to seeke CHRIST at his Sepulchre. Finally, no power externall or internall ought woman to keep idle, but to imploy it in some seruice of GOD, to the glorie of her Creator, and comfort of her owne soule.

The other end for which woman was made, was to be a Companion and *helper* for man; and if shee must be an *helper*, and but an *helper*, then are those husbands to be blamed, which lay the whole burthen of domesticall affaires and maintenance on the shoulders of their wiues. For, as yoake-fellowes they are to sustayne part of ech others cares, griefs, and calamities: But as if two Oxen be put in one yoke, the one being bigger then the other, the greater beares most weight; so the Husband being the stronger vessell is to beare a greater burthen then his wife; And therefore the Lord said to *Adam*, *In the sweate of thy face shalt thou eate thy bread,*
till

till thou returne to the dust. And Saint *Paul* saith, *That he that provideth not for his houshold is worse then an Infidel.* Nature hath taught senselesse creatures to helpe one another; as the Male Pigeon, when his Hen is weary with sitting on her egges, and comes off from them, supplies her place, that in her absence they may receiue no harme, vntill such time as she is fully refreshed. Of small Birds the Cocke alwaies helpes his Hen to build her nest; and while she sits vpon her egges, he flies abroad to get meat for her, who cannot then prouide any for her selfe. The crowing Cockrell helpes his Hen to defend her Chickens from perill, and will indanger himselfe to saue her and them from harme. Seeing then that these vnreasonable creatures, by the instinct of nature, beare such affection each to other, that without any grudge, they willingly, according to their kind, helpe one another, I may reason *à minore ad maius*, that much more should man and woman, which are reasonable creatures, be helpers each to other in all things lawfull, they hauing the Law of God to guide them, his Word to bee a Lanthorne vnto their feete, and a Light vnto their pathes, by which they are excited to a farre more mutuall participation of each others burthen, then other creatures. So that neither the wife may say to her husband, nor the husband vnto his wife, I haue no need of thee, no more then the members of the body may

1.Tim.5.8.

*so say each to other, betweene whom there is such a sympathie, that if one member suffer, all suffer with it: Therefore though God bade *Abraham* forsake his Countrey and Kindred, yet he bade him not forsake his wife, who being *Flesh of his flesh, and bone of his bone*, was to bee copartner with him of whatsoeuer did betide him, whether ioy or sorrow. Wherefore *Salomon* saith, *Woe to him that is alone*; for when thoughts of discomfort, troubles of this world, and feare of dangers do possesse him, he wants a companion to lift him vp from the pit of perplexitie, into which hee is fallen: for a good wife, saith *Plautus*, is the wealth of the minde, and the welfare of the heart; and therefore a meete associate for her husband; And *Woman*, saith *Paul, is the glorie of the man*.

Marriage is a merri-age, and this worlds Paradise, where there is mutuall loue. Our blessed Sauiour vouchsafed to honour a marriage with the first miracle that he wrought, vnto which miracle matrimoniall estate may not vnfitly bee resembled: For as Christ turned water into wine, a farre more excellent liquor; which, as the Psalmist saith, *Makes glad the heart of man*; So the single man is by marriage changed from a Batchelour to a Husband, a farre more excellent title: from a solitarie life vnto a ioyfull vnion and coniunction, with such a creature as God hath made meete for man, for whom none was meete till she was made. The enioying of this

this great blessing made *Pericles* more vnwilling to part from his wife, then to die for his Countrie; And *Antonius Pius* to poure forth that patheticall exclamation against death, for depriuing him of his deerely beloued wife, *O cruell hard-hearted death in bereauing mee of her whom I esteemed more then my owne life! A vertuous woman,* faith *Salomon, is the Crowne of her husband;* By which metaphor hee sheweth both the excellencie of such a wife, and what account her husband is to make of her: For a King doth not trample his Crowne vnder his feete, but highly esteemes of it, gently handles it, and carefully laies it vp, as the euidence of his Kingdome; and therefore when *Dauid* destroyed *Rabbah* hee tooke off the Crowne from their Kings head: So husbands should not account their wiues as their vassals, but as those that are heires together of the grace of life, and with all lenitie and milde perswasions set their feete in the right way, if they happen to tread awry, bearing with their infirmities, as *Elkanah* did with his wiues barrennesse. Prou.12.4.

1.Chron.20.2.

1.Pet.3.7.

1.Sam.1.17.

The Kingdome of God is compared vnto the marriage of a Kings sonne: *Iohn* calleth the coniunction of Christ and his Chosen, a Marriage: And not few, but many times, doth our blessed Sauiour in the Canticles, set forth his vnspeakeable loue towards his Church vnder the title of an Husband reioycing with his Wife; and often vouchsafeth to call her his Sister   Math.22.

Reu. 19.7.

16 *A Meuzell for Melastomus.*

Rom.2.11.

Iohn 3.18.

Sister and Spouse, by which is shewed that with *God is no respect of persons*, Nations, or Sexes: For whosoeuer, whether it be man or woman, that doth *beleeue in the Lord Iesus*, *such shall bee saued*. And if Gods loue euen from the beginning, had not beene as great toward woman as to man, then would hee not haue preserued from the deluge of the old world as many women as men; nor would Christ after his Resurrection haue appeared vnto a woman first of all other, had it not beene to declare thereby, that the benefites of his death and resurrection, are as auaileable, by beleefe, for women as for men; for hee indifferently died for the one sex as well as the other: Yet a truth vngainesay-

1.Cor.11.3.

able is it, that the *Man is the Womans Head*; by which title yet of Supremacie, no authoritie hath hee giuen him to domineere, or basely command and imploy his wife, as a seruant; but hereby is he taught the duties which hee oweth vnto her: For as the head of a man is the imaginer and contriuer of proiects profitable for the safety of his whole body; so the Husband must protect and defend his Wife from iniuries: For

Ephe.5.23.

Iob 2.4.

Iohn 15.13.

he is her *Head, as Christ is the Head of his Church*, which hee entirely loueth, and for which hee gaue his very life; the deerest thing any man hath in this world; *Greater loue then this hath no man, when he bestoweth his life for his friend*, saith our Sauiour: This president passeth all other patternes, it requireth great benignity, and

and enioyneth an extraordinary affection, For *men must loue their wiues, euen as Christ loued his Church.* Secondly, as the Head doth not iarre or contend with the members, which *being ma-ny,* as the Apostle saith, *yet make but one bodie*; no more must the husband with the wife, but expelling all bitternesse and cruelty hee must liue with her louingly, and religiously, honouring her as the weaker vessell. Thirdly, and lastly, as hee is her Head, hee must, by instruction, bring her to the knowledge of her Creator, that so she may be a fit stone for the Lords building. Women for this end must haue an especiall care to set their affections vpon such as are able to teach them, that as they *grow in yeares, they may grow in grace, and in the knowledge of Christ Iesus our Lord.*

    1.Cor.11.10.
    Col.3.19.
    1.Pet.3.7.
    1.Cor.14.35.
    1.Pet.3.18.

Thus if men would remember the duties they are to performe in being heads, some would not stand a tip-toe as they doe, thinking themselues Lords & Rulers, and account euery omission of performing whatsoeuer they command, whether lawfull or not, to be matter of great disparagement, and indignity done them; whereas they should consider, that women are enioyned to submit themselues vnto their husbands no otherwaies then as to *the Lord*; so that from hence, for man, ariseth a lesson not to bee forgotten, that as the Lord commandeth nothing to be done, but that which is right and good, no more must the husband; for if a wife

    Ephes 5.

E   fulfill

fulfill the euill command of her husband, shee obeies him as a tempter, as *Saphira* did *Ananias*. But least I should seeme too partiall in praysing women so much as I haue (though no more then warrant from Scripture doth allow) I adde to the premises, that I say not, all women are vertuous, for then they should be more excellent then men, sith of *Adams* sonnes there was *Cain* as well as *Abel*, and of *Noahs*, *Cham* as well as *Sem*; so that of men as of women, there are two sorts, namely, good and bad, which in *Mathew* the fiue and twenty chapter, are comprehended vnder the name of *Sheepe* and *Goats*. And if women were not sinfull, then should they not need a Sauiour: but the Virgin *Mary* a patterne of piety, *reioyced in God her Sauiour*: *Ergo*, she was a sinner. In the *Reuelation* the Church is called the Spouse of Christ; and in *Zachariah*, wickednesse is called a woman, to shew that of women there are both godly and vngodly: For Christ would not *Purge his Floore* if there were not Chaffe among the Wheate; nor should gold neede to bee fined, if among it there were no drosse. But farre be it from any one, to condemne the righteous with the wicked, or good women with the bad (as the Bayter of women doth:) For though there are some scabbed sheepe in a Flocke, we must not therefore conclude all the rest to bee mangie: And though some men, through excesse, abuse Gods creatures, wee must not imagine that all men are

Actes 5.2.

Luke 1.47.

Zach. 5.7.

Gen.18.25.

are Gluttons; the which wee may with as good reason do, as condemne all women in generall, for the offences of some particulars. Of the good sort is it that I haue in this booke spoken, and so would I that all that reade it should so vnderstand me: for if otherwise I had done, I should haue incurred that woe, which by the Prophet *Isaiah* is pronounced against them that *speake well of euill*, and should haue *iustified the wicked, which thing is abhominable to the Lord.*

Esay 5.20.
Prou.17.15.

The Epilogue or vpshut of the premises.

Gen.40.23.

GReat was the vnthankefulnesse of *Pharaohs* Butler vnto *Ioseph*; for though hee had done him a great pleasure, of which the Butler promised requitall, yet was hee quite forgotten of him: But farre greater is the ingratitude of those men toward God, that dare presume to speake and exclaime against *woman*, whom God did create for mans comfort. What greater discredit can redound to a worke man, then to haue the man, for whom hee hath made it, say, it is naught? or what greater discurtesie can be offered to one, that bestoweth a gift, then to haue the receiuer giue out, that hee cares not for it: For he needes it not? And what greater ingratitude can bee shewed vnto God then the opprobrious speeches and disgracefull inuectiues, which some diabolicall natures doe frame against women?

Ingratitude is, and alwayes hath beene accounted so odious a vice, that *Cicero* saith, *If one doubt what name to giue a wicked man, let him call him an vngratefull person, and then hee hath said enough*. It was so detested among the *Persians*, as that by a Law they prouided, that such should suffer death as felons, which prooued

vnthanke-

The Epilogue.

vnthankefull for any gift receiued. And *Loue* (faith the Apostle) *is the fulfilling of the Lawe:* But where Ingratitude is harbored, there Loue is banished. Let men therefore beware of all vnthankefulnesse, but especially of the superlatiue ingratitude, that which is towards God, which is no way more palpably declared, then by the contemning of, and rayling against women, which sinne, of some men (if to be termed men) no doubt but God will one day auenge, when they shall plainely perceiue, that it had been better for them to haue been borne dumbe and lame, then to haue vsed their tongs and hands, the one in repugning, the other in writing against Gods handie worke, their owne flesh, women I meane, whom God hath made equall with themselues in dignity, both temporally and eternally, if they continue in the faith: which God for his mercie sake graunt they alwayes may, to the glory of their Creator, and comfort of their owne soules, through Christ Amen.

Rom.13.10.

To God onely wise be glorie now and for euer, AMEN.

Certaine
QVAERES
to the bayter of
Women.

WITH

CONFVTATION
of some part of his Dia-
bolicall Disci-
pline.

LONDON,
Printed by N. O. for *Thomas Archer*,
and are to be sold at his shop in
Popes-head-Pallace.
1 6 1 7.

To the Reader.

Lthough (curteous Reader) I am young in yeares, and more defectiue in knowledge, that little smattering in Learning which I haue obtained, being onely the fruit of such vacant houres, as I could spare from affaires befitting my Sex, yet am I not altogether ignorant of that Analogie which ought to be vsed in a literate Responsarie: But the Beare-bayting of Women, vnto which I haue framed my Apologeticall answere, beeing altogether without methode, irregular, without Grammaticall Concordance, and a promiscuous mingle mangle, it would admit no such order to bee obserued in the answering thereof, as a regular Responsarie requireth.

Wherfore (gentle Reader) fauorably cõsider, that as that Painter is not to be held vnskilfull, which hauing a deformed Obiect, makes the like portraiture; no more am I iustly to be blamed for my immethodicall Apologie, sith any iudicious Reader may plainely see, that the Bayter of Women his pestiferous obtrectation is like a Taylers Cushion, that is botcht together

To the Reader.

gether of shreddes, so that, were it not to preuent future infection with that venome, which he hath, and daily doth sweate out, I would haue beene loath to haue spent time so idlely, as to answere it at all: but a crooked pot-lid well enough fits a wrie-neckt pot, an vnfashioned shooe a mis-shapen foote, and an illiterate answere an vnlearned irreligious prouocation. His absurdities therein contayned, are so many, that to answere them seuerally, were as friuolous a worke, as to make a Trappe for a Flea, and as tedious as the pursuite of an Arrow to an impotent man. Yet to preuent his hauing occasion to say, that I speake of many, but can instance none, I haue thought it meete to present a few of them to his view, as followeth, that if Follie haue taken roote in him, he may seeke to extirpate it, and to blush at the sight of that fruit, which he hath already brought foorth; a fruite I call it (not vnfitly I hope) because a Crabbe may so be termed, as well as a good Apple. Thus, not doubting of the fauour of well affected, and of their kinde acceptance of my indeuours, of which I desire not applaud, but approbation: I rest,

Your friend,
RACHEL SPEGHT.

¶ The Preface vnto the Subseqnent.

With edged tooles (saith the old Prouerbe) it is ill sporting; but farre more dangerous: yea damnable is it to dally with Scripture, the two-edged Sword of the Eternall: for so to doe is a breach of the third Commandement; and he that failes in one point, is guiltie of all. If the magnitude of this sinne had beene considered by the Bayter of Women, the lamentable, yet iust reward thereof, as of all other sinnes without repentance, would, if he had but a seruile feare, haue restrained him from transgressing herein. But as one deuoide of all true feare of Gods indignation against wilfull sinners (for as ignorance doth somewhat extenuate a fault, so doth knowledge much aggrauate it) he hath made the exordium of his brainesicke exhalation against women, to bee a peruerting of a part of holy Writ; ex vnguibus leonem, *iudge of this Lion by his pawe.* For if the fore foot be monstrous, doubtlesse the whole bodie is correspondent thereto.

Hebr. 4.12.

Iames 2.10.

F 2

The Preface.

thereto. The Porch indeede is fowle, but hee that viewes the sequel, as I haue done, shall find a lay-stall of heathenish Assertions, Similies, and Examples, illiterate composition, irreligious inuectiues, and (which is worst) impious blasphemies therein included, filthy rubbish, more fitte to be heaped vp by a Pagan, then one that beareth the name of a Christian.

But lest it should not onely be thought, but also said, that I finde fault where none is; or that I do ill to mislike the Worke, and not make the Author therewith acquainted, that if he please, hee may answer for himselfe: I thinke it not amisse to propose some few Quæres vnto the Bayter of Women, which I haue abstracted out of his infamous Booke, as himselfe confesseth it to be in his Epistle to Women.

Certaine Quæres to the Bayter of women, with confutation of some part of his Diabolicall Discipline.

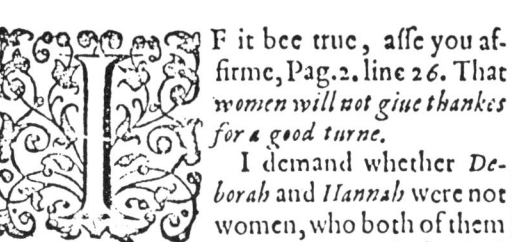

IF it bee true, asse you affirme, Pag. 2. line 26. That *women will not giue thankes for a good turne.*

I demand whether *Deborah* and *Hannah* were not women, who both of them sang hymnes of thankesgiuing vnto the Lord; the one for his mercy in granting her victory ouer *Israels* enemies, the other for his fauourable giuing vnto her a son, which she full oft and earnestly had desired?

Iudg. 5.
1. Sam. 1. 11.
& 2. 1.

And where-asse you say, Page 4. line 22. *that a woman that hath a faire face, it is euer matched with a cruel heart, and her heauenly lookes with hellish thoughts:* You therein shew your selfe a con-

contradictor of Scriptures presidents: For *Abigail* was a beautifull woman, and tender-hearted; *Rebekah* was both faire of face and pittifull. Many examples seruing to confute your vniuersall rule might bee produced, but these are sufficient to dispell this your cloud of vntruth. As for your audacitie in iudging of womens thoughts, you thereby shew your selfe an vsurper against the King of heauen, the true knowledge of cogitations being appropriate vnto him alone.

 If your assertion, That *a woman is better lost then found, better forsaken then taken* (Page 5. line 4.) be to be credited, me thinkes, great pitty it is, that afore you were borne, there was none so wise as to counsell your father not to meddle with a woman, that hee might haue escaped those troubles, which you affirme, that all married men are cumbred with, Page 2. line 20. As also that hee might not haue begotten such a monster in nature *Asse* your selfe, who (like the Priest which forgot he was Parish Clearke) defame and exclaime against women, as though your selfe had neuer had a mother, or you neuer beene a child.

 You affirme (Page 10. line 18.) that *for the loue of women, Dauid purchased the displeasure of his God*: It had beene good that you had cited the place of story where you finde it, For I neuer yet in Scripture read, that the Almighty was displeased with *Dauid* for his loue to women,

marginalia: 1. Sam. 25. 3. 18. Gen. 24. 16. 18.

Math. 12. 25.

A Mouzell for Melastomus.

men, but for his lust to *Bathsheba*, which afterward brought forth his adulterous act, and his causing *Vriah* to be murthered.   2. Sam. 11.

In saying (Page 10. line 25.) that *Iobs wife counselled her husband to curse God*, you misconster the Text; for the true construction thereof will shew it to bee a *Scareasmus* or *Ironicall* speech, and not an instigation to blasphemie.

Page 11. line 8. you count it *wonderfull to see the mad feates of women, for shee will now bee merry, then sad*: but me thinkes it is farre more *wonder-foole* to haue one, that aduentures to make his Writing as publique as an In-keepers Signe, which hangs to the view of all passengers, to want Grammaticall Concordance in his said Writing, and ioyne together *women* plurall, and *shee* singular, *Asse* you not onely in this place, but also in others haue done.

Albeit the Scripture verifieth, that God made woman and brought her to man; and that a prudent wife commeth of the Lord: yet haue you not feared blasphemously to say, *that women sprung from the diuell*, Page 15. line 26. But being, as it seemes, defectiue in that whereof you haue much need (for *mendacem oportet esse memorem*) you suddainely after say, That *women were created by God, and formed by nature, and therefore by policie and wisedome to be auoyded*, Page 16. line 12. An impious conclusion to inferre, that because God created, therefore to be auoyded: Oh intollerable absurdity!   Gen 2. 22. Prou. 19. 14.

Men

Men I say may liue without women, but women cannot liue without men, Page 14. line 18. If any Religious Author had thus affirmed, I should haue wondred, that vnto Satans suggestions he had so much subiected himselfe, as to crosse the Almighties prouidence and care for mans good, who positiuely said, *It is not good for man to bee alone;* But being that the sole testimony heereof is your owne *dico,* I maruell no whit at the errour, but heartily wish, that vnto all the vntruths you haue vttered in your infamous booke, you had subscribed your *Dico,* that none of them might bee adiudged truths: For *mendacis præmium est verbis eius non adhiberi fidem.*

Gen. 2.18.

Page 17. line 5. you affirme, that *Hosea was brought vnto Idolatrie by marrying with a lewd woman,* which is as true as the sea burnes; and for proofe thereof you cite *Hosea* 1. in which chapter is no such matter to be found, it onely containing a declaration of the Lords anger against the adulterous Iewes, who had gone a whoring after other Gods, set forth in a parable of an husband and an adulterous wife.

Page 19. *Theodora a monstrous strumpet, Lavia, Floria, and Lais, were three notable Curtizans.*

Was not that noble Citie of Troy, sacked and spoyled for the faire Helena? Page 21. *Therefore stay not alone in the company of a woman, trusting to thy owne chastity, except thou bee more strong then* Sampson, *more wise then* Salomon, *or more holy*

holy then Dauid, for these, and many more haue beene ouercome by the sweete intisements of women, Page 22.

I may as well say *Barrabas* was a murtherer, *Ioab* killed *Abner* and *Amasa*, and *Pharaoh Necho* slew *Iosiah*; therefore stay not alone in the companie of a man, trusting to thy owne strength, except thou bee stronger then *Iosiah*, and more valiant then *Abner* and *Amasa*, for these and many more haue beene murthered by men. The forme of argumentation is your owne, the which if you dislike, blame your selfe for proposing such a patterne, and blush at your owne folly, *Quod te posse non facile credo*: for it is an old saying, how true I know not, that blushing is a signe of grace.

Luke 23. 19.
2. Sam. 3. 27.
2. Sam. 20 10.
2. King 23. 29.

Page 31. line 15. *If God had not made women onely to bee a plague to man, hee would neuer haue called them necessarie euils.* Albeit I haue not read *Seaton* or *Ramus*, nor so much as seene (though heard of) *Aristotles Arganox*, yet by that I haue seene and reade in compasse of my apprehension, I will aduenture to frame an argument or two, to shew what danger, for this your blasphemy your are in.

To fasten a lie vpon God is blasphemy: But the *Bayter of women* fastens a lie vpon God: *ergo*, the *Bayter* is a blasphemer.

The Proposition, I trowe, none will gaine-say, the assumption I thus proue,

Whosoeuer affirmes God to haue called women

men neceſſary euils, faſtens a lie vpon God: For from the beginning of *Geneſis* to the end of the *Reuelation* is no ſuch inſtance to be found: But the *Bayter* affirmes God ſo to haue called women, *Ergo*, the *Bayter* faſtens a lie vpon God.

The reward according to Law Diuine due vnto the Bayter of women.

Whoſoeuer blaſphemeth God, ought by his Law, to die; The *Bayter of women* hath blaſphemed God, *Ergo*, he ought to die the death.

*The Propoſition is vpon record, Leuit.*24.14.16. *The Aſſumption is formerly proued.*

If thou marryeſt a ſtill and a quiet woman, that will ſeeme to thee that thou rideſt but an ambling horſe to hell, but if with one that is froward and vnquiet, then thou wert as good ride a trotting horſe to the diuell. Page 35. line 13.

If this your affirmation be true, then ſeemes it, that hell is the period of all married mens trauailes, and the center of their circumference. A man can but haue either a good wife or a bad; and if he haue the former, you ſay he doth but ſeeme to amble to hell; if the latter, he were as good trot to the diuell: But if married men ride, how trauaile Batchelours? ſurely, by your rule they muſt go on foote, becauſe they want wiues; which (incluſiuely) you ſay are like horſes to carry their husbands to hell. Wherefore in my minde, it was not without mature conſideration

deration that you married in time, becaufe it would be too irkefome for you to trauaile fo tedious a iourney on foote.

Now the fire is kindled, let vs burne this other faggot. Page 38. line 4.

Beware of making too great a fire, left the furpluffage of that fires effect which you intended for others, finge your felfe.

Shee will make thee weare an Oxe feather in thy Cappe. Page 44. line 4.

If Oxen haue feathers, their haires more fitly may be fo termed then their hornes.

Page 50. *line 28. There is no ioy nor pleafure in this world which may be compared to Marriage, for if the husband be poore and in aduerfitie, then hee beares but the one halfe of the griefe: and furthermore, his wife will comfort him, with all the comfortable meanes fhe can deuife.*

Page 51. *line 16. Many are the ioyes and fweete pleafures in Marriage, as in our children, &c.*

Page 34. *line 5. There are many troubles comes gallopping at the heeles of a woman. If thou wert a Seruant, or in bondage afore, yet when thou marieft, thy toyle is neuer the nearer ended, but euen then, and not before, thou changeft thy golden life, which thou didft leade before (in refpect of the married) for a droppe of hony, which quickely turnes to be as bitter as wormewood.*

Page 53. *line 19. The husband ought (in figne of loue) to impart his fecrets and counfell vnto his wife, for many haue found much comfort and pro-*

G 2 *fite*

fite by taking their wiues counfell; and if thou impart any ill happe to thy wife, fhee lighteneth thy griefe, either by comforting thee louingly, or elfe, in bearing a part thereof patiently.

Page 41. line 12. If thou vnfouldeft any thing of fecret to a woman, the more thou chargeft her to keepe it clofe, the more fhee will feeme, as it were, with childe, till fhee haue reuealed it.

It was the faying of a iudicious Writer, that whofo makes the fruit of his cogitations extant to the view of all men, fhould haue his worke to be as a well tuned Inftrument, in all places according and agreeing, the which I am fure yours doth not: For how reconcile you thofe diffonant places aboue cited? or how make you a confonant diapafon of thofe difcords wanting harmony?

Page 34. line 19. You counfell all men, to *fhunne idleneffe*, and yet the firft words of your Epiftle to Women are thefe, *mufing with my felfe being idle*: Heerein you appeare, not vnlike vnto a Fencer, which teacheth another how to defend himfelfe from enemies blowes, and fuffers himfelfe to be ftricken without refiftance: for you warne others, to efchew that dangerous vice, wherewith (by your owne confeffion) your felfe is ftained.

Page 57. line 5. If thou like not my reafons to expell loue, then thou mayeft trie Ouids *Art, for he counfells thofe that feele this horrible heate to coole their flames with hearbes which are colde of nature*

nature as Rew, &c.

Albeit you doubt not but by some to be reputed for a good Archer, yet heere you shot wide from the truth, in saying without contradiction of *Ouids* errour, that Rew is of a cold nature: For most Physitions (if not all) both ancient and moderne, holde it to be hote and drie in the third degree: and experience will tell the vser thereof, that the temperature is hote, not colde. And though the sense of tasting, without further triall, doth repell this errour, I doubt not but in citing this prescription, you haue verified the opinion of that philosopher, which said, That there are some, who thinke they speake wisest, and write most iudiciously, when they vnderstand not themselues.

But, *vt opus ad finem perducam*, sith I haue trode my vtmost intended steppe, though left one path vngone, I meane the *Beare-bayting of Widdowes* vnviewed, in that I am ignorant of their dispositions, accounting it a follie for me to talke of *Robin-hood*, as many doe, that neuer shot in his Bowe, I leaue the speculation (with approbation of their *Beare-bayting*) to those that regard neyther affabilitie nor humanitie, and wishing vnto euery such *Misogunes*, a *Tiburne Tiffenie* for curation of his swolne necke, which onely through a Cynicall inclination will not indure the yoke of lawfull Matrimony, I bid farewell.

F ret, fume, or frumpe at me who will, I care not,
I will thrust forth thy sting to hurt, and spare not:
N ow that the taske I vndertooke is ended,
I dread not any harme to me intended,
S ith iustly none therein I haue offended.

Page 7. line 7. for *Herods* reade *Henahs*

Ester hath hang'd Haman:
OR
AN ANSVVERE TO
a lewd Pamphlet, entituled,
The Arraignment of Women.
With the arraignment of lewd, idle,
froward, and vnconstant men, and
HVSBANDS.

Diuided into two Parts.

The first proueth the dignity and worthinesse
of *Women, out of diuine Testimonies.*
The second shewing the estimation of the Fœminine Sexe, in ancient and Pagan times; all which
is acknowledged by men themselues in their
daily actions.

VVritten by *Ester Sowernam,* neither Maide,
Wife nor Widdowe, yet really all, and therefore experienced to defend all.

IOHN 8.7:
He that is without sinne among you, let him first cast a stone at her.

Neque enim lex iusticior vlla
——— *Quam necis Artificem arte perire sua.*

LONDON,
Printed for *Nicholas Bourne,* and are to be sold at his shop
at the entrance of the Royall Exchange. 1617.

TO ALL RIGHT HONOVrable, Noble, and worthy Ladies, Gentlewomen, and others, vertuously disposed, of the Fæminine Sexe.

Ight Honourable, and all others of our Sexe, vpon my repaire to *London* this last *Michaelmas* Terme; being at supper amongst friends, where the number of each sexe were equall; As nothing is more vsuall for table-talke; there fell out a discourse concerning women, some defending, others obiecting against our Sex: Vpon which occasion, there happened a mention of a Pamphlet entituled *The Arraignment of Women*, which I was desirous to see. The next day a Gentleman brought me the Booke, which when I had superficially runne ouer, I found the discourse as far off from performing what the Title promised, as I found it scandalous and blasphemous: for where the Authour pretended to write against lewd, idle, and vnconstant women, hee doth most impudently rage and rayle generally against all the whole sexe of women. Whereupon, I in defence of our Sexe, began an answer to that

shamefull

The Epistle Dedicatory.

full Pamphlet. In which, after I had spent some small time, word was brought mee that an Apologie for women was already vndertaken, and ready for the Presse, by a Ministers daughter: Vpon this newes I stayed my pen, being as glad to be eased of my entended labour; as I did expect some fitting performance of what was vndertaken: At last the Maidens Booke was brought me, which when I had likewise runne ouer, I did obserue, that whereas the Maide doth many times excuse her tendernesse of yeares, I found it to be true in the slendernesse of her answer, for she vndertaking to defend women, doth rather charge and condemne women, as in the ensuing discourse shall appeare: So that wheras I expected to be eased of what I began, I do now finde my selfe double charged, as well to make reply to the one, as to adde supply to the other.

In this my Apologie, Right Honourable, Right Worshipfull, and all others of our Sexe, I doe in the first part of it plainely and resolutely deliuer the worthinesse and worth of women; both in respect of their Creation, as in the worke of Redemption. Next I doe shew in examples out of both the Testaments: what blessed and happy choyse hath beene made of women, as gratious instruments to deriue Gods blessings and benefits to mankinde.

In my second part I doe deliuer of what estimate women haue been valued in all ancient and moderne times, which I prooue by authorities, customes, and daily experiences. Lastly, I doe answer all materiall obiections which haue or can be alledged against our Sexe: in which also I doe arraigne such kind of men, which

The Epistle Dedicatory.

which correspond the humor and disposition of the Author; lewd, idle, furious and beastly disposed persons.

This being performed, I doubt not but such as heretofore haue beene so forward and lauish against women, will hereafter pull in their hornes, and haue as little desire, and lesse cause so scandalously and slanderously to write against vs then formerly they haue.

The ends for which I vndertooke this enterprise, are these. First, to set out the glory of Almightie God, in so blessed a worke of his Creation. Secondly, to encourage all Noble, Honourable, and worthy Women, to expresse in their course of life and actions, that they are the same Creatures which they were designed to be by their Creator, and by their Redeemer: And to parallell those women, whose vertuous examples are collected briefly out of the Olde and New Testament. Lastly, I write for the shame and confusion of such as degenerate from woman-hoode, and disappoint the ends of Creation, and Redemption.

There can be no greater encouragement to true Nobility, then to know and stand vpon the honour of Nobility, nor any greater confusion and shame, then for Nobility to dismount and abase it selfe to ignoble and degenerate courses.

You are women; in Creation, noble; in Redemption, gracious; in vse most blessed; be not forgetfull of your selues, nor vnthankefull to that Author from whom you receiue all.

A 3   To

TO ALL WORTHY AND HOPE full young youths of *Great-Brittaine*; But respectiuely to the best disposed and worthy Apprentises of LONDON.

Hopefull and gallant youths of Great-Brittaine, and thus so famous a Citie. There hath been lately published a Pamphlet, entituled The Arraignment of lewd, idle, froward and inconstant Women. This patched and mishapen hotch-potch, is so directed, that if Socrates did laugh but once to see an Asse eate Thistles, he would surely laugh twice to see an addle-brain like direct his misshapen Labours to giddy-headed young men: he would say, as he did when the Asse did eate Thistles, like lips, like Lance, so a franticks writer doth aptly chuse giddy sawcebox.

The Author of the Arraignment, and my selfe, in our labours doe altogether disagree; he raileth without cause, I defend vpon direct proofe. He saith, women are the worst of all Creatures, I prooue them blessed aboue all Creatures: He writeth, that men should abhorre them for their bad conditions: I proue, that men should honour them for their best dispositions. he saith, women are the cause of mens ouerthrow, I praue, if there be any, by seruice in a woman, men were the beginners. Now, in that it is farre more woman-like to maintaine a right, than it is man-like to offer a wrong, I conceiued that I could not erre in my choyse, if I did direct a labour well intended, to worthy young youths, which are well disposed.

When you haue past your minority, or serued your Apprentiships vnder the gouernment of others, when you begin the world

for

To the Reader.

for your selues, the chiefest thing you looke for is a good Wife.

The world is a large field, and it is full of brambles, bryers, and weedes: If there be any more tormenting, more scratting, or more poysonable weede then other, the Author hath collected them in his lothsome Pamphlet, and doth utter them to his giddy company.

Now my selfe presuming vpon your worthy and honest dispositions, I haue entred into the Garden of Paradice, and there haue gathered the choysest flowers which that Garden may affoord, and those I offer to you.

If you beleeue our aduersary, no woman is good, howsoeuer she be vsed: if you consider what I haue written, no woman is bad, except she be abused.

If you beleeue him that women are so bad Creatures, what a dangerous and miserable life is marriage?

If you examine my proofes to know directly what women are, you shall then finde there is no delight more exceeding then to be ioyned in marriage with a Paradisian Creature. Who as shee commeth out of the Garden, so shall you finde her a flower of delight, answerable to the Countrey from whence she commeth.

There can be no loue betwixt man and wife, but where there is a respectiue estimate the one towards the other. How could you loue? nay, how would you loath such a monster, to whom Ioseph Swetnam poynteth?

Whereas in view of what I haue described, how can you but regardfully loue with the vttermost straine of affection so incomparable a Iewell.

Some will perhaps say, I am a woman and therefore write more for women then they doe deserue: To whom I answere, if they misdoubt of what I speake, let them impeach my credit in any one particular: In that which I write, Eue was a good woman before she met with the Serpent, her daughters are good Virgins, if they meet with good Tutors.

You my worthy youths are the hope of Man-hoode, the principall poynt of Man-hoode is to defend, and what more man-like defence, then to defend the iust reputation of a woman. I know that you the Apprentises of this Citie are as forward to main-

taine

To the Reader.

taine the good, as you are vehement to put downe the bad.

That which is worst I leaue to our aduersary, but what is excellently best, that I commend to you: doe you finde the gold, I doe here deliuer you the Iewell, a rich stocke to begin the world withall, if you be good husbands to vse it for your best aduantage.

Let not the title of this Booke in some poynt distaste you, in that men are arraigned, for you are quit by Non-age. None are here arraigned, but such olde fornicators as came with full mouth and open cry to Iesus, and brought a woman to him taken in adultery, who when our Sauiour stoopt downe and wrote on the ground, they all fled away. Ioseph Swetnam saith, A man may finde Pearles in dust, Pag. 47. But if they who fled had seene any Pearles, they would rather haue stayed to haue had share, then to flye and to leaue the woman alone, they found some fowle reckoning against themselues in our Sauiours writing, as they shall doe who are heare arraigned. And if they dare doe like, as our Sauiour bad the womans accusers, He that is without sinne throw the first stone at her; so let them raile against women, who neuer tempted any woman to be bad: Yet this is an hard case. If a man raile against a woman, and know no lewdnesse by any, be shall proue himselfe a compound foole. If he rayle at women, who in his owne experience tryall had made many bad, he shall shew himselfe a decompounded K. I doe not meane Knight: The best way is, he that knoweth none bad, let him speake well of all: he who hath made more bad then he euer intended to make good, let him hold his peace least hee shame himselfe. Farewell.

Ester Sowrenam.

AN

AN ANSVVERE TO THE FIRST CHAPTER OF THE *Arraignment of Women.*

CHAP. I.

IF the Author of this *Arraignment* had performed his discourse either answerable to the Title, or the Arguments of the Chapters; hee had beene so farre off from being answered by me, that I should haue commended so good a labour, which is imployed to giue vice iust reproofe, and vertue honourable report. But at the very first entrance of his discourse, in the very first page, he discouereth himselfe neither to haue truth in his promise, nor religious performance. If in this answere I doe vse more vehement speeches then may seeme to correspond the naturall disposition of a Woman; yet all iuditious Readers shall confesse that I vse more mildnesse then the cause I haue in hand prouoketh me vnto.

I am not onely prouoked by this Authour to defend women, but I am more violently vrged to defend diuine Maiestie, in the worke of his Creation. In

Ester *hath hang'd* Haman.

Epist. ad Ciprianum.
Sup. Math.

which respect I say with Saint *Ierome*, *Meam iniuriam patienter sustinui,impietatem contra deum ferre non potui.* For as Saint *Chrisostome* saith, *iniurias Dei dissimulare impium est.*

If either *Iulian* the Apostata, or *Lucian* the Atheist should vndertake the like worke, could the owne deuise to write more blasphemously, or the other to scoffe and flout at the diuine Creation of Woman, more prophanely then this irreligious Author doth?

Homer doth report in his Illiads, that there was at the siege of *Troy*, a Græcian, called *Thersites*, whose wit was so blockish, he was not worthy to speake: yet his disposition was so precipitate, hee could not hold his tongue. *Ioseph Swetnam* in all record of Histories cannot be so likely paraleld as with this *Thersites*. What his composition of body is I know not, but for his disposition otherwise, in this Pamphlet I know, he is as monstrous as the worke is mishapen, which shall plainely appeare in the examination of the first page onely.

The Argument of the first Chapter is, *to shew to what vse Women were made*; it also sheweth, *That most of them degenerate from the vse they were framed vnto*, &c.

Now, to shew to what vse woman was made, hee beginneth thus. *At the first beginning a Woman was made to bee an helper to Man: And so they are indeed, for they helpe to consume and spend*, &c. This is all the vse, and all the end which the Authour setteth downe in all his discourse for the creation of woman. Marke a ridiculous ieast in this: Spending and consuming of that which Man painfully getteth, is by this

this Authour the vſe for which Women were made. And yet (ſaith hee in the Argument) *moſt of them degenerate from the vſe they were framed vnto.* Woman was made to ſpend and conſume at the firſt: But women doe degenerate from this vſe, *Ergo*, *Midaſſe* doth contradict himſelfe. Beſide this egregious folly, he runneth into horrible blaſphemy. VVas the end of Gods creation in VVoman to ſpend and conſume? Is *helper* to be taken in that ſence, to helpe to *ſpend?* &c. Is ſpending and conſuming, *helping?*

He runneth on, and ſaith, *They were made of a Rib, and that their froward and crooked nature doth declare, for a Rib is a crooked thing,* &c.

VVoman was made of a crooked rib, ſo ſhe is crooked of conditions. *Ioſeph Swetnam* was made as from *Adam* of clay and duſt, ſo he is of a durty and muddy diſpoſition: The inferences are both alike in either; woman is no more crooked, in reſpect of the one; but he is blaſphemous in reſpect of the other. Did Woman receiue her ſoule and diſpoſition from the rib, Or as it is ſaid in *Geneſis*, *God did breath in them the ſpirit of life?* Admit that this Authors doctrine bee true, that woman receiueth her froward and crooked diſpoſition from the rib, Woman may then conclude vpon that Axiome in Philoſophy, *Quicquid efficit tale, illud eſt magis tale,* That which giueth quality to a thing, doth more abound in that quality; as fire which heateth, is it ſelfe more hot: The Sunne which giueth light, is of it ſelfe more light: So, if Woman receaued her crookedneſſe from the rib, and conſequently from the Man, how doth man excell in crookedneſſe, who hath more of thoſe crooked ribs?

To take a vantage vpon a diſaduantage.

Ester *hath hang'd* Haman.

See how this vaine, furious, and idle Authour furnisheth woman with an Argument against himselfe, and others of his Sexe.

The Authour hauing desperately begunne, doth more rashly and impudently runne on in blasphemy, which he doth euidently shew in the inference vpon his former speeches: And therefore (saith he) *Euer since they haue beene a woe vnto Man, and follow the liue of the first leader.* Now let the Christian Reader please to consider how dishonestly this Authour dealeth, who vndertaking a particular, prosecuteth and persecuteth a generall, vnder the cloake and colour of lewd, idle, and froward women, to rage and raile against all women in generall.

Now, hauing examined what collections *Ioseph Swetnam* hath wrested out of Scriptures, to dishonor and abuse all women: I am resolued, before I answere further particulars made by him against our sexe, to collect and note out of Scriptues; First, what incomparable and most excellent prerogatiues God hath bestowed vpon women, in honour of them, and their Creation: Secondly, what choyse God hath made of women, in vsing them as instruments to worke his most gracious and glorious designes, for the generall benefit of man-kind, both during the law of Nature, and of *Moyses*: Thirdly, what excellent and diuine graces haue beene bestowed vpon our Sexe, in the law of Grace, and the worke of Redemption: With a conclusion, that to manifest the worthinesse of women, they haue beene chosen to performe and publish the most happy and ioyfull benefits which euer came to man-kinde.

CHAP.

Chapter II.

What incomparable and excellent prerogatives God hath bestowed upon Women, in their first Creation.

IN this ensuing Chapter I determine briefly to obserue (not curiously to discourse at large) the singuler benefits and graces bestowed vpon Women: In regard of which, it is first to bee considered; That the Almighty God in the worlds frame in his Diuine wisedome, designed to himselfe a maine end to which he ordayned all the workes of his Creation, in which hee being a most excellent worke-master, did so Create his workes, that euery succeeding worke was euer more excellent then what was formerly Created: hee wrought by degrees, prouiding in all for that which was and should be the end.

It appeareth by that Soueraignty which God gaue to *Adam* ouer all the Creatures of Sea and Land, that man was the end of Gods creation, wherevpon it doth necessarily, without all exception follow, that *Adam*, being the last worke, is therefore the most excellent worke of creation: yet *Adam* was not so absolutly perfect, but that in the sight of God, he wanted an *Helper*: Wherevpon God created the woman his last worke, as to supply and make absolute that imperfect building which was vnperfected in man, as all Diuines do hold, till the happy creation of

The prerogatiues giuen to women in their Creation.

Ester hath hang'd Haman.

the woman. Now of what estimate that Creature is and ought to be, which is the last worke, vpon whom the Almighty set vp his last rest: whom he made to to adde perfection. to the end of all creation I leaue rather to be acknowledged by others, then resolued by my selfe.

The last worke.

It is furthermore to be considered, as the Maide, *in her Mussell for Melastomus* hath obserued: that God intended to honour woman in a more excellent degree, in that he created her out of a subiect refined, as out of a Quintissence: For the ribbe is in Substance more solid, in place as most neare, so in estimate most deare, to mans heart, which doth presage that as she was made for an helper, so to be an helper to stay, to settle all ioy, all contents, all delights, to and in mans heart, as hereafter shall be shewed.

Created vpon a refined subiect.

That delight, solace, and pleasure, which shall come to man by woman, is prognosticated by that place wherein woman was created: for she was framed in Paradice, a place of all delight and pleasure, euery element hath his creatures, euery creature doth corresponde the temper and the inclination of that element wherein it hath and tooke his first and principall *esse*, or being. So that woman neither can or may degenerate in her disposition from that naturall inclination of the place, in which she was first framed, she is a Paradician, that is, a delightfull creature, borne in so delightfull a country.

A better countrey.

When woman was created, God brought her vnto *Adam*, and then did solempnise that most auspicious Marriage betwixt them, with the greatest Maiestie, and magnificence that heauen, or earth might afford.

Men are worldlings, Women paradicians.

God

Ester hath hang'd Haman.

God was the Father, which gaue so rich a iewell: God was the Priest which tied so inseperable a knot. God was the Steward which prouided all the pleasures, all the dainties, all the blessings, which his deuine wisdome might affoord, in so delightfull a place.

Woman marriage

The woman was married to *Adam*, as with a most sure and inseparable band, so with a most affectionate and dutifull loue: *Adam* was enioyned to receaue his wife, as is noted in the Bible printed 1595.

There is no loue (alwayes excepting the transcending loue) which is so highly honoured, so gratiously rewarded, so straightly commanded, or which being broken, is so seuerely punished, as the loue and duty which Children owe to their Parents: Yet this loue albeit neuer so respectiue, is dispensed withall in respect of that loue which a man is bound to beare to his wife: *For this cause*, saith *Adam*, (as from the mouth of God) *shall a man leaue Father and Mother, and cleaue onely to his Wife*. This word *cleaue* is vttered in the Hebrew with a more significant emphasie, then any other Language may expresse; such a cleauing and ioyning together, which admitteth no seperation. It may be necessarily obserued, that that gift of the woman was most singularly excellent, which was to bee accepted and entertained with so inestimable a loue, and made inseparable by giuing and taking the Ring of Loue, which should be endlesse.

The wedding Ring.

Now, the woman taking view of the Garden, shee was assaulted with a Serpent of the masculine gender; who maliciously enuying the happinesse in which man was at this time, like a mischieuous Politician,

Ester hath hang'd Haman.

Womans temptation. Politician, hee practised by supplanting of the woman, to turne him out of all: For which end he most craftily and cunningly attempteth the woman; and telleth her, that therefore they were forbidden to eate of the fruit which grew in the middest of the Garden, that in eating, they should not be like vnto God: Wherevpon the woman accepted, tasted, and gaue to her Husband. In accepting the Serpents offer, there was no sinne; for there was no sinne till the fruit was eaten: Now, albeit I haue vndertaken the defence of women, and may in that respect be fauoured, in taking all aduantages I may, to defend my sexe.

There are many pregnant places in the Scripture which might be alleaged to extenuate the sin of the Woman, in respect of the sinne of *Adam*: it is said *Ecclesiast.* 25. *Sinne had his beginning in woman, Ergo,* his fulnesse in man.

Chap. 5. Saint *Paul* saith, *Rom.* 5. *By one mans sinne death came into the world,* without mention of the woman:

Chap. 9. The same Saint *Paul* writeth to the *Corinthians*, to whom he affirmeth, *that all die in Adam,* in which the fulnesse and effects of sinne are charged vpon *Adam* alone, not but that woman had her part in the Tragedy, but not in so high a degree as the man.

Adam his offences vpon his fall. When *Adam* had eaten, and sinne was now in fulnesse, hee beginneth to multiply sinne vpon sinne: first he flieth from the sight of God; next, being called to account, he excuseth his sinne; and doth expostulate (as it were) with Almightie God, and telleth him, *That woman which thou gauest mee, gaue me, and I did eate:* As who should say, if thou hadst not giuen

giuen the cause, I had not beene guilty of the effect; making (heerein) God the Authour of his fall.

Now what is become of that loue, which *Adam* was bound to beare towards his wife? He chargeth her with all the burden; so he may discharge himselfe, he careth little how hee clog her.

Adams loue like his childrens in these dayes.

God hauing examined the offendors, and hauing heard the vttermost they could alledge for themselues, he pronounceth sentence of death vpon them, as a punishment in iustice due and deserued. Iustice he administred to *Adam*: Albeit the woman doth taste of iustice, yet mercy is reserued for her, and of all the workes of mercy which mankinde may hope for, the greatest, the most blessed, and the most ioyfull is promised to woman.

Adam punished with iustice.

Woman punished by Iustice, relieued by Mercy.

Woman supplanted by tasting of fruit, she is punished in bringing forth her owne fruit. Yet what by fruit she lost, by fruit she shall recouer.

What more gratious a gift could the Almightie promise to woman, then to bring forth the fruit in which all nations shall be blessed? so that as woman was a meanes to loose Paradice, she is by this, made a meanes to recouer Heauen. *Adam* could not vpbraid her for so great a losse, but he was to honour her more for a greater recouery: all the punishments inflicted vpon women, are encountred with most gratious blessings & benefits; she hath not so great cause of dolour in one respect, as shee hath infinite cause of ioy in another. She is commanded to obey her husband; the cause is, the more to encrease her glorie. Obedience is better then Sacrifice: for nothing is more acceptable before God then to obey:

The incomparable inuentions of womens wits.

1 Sam. 12.

C   Woman

women are much bound to God, to haue so acceptable a vertue enioyned them for their pennance.

Amongst the curses and punishments heaped vpon the Serpent, what greater ioy could she heare, or what greater honour could be done vnto her, then to heare from the voyce of God these words; *I will put enmitie betwixt the woman and thee, betwixt thy seede and her seede,* and that her seed should breake the Serpents head? This must perforce be an exceeding ioy for the woman, to heare and to be assured that her fruit should reuenge her wrong.

After the fall, and after they were all arraigned and censured, and that now *Adam* saw his wiues dowrie, and what blessings God hath bestowed vpon her, hee being now a bondslaue to death and hell, stroke dead in regard of himselfe, yet hee comforts himselfe, he taketh heart from grace, he engageth his hope vpon that promise which was made to the woman. Out of this most comfortable and blessed hope bee now calleth his wife by a name, in whose effects not onely he, but all mankinde should most blessedly share: hee calleth her *Eue*, which is, the mother of the liuing: which is sutable as well in respect of the promise made to her and her seede, as in respect of those imployments for which in her creation she and all women are designed, to be helpers, comforters, Ioyes, and delights, and in true vse and gouerment they euer haue beene and euer will be, as hereafter shall be shewed, maugre the shamefull, blasphemous and prophane speach of *Ioseph Swetnam*, page 31. begining line 15. as followeth.

If God had not made them onely to be a plague to a man,

Womans name answerable to her nature.

man, hee would neuer haue called them necessary euils.
Out of what Scripture, out of what record, can hee proue these impious and impudent speeches? They are onely faigned and framed out of his owne idle, giddie, furious, and franticke imaginations. If he had cited *Euripides* for his Author, hee had had some colour, for the prophane Poet in *Medea*, vseth these speeches, *Quod si Deorum aliquis mulierem formauit, opificem se malorum sciat, maximum & hominibus inimicum.* If any of the Gods framed woman, let him know he was the worker of that which is naught, and what is most hurtfull to men. Thus a Pagan writeth prophanely, but for a Christian to say, that God calleth women *necessary euils*, is most intolerable and shamefull to be written and published.

Chap. III.

What choise God hath made of women to be instruments to deriue his benefits to Mankinde.

Abraham being in danger, was blessed and preserued in respect of *Sara*. — Genes. 20.

Rebecca by Gods prouidence was the meanes to bring the blessing of *Isaac* to fall vpon *Iacob*. — Genes. 27.

The Ægyptian Mid-wiues were a meanes to preserue the male children of the *Israelites* from the murther entended by *Pharao*. — Exod. 1.

Moses

Ester *hath hang'd* Haman.

Exod. 2. *Moses* was preserued by the daughter of *Pharao.*

Iosua 2. 6: The Messengers sent by Duke *Iosuah* to view the Land of Promise, were harboured and freed from danger by a woman.

Iudges 4. When the Children of *Israell* had beene twentie yeres oppressed by *Iabin* King of *Canaan*, *Debbora* and *Iahell*, two women; the one wonne the battell, the other slew the Generall.

Iudges 9. When *Abimilech* had murthered seauenty of his Brethren, he was punished and slaine by a woman at the siege of *Thebes.*

1 Kings 19. *Micholl* aduentured the hazard of her Fathers displeasure to preserue her Husband *Dauid.*

1 Kings 25. *Abigail* by incomparable wisedome with-held *Dauid* from shedding of innocent bloud.

2 Kings 20. The Citie of *Abdela* being in danger, was preserued by a wise woman of that Citie.

3 Kings 17. In the great famine of *Samaria*, the widow of *Sarepta* was chosen to preserue *Elias*, and *Elias* to preserue her.

4 Kings 4. The like prouision did the woman, a *Sunamite*, make for *Elizeus*, and *Elizeus* for the woman.

4 Kings 11. When the bloud-Royall of *Iudah* had beene all murthered, *Ioas* afterwards King, was preserued by a woman.

Iudith. What was that noble aduenture so blessedly performed by *Iudith*, in cutting off the head of *Holofernes*?

Hester. With what wisedome did Queene *Hester* preserue her people, and caused their enemies to be hanged?

Susanna. What a chast mirrour was *Susanna*, who rather hazarded her life, then offend against God?

Neuer

Ester hath hang'd Haman.

Neuer was greater magnanimity shewed by a wo- *2 Mach.7.*
man, then by that Mother which saw her seauen children tormented most cruelly, yet she encouraged
them to the death.

Chap. IIII.

*What excellent blessings and graces haue beene be-
stowed vpon women in the Lawe of
Grace.*

THe first which commeth in this place, to be mentioned, is that blessed mother and mirrour of al woman-hood, the Virgin *Marie*, who was magnified in the birth of *Iesus*, glorified by Angels, chosen by the Almighty to beare in her wombe the Saviour of mankinde.

With what a faithfull salutation did *Elizabeth*, Saint *Luke 1.*
Iohn Baptist Mother, entertaine the Virgin vpon her
repaire vnto her?

Anna the old Prophetesse did miraculously de- *Luke 2.*
monstrate our Saviour.

The woman which had the issue of bloud: the *Math. 9 19.*
woman of *Canaan, Ioh.* 4. The *Samaritan* woman.
Martha, the 11. of *Iohn*: all these and sundry others
are saued, healed, and haue their sinnes forgiuen, in
respect of their true and liuely faith.

VVhat faith? what zeale? what deuotion did

Marie

Ester *hath hang'd* Haman.

Marie Magdelen shew toward Iesus, in prostrating her selfe at the feete of Iesus, annoynting them with pretious oyntment, washing them with teares, and drying them with the haire of her head? *Luke 7.*

With what bountie and deuotion did the *Maryes*, the wife of *Herods* steward, did *Ioanna*, with other women contribute of their goods to Iesus? *Luke 8.*

How charitable was that poore widdow, whose two Mites our Sauiour valued at a greater estimate, then any gift of any other whatsoeuer? *Luke 2.1.*

In all dangers, troubles, and extremities, which fell to our Sauiour, when all men fled from him, liuing or dead, women neuer forsooke him. *Luke 2.3.*

I should be ouer-tedious to repeate euery example of most zealous, faithfull, and deuout women, which I might in the new Testament, whose faith and deuotion was censured by our Sauiour to be without compare.

I will conclude for women that they haue beene chosen both to set out Gods glory, and for the benefit of all mankinde, in more glorious and gratious imployments then men haue beene.

The first promise of a Messias to come was made to a woman: the birth and bearing of that promised Messias was performed by a woman.

The triumphant resurrection with the conquest ouer death and hell, was first published and proclaymed by a woman.

I might hereunto adde those wiues, widdowes, and virgins, which flourished in the primatiue Church, and all succeeding ages sithence, who in all vertues haue excelled, and honoured both their sexe in generall,

Ester *hath hang'd* Haman.

rall, and themselues in particular, who in their martyrdomes, in their confession of Iesus, and in all Christian, and deuine vertues, haue in no respect beene inferiour vnto men.

THus out of the second and third Chapters of *Genesis*, and out of the Old and New Testaments, I haue obserued in proofe of the worthinesse of our Sexe: First, that woman was the last worke of Creation, I dare not say the best: She was created out of the chosen and best refined substance: She was created in a more worthy country: She was married by a most holy Priest: She was giuen by a most gratious Father: Her husband was enioyned to a most inseperable and affectionate care ouer her: The first promise of saluation was made to a woman: There is inseperable hatred and enmitie put betwixt the woman and the Serpent: Her first name, *Eua*, doth presage the nature and disposition of all women, not onely in respect of their bearing, but further, for the life and delight of heart and soule to all mankinde.

The summon of womans blessings and graces.

I haue further shewed the most gratious, blessed, and rarest benefits, in all respects, bestowed vpon women; all plainely and directly out of Scriptures.

All which doth demonstrate the blasphemous impudencie of the authour of the *Arraignement*, who would or durst write so basely and shamefully, in so generall a manner, against our so worthy and honored a sexe.

To the courteous and friendly
Reader.

Entle READER, in my first Part I haue (what I might) strictly obserued a religious regard, not to entermingle any thing vnfitting the grauitie of so respectiue an Argument.

Now that I am come to this second Part, I am determined to solace my selfe with a little libertie: What aduantages I did forbeare to take in the former, I meane to make vse of in this second. Ioseph Swetnam hath beene long vnanswered, which had beene performed sooner, if I had heard of his Booke before this last Terme: Or if the report of the Maidens answere had not stayed me. I haue not so amply and absolutely discharged my selfe in this Apologie as I would haue done, if either my leisure had beene such, as I could haue wished, or the time more fauourable, that I might haue stayed. What my repaire into the Countrey enforceth me to leaue rather begunne then finished; I meane (by Gods grace) to make perfect the next Terme: In the meane time (gentle READER) I bid thee kindly farewell.

Ester Sowrenam.
Chap.

Ester hath hang'd Haman.

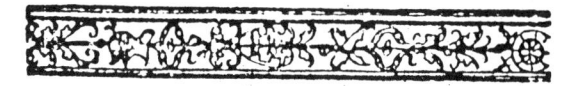

Chap. IIII.

At what estimate Women were valued in ancient and former times.

Plato in his Bookes *de Legibus*, estimateth of Women, which doe equall Men in all respects, onely in bodie they are weaker, but in wit and disposition of minde nothing inferiour, if not superiour. Whereupon he doth in his so absolute a Common-wealth, admit them to gouernment of Kingdomes and Common-weales, if they be either borne thereunto by Nature, or seated in gouernment by Election.

It is apparent, that in the prime of antiquity, women were valued at highest estimate, in that all those most inestimable and incomparable benefites which might either honour or preserue Mankinde, are all generally attributed to the inuention of women, as may appeare in these few examples following.

When *meum & tuum*, Mine and Thine, when right and wrong were decided by warres, and their weapons then were the furniture of Nature, as Fists, Teeth, Stones, Stakes, or what came next to hand: A Ladie of an heroicall disposition, called *Bellona*, did first inuent a more man-like and honourable weapon

The incomparable inuentions of women.

for warre, which was the sword, with other Armour correspondent, for which she was at first (and so euer since) honoured, as the Goddesse of warre.

When at the first the finest Manchet and best bread in vse was of Acorns, by the singular and practicall wit of a Lady called *Ceres*, the sowing of Corne, and Tillage was inuented.

The inuention of the seauen liberall Sciences, of all Arts, of all Learning, hath beene generally with one consent ascribed to the inuention of *Iupiters* daughters, the nine Muses, whose Mother was a royall Ladie *Mnemosum*.

Carmentis a Ladie, first inuented Letters, and the vse of them by reading and writing.

The royall and most delightfull exercise of Hunting was first found out and practised by *Diana*, who thervpon is celebrated for the Goddesse of Hunting.

The three Graces, which adde a *decorum*, and yeeld fauour to Persons, Actions, and Speaches, are three Ladies, *Aglaia*, *Thalia*, and *Enphrosune*.

The heroicall exercises of *Olimpus*, were first found and put in practife by *Palestra* a woman.

The whole world being diuided into three parts in more ancient times, euery diuision to this day keepeth the name in honour of a woman.

The foeminine Sexe is exceeding y honoured by Poets in their writings: They haue Gods as well for good things, as for bad; but they haue no women-Goddesses, but in things which are especially good. They haue *Bacchus* for a drunken God, but no drunken Goddesse. They haue *Priapus* the lustfull God of Gardens, but no garden-Goddesses, except of late in the

Ester hath hang'd Haman.

the garden-Allies. They will obiect here vnto mee *Venus*, she indeed is the Goddesse of Loue, but it is her blinde Sonne which is the God of Lust; poore Ladie, she hath but her ioynture in the Mannor of Loue, *Cupid* is Lord of all the rest, hee hath the royalty; she may not strike a Deare, but she must imploy her Sonne that sawcie Boy.

For Pride, they held it so farre from women, that they found out *Nemesis* or *Rhamnusia*, to punish and reuenge pride, but none to infect with pride.

They haue *Pluto* the God of Hell, but no proper Goddes of hell; but *Proserpina*, whom *Pluto* forcibly tooke from Mount *Ætna*, and carried her away, and made her Queene of Hell; yet she doth not remaine in Hell but one halfe of the yeare, by a decree from *Iupiter*.

If I should recite and set downe all the honourable records and Monuments for and of women, I might write more Bookes then I haue yet written lines. I will leaue and passe ouer the famous testimonies of forreine Kingdomes and Common-wealths, in honour of our Sexe: and I will onely mention some few examples of our owne Countrey and Kingdome, which haue been incomparably benefited and honoured by women.

Amongst the olde Britaines, our first Ancestors, the valiant *Boadicea*, that defended the liberty of her Countrey, against the strength of the *Romans*, when they were at the greatest, and made them feele that a woman could conquer them who had conquered almost all the men of the then known world.

The deuout *Helen*, who besides that, she was the

mother

Mother of that religious and great *Constantine*, who first seated Christian Religion in the Imperiall throne, & in that respect may be stiled the mother of Religion, is still more honoured for her singular pietie and charitie towards him and his members, who dyed for vs vpon the Crosse, then for her care and industry in finding out the wood of that Crosse on which he dyed.

In the time of the *Danes*, chaste *Æmma*, whose innocency carried her naked feete ouer the fire-hot Plow-shares vnfelt; with the *Saxons* Queene *Elfgiue* the holy widdow, and the Kings daughter *Edith* a Virgin Saint, both greater Conquerers then *Alexander* the great, that men so much boast of, who could not conquere himselfe.

Since the *Normans*, the heroicall vertues of *Elenor* wife to *Edward* the first, who when her Husband in the Holy Land was wounded with a poysoned Arrow, of which ther was no hope of recouery from the Chyrurgions, she suckt the poyson into her own bodie to free him: together, curing that mortall wound, and making her owne fame immortall: so that I thinke this one act of hers may equall all the acts that her great Husband did in those warres besides.

Philip, wife to *Edward* the third, no lesse to be honoured for being the Mother of so many braue children, then of so many good deeds, which worthily got her the title of good.

Margaret the wise, wife to *Henrie* the sixt, who if her Husbands fortune, valour, and foresight, had beene answerable to hers, had left the Crowne of *England* to their owne Sonne, and not to a stranger.

The

The other *Margaret* of *Richmond*, mother to *Henrie* the seuenth, from whose brests he may seeme to haue deriued as well his vertues as his life, in respect of her heroicall prudence and pietie; whereof, besides other Monuments, both the Vniuersities are still witnesses.

Besides this, it was by the blessed meanes of *Elizabeth*, wife to *Henrie* the seuenth, that the bloudy wars betwixt the houses of *Yorke* and *Lancaster* were ended, and the red Rose and the white vnited, &c.

It was by the meanes of the most renowmed Queene (the happy Mother of our dread Soueraigne) that the two Kingdomes once mortall foes, are now so blessedly contyned.

And that I may name no more (since in one onely were comprized all the qualities and endowments that could make a person eminent) *Elizabeth* our late Soueraigne, not onely the glory of our Sexe, but a patterne for the best men to imitate, of whom I will say no more, but that while she liued, she was the mirrour of the world, so then knowne to be, and so still remembred, and euer will be.

Daily experience, and the common course of Nature, doth tell vs that women were by men in those times highly valued, and in worth by men themselues preferred, and held better then themselues,

I will not say that women are better then men, but I will say, men are not so wise as I would wish them to be, to wooe vs in such fashion as they do, except they should ho'd and account of vs as their betters.

What trauaile? what charge? what studie? doe not men vndertake to gaine our good-will, loue, and liking? *Men sue to Women.*

liking? what vehement suits doe they make vnto vs? with what solemne vowes and protestations do they solicite vs? they write, they speake, they send, to make knowne what entire affection they beare vnto vs, that they are so deepely engaged in loue, except we doe compassion them with our loue and fauour, they are men vtterly cast away. One he will starue himselfe, another will hang, another drowne, another stab, another will exile himselfe from kinred and country, except they may obtaine our loues: What? will they say that we are baser then themselues? then they wrong themselues exeedingly, to prefer such vehement suits to creatures inferiour to themselues: Sutors doe euer in their suites confesse a more worthinesse in the persons to whom they sue. These kind of suits are from Nature, which cannot deceiue them: Nature doth tell them what women are, and custom doth approue what nature doth direct. *Aristotle* saith, *Omnia appetunt bonum*, euery thing by nature doth seeke after that which is good. Nature then doth cary men with violence, to seeke and sue after women: They will answere, and seeke to elude this *Maxime* with a distinction, that *bonum* is duplex, *aut verum, aut apparens*; that goodnesse or the thing which is good, is either truely good, or but apparantly good; so they may say, women are but apparantly good. But the heathen Orator and the deuine philosopher to, affirme, if we follow the true direction of nature we shall neuer be deceiued. Nature in her vehement motions is not deceiued with apparant shewes. It is naturall, they will say, for the Male to follow the Female; so it is as naturall, for the Female to be better then

Suit is alwaies preferred to the better.

then the Male, as appeareth to be true in obseruation of Hawkes: the Spar-hawke is of more esteeme then the Musket; the Goshawke more excellent then the Tersell; so in Falcons, the females doe excell: The like men are bound to acknowledge women; the rather in respect of their owne credit and honour. To what obsequious duty and seruice doe men binde themselues, to obtaine a fauour from their deuoted Mistresse, which if he may obtaine he thinketh himselfe to be much honoured, & puts in place of most noted view, that the world may take note: He weareth in his hat, or on his brest, or vpon his arme, the Gloue, the Scarfe, or Ring of his Mistrisse: If these were not relickes from Saintly creatures, men would not sacrifice so much deuotion vnto them. *Womens fauours estimated as relicks.*

Amongst diuers causes which proceede from nature and custome, why men are so earnest Sutors to women, I haue obserued one, which by practise is daily confessed. *Plato* sayth, that Honestie is of that worthinesse, that men are greatly enflamed with the loue of it; and as they doe admire it, so they studie how to obtaine it: it is apparant, yong men which are vnmarried, and called batchelers, they may haue a disposicion, or may serue an apprentiship to honesty, but they are neuer free-men, nor euer called honest men, till they be married: for that is the portion which they get by their wiues. When they are once married, they are forthwith placed in the ranke of honest men, If question be asked, what is such a man? it is presently resolued, he is an honest man: And the reason presently added, for hee hath a wife; shee is the sure signe and seale of honestie. It is vsuall amongst *Honestie comes by marriage, the womans dowrie.*

Ester hath hang'd Haman.

amongst old and graue fathers, if they haue a sonne giuen to spending and companie-keeping, who is of a wild and riotous disposition, such a father shall presently be counselled, helpe your sonne to a good wife, marry him, marry him, that is the onely way to bring him to good order, to tame him, to bring him to be an honest man: The auncient fathers doe herein acknowledge a greater worthinesse in women then in men; the hope which they haue of an vntowardly sonne, to reclaime him, is all engaged vpon the woman.

In no one thing, men doe acknowledge a more excellent perfection in women then in the estimate of the offences which a woman doth commit: the worthinesse of the person doth make the sinne more markeable. What an hatefull thing is it to see a woman ouercome with drinke, when as in men it is noted for a signe of goodfellowship? and whosoeuer doth obserue it, for one woman which doth make a custome of drunkennesse, you shall finde an hundred men: it is abhorred in women, and therefore they auoyd it: it is laughed at and made but as a iest amongst men, and therefore so many doe practise it: Likewise if a man abuse a Maide & get her with child, no matter is made of it, but as a trick of youth; but it is made so hainous an offence in the maide, that she is disparaged and vterly vndone by it. So in all offences those which men commit, are made light and as nothing, slighted ouer; but those which women doe commit, those are made grieuous and shamefull, and not without iust cause: for where God hath put hatred betwixt the woman and the serpent,

Womens faults more markable because they are the better.

it

Ester hath hang'd Haman.

it is a foule shame in a woman to carry fauour with the deuill, to stayne her womanhoode with any of his damnable qualities, that she will shake hands where God hath planted hate.

Ioseph Swetnam in his Pamphlet aggrauateth the offences of women in the highest degree, not onely exceeding, but drawing men into all mischeife. If I do grant, that woman degenerating from the true end of womanhood, prooue the greatest offenders, yet in graunting that, I doe thereby proue that women in their creation are the most excellent creatures: for corruption, *boni pessima*, the best thing corrupted proueth the worst, as for example, the most glorious creature in heauen is by his fall the most damned deuill in hell: all the Elements in their puritie are most pretious, in their infection and abuse most dangerous: so the like in women, in their most excellent puritie of nature, what creature more gratious! but in their fall from God, and all goodnesse, what creature more mischieuous? which the deuill knowing he doth more assault woman then man, becausehis gaine is greater, by the fall of one woman, then of twentie men. Let there be a faire maide, wife, or woman, in Countrie, towne or Citie, she shall want no resort of Serpents, nor any varietie of tempter: let there be in like sort, a beautifull or personable man, he may sit long enough before a woman will solicite him. For where the deuill hath good acquaintance, he is sure of entertainement there, without resistance: The Serpent at first tempted woman, he dare assault her no more in that shape, now he imployeth men to supply his part; and so they doe: for as the Serpent began

The deuill doth more violently tempt women then men. He is sure of them when he will.

began with *Eue* to delight her taste, so doe his instruments draw to wine and banqueting; the next, the Serpent enticed her by pride, and tolde her shee should be like to God; so doe his instruments; first, they will extoll her beauty, what a paragon she is in their eyes; next, they will promise her such maintenance, as the best woman in the Parish or Country shall not haue better: What care they, if they make a thousand oathes, and commit tenne thousand periuries, so they may deceiue a woman? When they haue done all and gotten their purpose, then they discouer all the womans shame, and imploy such an Author as this (to whose *Arraignment* I doe make haste) to raile vpon her and the whole Sexe.

Dissembling in men.

THE ARRAIGNMENT OF
Joseph Swetnam, who was the Author of the *Arraignment of Women*; And vnder his person, the arraignment of all idle, franticke, froward, and lewd men.

Chapter V.

Ioseph Swetnam hauing written his rash, idle, furious and shamefull discourse against Women, it was at last deliuered into my hands, presently I did acquaint some of our Sexe with the accident, with whom I did aduise what course wee should take with him. It was concluded (that his vnworthinesse being much like to that of *Thersites*, whom I haue formerly mentioned) wee would not answere him either with *Achilles* fist, or *Stafford*-law; neither p'ucke him in pieces as the *Thracian* woman did *Orpheus*, for his intemperate rayling against women: But as he had arraigned women at the barre of fame and report; wee resolued at the same barre where he did vs the wrong, to arraigne him, that thereby

E 2   wee

Ester hath hang'd Haman.

we might defend our assured right: And withall (respecting our selues) we resolued to fauour him so far in his triall that the world might take notice there was no partiall or indirect dealing, but that he had as much fauour as he could desire, and farre more then he did or could deserue.

The Iudgesses. So that wee brought him before two Iudgesses, *Reason,* and *Experience,* who being both in place, no man can suspect them with any indirect proceedings: For albeit, *Reason* of it selfe may be blinded by passion, yet when she is ioyned with *Experience,* shee is knowne to be absolute, and without compare. As for *Experience,* she is knowne of her selfe to be admirable excellent in her courses, she knoweth how to vse euery man in her practise; she will whip the foole to learne him more wit; she will punish the knaue to practise more honesty; she will curbe in the prodigall, and teach him to be warie; she will trip vp the heeles of such as are rash and giddy, and bid them hereafter looke before they leape. To be short, there is not in all the world, for all estates, degrees, qualities and conditions of men, so singular a Mistresse, or so fit to be a Iudgesse as she, onely one property she hath aboue all the rest, no man commeth before her but she maketh him ashamed, and shee will call and proue almost euery man a foole, especially such who are wise in their owne conceits.

The Iurie. For his Iurie, albeit we knew them to be of his dearest, and neirest inward familiar friends, in whose company he was euer, and did spend vpon them all that he cou'd get, or deuise to get; yet wee did challenge no one of them, but were well pleased that his

fiue

Ester *hath bang'd* Haman.

fiue Senses, and the seauen deadly sinnes should stand for his Iury.

The partie which did giue euidence against him, we knew to bee a sure Card, and one which would not faile in proofe of any thing, and such proofe which should be without all exception, *Conscience* is a sure witnesse.

So all things being accordingly prouided, the prisoner was brought to the barre, where he was called and bid hold vp his hand, which hee did, but a false hand God he knowes, his enditement was red, which was this which followeth.

The Euidence.

Chap. VI.

Ioseph Swetnam his Enditement.

Ioseph *Swetnam*, thou art endited by the name of *Ioseph Swetnam* of *Bedlemmore*, in the Countie of *Onopolie* *: For that thou the twentieth day of *December*, in the yeare &c. Diddest most wickedly, blasphemously, falsly, and scandalously publish a lewd Pamphlet, entituled the *Arraignment of Women*; In which, albeit thou diddest honestly pretend to arraigne lewd, idle, froward and vnconstant women, yet contrary to thy pretended promise thou diddest rashly, and malitiously raile and rage against all women, generally writing and publishing

*Pamphlet-maker.
An Inditement.

lishing most blasphemously that women by their Creator were made for *Helpers*, for *Helpers*. (thou sayest) *to spend and consume that which Man painefully getteth*; furthermore, thou dost write, *That being made of a rib, which was crooked, they are therefore crooked and froward in conditions, and that Woman was no sooner made, but her heart was set vpon mischiefe*; which thou doest deriue to all the Sexe generally, in these words, *And therefore euer since they haue beene a woe vnto man, and follow the line of their first leader:* Further then all this, thou doest affirme an impudent lye vpon Almighty God, in saying, that God calleth them *necessary euils, and that therefore they were created to bee a plague vnto man*. Thou writest also, *That women are prowde, lasciuous, froward, curst, vnconstant, idle, impudent, shamelesse, and that they decke and dresse themselues to tempt and allure men to lewdnesse*, with much and many more foule, intemperate, and scandalous speaches, &c.

When *Ioseph Swetnam* was asked what he said to his enditement, *Guilty, or not guiltie,* hee pleaded the generall issue, *not guiltie,* being asked how hee would be tryed, he stood mute, for *Conscience* did so confront him, that he knew vpon tryall there was no way but one; wherevpon hee thought it much better to put himselfe vpon our mercy, then to hazard the tryall of his owne Iurie.

Wherevpon we did consider if we should haue vrged him to be pressed, the disaduantage had beene ours: for then his fauourites would haue said as some did say, that *Ioseph Swetnam* did not stand mute, as misdoubting the proofe of what he had written: But

Standeth mute.

seeing

Ester hath hang'd Haman.

seeing the Iudgesses, the Iurie, the Accuser, and all others, most of them of the fœminine gender, he suspelled the question by vs, being made Generall, that they would rather condemne him to please a generall, although in particular respect of himselfe he knew they would fauour him. And besides that hee held it a strange course, that the selfe and the same persons should be Iudges and Accusers, whereupon we resolued to graunt him longer time to aduise with himselfe whether he would put himselfe to triall, or vpon better deliberation to recall his errours.

But that the world might be satisfied in respect of the wrongs done vnto vs, and to maintaine our honourable reputation, it was concluded, that my selfe should deliuer before the Iudges, to all the assembly, speaches to these effects following.

Chap. VII.

The answere to all obiections which are materiall, made against Women.

Right Honourable and Worshipfull, and you of all degrees; it hath euer beene a common custome amongst Idle, and humerous Poets, Pamphleters, and Rimers, out of passionate discontents, or hauing little otherwise to imploy themselues about, to write some bitter Satire-Pamphlet, or Rime, against women: in which argument he who could deuise any thing more bitterly,

terly, or spitefully, against our sexe, hath neuer wanted the liking, allowance, and applause of giddy headed people. Amongst the rable of scurill writers, this prisoner now present hath acted his part, whom albeit women could more willingly let passe, then bring him to triall, and as euer heretofore, rather contemn such authors thē deigne them any answere, yet seeing his booke so commonly bought vp, which argueth a generall applause; we are therfore enforced to make answere in defence of our selues, who are by such an author so extreamely wronged in publike view.

You all see hee will not put himselfe vpon triall: if we should let it so passe, our silence might implead vs for guiltie, so would his Pamphlet be receiued with a greater currant and credite then formerly it hath beene: So that as well in respect of our sexe, as for a generall satisfaction to the world, I will take this course with our prisoner, I will at this present examine all the obiections which are most materiall, which our aduersarie hath vomited out against woman, and not onely what he hath obiected, but what other authors of more import then *Ioseph Swetnam* haue charged vpon women: alas, seely man he obiecteth nothing but what he hath stolne out of English writers, as *Euphues*, the *Palace of Pleasure*, with the like, which are as easily answered as vaynly obiected. He neuer read the vehement and profest enemies against our sexe, as for *Gracians, Euripides, Menander, Simonides, Sophocles*, with the like, amongst Latine writers *Iuuenall, Plautus*, &c.

But of all that euer I read, I did neuer obserue such
generall

Ester *hath hang'd* Haman.

generall sinceritie in any, as in this aduersarie, which you shall finde I will make as manifest as the Sunne to shine at mid-day.

It is the maine end that our aduersarie aimeth at in all his discourse, to proue and say that women are bad; if he should offer this vpon particulers, no one would denie it: but to lauish generally against all women, who can endure it? You might *M*[r]. *Swetnam*, with some shew of honestie haue sayd, some women are bad, both by custome and company, but you cannot avoide the brand, both of blasphemie and dishonestie, to say of women generally they are all naught, both in their creation and by nature, and to ground your inferences vpon Scriptures.

I let passe your obiections in your first page; because they are formerly answered, onely whereas you say, *woman was no sooner made, but her heart was set vpon mischiefe*: if you had then said, she had no sooner eaten of the fruit, but her heart was set vpon mischiefe, you had had some colour for your speaches; not in respect of the womans disposition, but in consideration both of her first Tutor and her second instructor: For whereas scripture doth say, *Woman was supplanted by a Serpent, Ioseph Swetnam* doth say, *she was supplanted by the deuill, which appeared to her in the shape of a beautifull yong man.* Men are much beholding to this author, who will seeme to insinuate, that the deuill would in so friendly and familier a manner, put on the shape of man, when he first began to practise mischiefe: The deuill might make bold of them, whom he knew in time would proue his famil-

The Deuill tooke the shape of man.

F lier

Ester hath hang'd Haman.

lier friends. Herevpon it may be imagined it commeth to passe that Painters, and Picture-makers, when they would represent the deuill, they set him out in the deformed shape of a man; because vnder that shape he began first to act the part of a diuell: and I doubt he neuer changed his suite sithence. Here it is to be obserued, that which is worst is expressed by the shape of a man; but what is the most glorious creature is represented in the beautie of a woman, as Angels. Woman at the first might easily learne mischeife, where or how should the learne goodnes? her first Schoole-master was aboundant in mischiefe, and her first husband did exceede in bad examples. First, by his example he taught her how to flye from God: next how to excuse her sinne: then how to cample and contest with God, and to say as *Adam* did, thou art the cause, for, the woman whom thou gauest me, was the cause I did eate. What *Adam* did at the first, bad husbands practise with their wiues euer sithence, i meane in bad examples. It was no good example in *Adam*, who hauing receiued his wife from the gift of God, and bound to her in so inseperable a bond of loue, that forthwith he being taken tardie would presently accuse his wife & put her in all the danger; but the woman was more bound to an vpright iudge, then to a louing husband: it would not serue *Adams* turne, to charge her, therby to free himselfe: It was an hard and strange course, that he who should haue beene her defender, is now become her greatest accuser. I may heare say with Saint *Paul, by one mans sinne, death,* &c. So by the contagion

Serpent gaue the woman bad counsell and her husband bad example.

Men doe shew themselues the children of Adam.

Ester *hath hang'd* Haman.

tagion of originall sinne in *Adam*, all men are infected with his diseases; and looke what examples he gaue his wife at the first, the like examples and practises doe all men shew to women euer sithence. Let mee speake freely, for I will speake nothing but truly, neither shall my words exceede my proofe.

In your first and second Page, you alledge *Dauid* and *Salomon*, for exclaiming bitterly against women: And that *Salomon* saith, *Women (like as Wine) doe make men drunke with their deuices*. What of all this?

Ioseph Swetnam, a man which hath reason, will neuer obiect that vnto his aduersary, which when it commeth to examination will disaduantage himselfe. Your meaning is, in the disgrace of women to exalt men: but is this any commendation to men, that they haue been and are ouer-reacht by women? Can you glory of their holinesse, whom by women proue sinfull? or in their wisedome, whom women make fooles? or in their strength, whom women ouercome? can you excuse that fall which is giuen by the weaker? or colour that foyle which is taken from women? Is holinesse, wisedome, and strength, so slightly seated in your Masculine gender, as to be stained, blemished, and subdued by women? But now I pray you let vs examine how these vertues in men so potent, came by women to be so impotent. Doe you meane in comparatiue degree, that women are more holy, more wise, more strong, then men? if you should graunt this, you had small cause to write against them. But you will not admit this: What is, or are the causes then why men are so ouertaken by women?

Foolish men tempted with outward shewes.

Ester *bath hang'd* Haman.

women? You set downe the causes in your fourth Page; there you say, *They are dangerous for men to deale withall, for their faces are Lures, their beauties baytes, their lookes are nets, and their words are charmes,* and all to bring men to ruine: *Incidit in Scyllam qui vult vitare Charibdim,* whil'ft he seeketh to auoide one mischiefe, he falleth into another. It were more credit for men to yeeld our sexe to be more holy, wise, and strong, then to excuse themselues by the reasons alleaged: for by this men are proued to haue as ltle wit as they are charged to exceed in wickednesse. Are external & dumbe shews such potent baites, nets, lures, charmes, to bring men to ruine? Why? wilde Asses, dotterels, and woodcockes, are not so easily entangled and taken? are men so idle, vaine, and weake, as you seeme to make them? Let mee now see how you can free these men from dishoneft mindes, who are ouertaken thus with beautie, &c. How can beautie hurt? how can it be a cause of a mans ruine, of it selfe? what, do women forcibly draw? why, men are more strong? are they so eloquent to perswade? why, men are too wise; are they mischieuous to entise? men are more holy; how then are women causes to bring men to ruine? direct causes they cannot be in any respect; if they be causes, they are but accidentall causes: A cause as Philosophers say, *causa sine qua non*: a remote cause, which cause is seldome alleaged for cause, but where want of wit would say somewhat, and a guilty conscience wou'd excuse it selfe by something. Philosophers say, *Nemo leditur nisi à seipso,* no man is hurt but the cause is in himselfe. The

If men be hurt thanke themselues.

prodi-

Ester hath hang'd Haman.

prodigall person amongst the *Græcians* is called *Asotos*, as a destroyer, an vndoer of himselfe: When an heart fraughted with sinne doth prodigally lauish out a lasciuious looke out of a wanton eye; when it doth surfeit vpon the sight, who is *Asotos*? who is guiltie of his lasciuious disease but himselfe? *Volenti non fit iniuria*, hee who is wounded with his owne consent, hath small cause to complaine of anothers wrong: Might not a man as easily, and more honestly, when hee seeth a faire woman, which doth make the best vse that she can to set out her beautie, rather glorifie God in so beautifull a worke, then infect his soule with so lasciuious a thought? And for the woman, who hauing a Iewell giuen her from so deare a friend, is she not to be commended rather that in the estimate which she sheweth, shee will as carefully and as curiously as she may set out what she hath receiued from Almighty God, then to be censured that she doth it to allure wanton and lasciuious lookes? The difference is in the minds, things which are called *Adiaphora*, things indifferent, whose qualities haue their name from the vses, are commonly so censured, and so vsed, as the minde is inclined which doth passe his verdict. A man and a woman talke in the fields together, an honest minde will imagine of their talke answerable to his owne disposition, whereas an euill dispos'd minde will censure according to his lewd inclination. When men complaine of beautie, and say, *That womens dressings and attire are prouocations to wantonnesse, and baites to allure men*, It is a direct meanes to know of what dispositi-

Womans beauty is good, but the heart which doth surfeit is naught.

on

on they are, it is a shame for men in censuring of women to condemne themselues; but a common Inne cannot be without a common signe; it is a common signe to know a leacher, by complaining vpon the cause and occasion of his surfeit; who had knowne his disease but by his owne complaint? It is extreme folly to complaine of another, when the roote of all resteth within himselfe; purge an infected heart, and turne away a lacinious eye, and then neither their dressings, nor their beautie can any waies hurt you. Doe not men exceede in apparell, and therein set themselues out to the view? Shall women betray themselues and make it knowne that they are either so bad in their disposition, or so wanton in their thoughts, or so weak in their gouernment as to complaine that they are tempted and allured by men? Should women make themselues more vaine then yongest children, to fall in loue with babyes. Women are so farre off from being in any sort prouoked to loue vpon the view of mens apparell, and setting forth themselues, that no one thing can more draw them from loue, then their vanitie in apparell. Women make difference betwixt colours and conditions, betwixt a faire shew, and a foule substance: It shewes a leuitie in man to furnish himselfe more with trim colours, then manlike qualities: besides that, how can we loue at whom we laugh? We see him gallant it at the Court one day, & braue it in the Country the next day; we see him weare that on his backe one week, which we heare is in the brokers shop the next: furthermore we see diuers weare apparell and colours

Women doe not fall in loue with men for their apparell.

made

Ester *hath hang'd* Haman. 39

made of a Lordſhip, lined with Farmes and Granges, embrodered with all the plate, gold, and wealth, their Friends and Fathers left them : Are theſe motiues to loue or to laughter? Will or dare a woman truſt to their loue for one Moneth, who will turne her of the next? This is the ſurfeit which women take by braue apparell. They rather ſuſpect his worth, then wiſh his loue, who doth moſt exceede in brauerie. So Mr. *Swetnam*, doe you and all yours forbeare to cenſure of the dreſſings and attires of women for any ſuch lewd intent, as you imagine: Bad minds are diſcouered by bad thoughts and hearts. Doe not ſay and rayle at women to be the cauſe of mens ouerthrow, when the originall roote and cauſe is in your ſelues. If you bee ſo affected that you cannot looke but you muſt forthwith be infected, I doe maruaile (*Ioſeph Swetnam*) you ſet downe no remedies for that torment of Loue, as you call it: You bid men ſhunne and auoyde it, but thoſe be common and ordinary rules and inſtructions : yet not ſo ordinary, as able to reſtraine the extraordinary humors of your giddy company. I will do you and your friends a kindneſſe if you be ſo ſcorched with the flames of loue. *Diogines* did long ſince diſcouer the ſoueraigne ſalue for ſuch a wound : The receipt is no great charge, your ſelfe may be the Apothecarie, it is comprehended in three words : Firſt, trie with χεονος, next with λιμος, if both theſe faile, the third is ſure, βροχος. This was *Diogenes* Antidote againſt that venemous infection. There are more milder remedies which you may put in practiſe : If your hearts be ſo fleſhly, or your eies

A medicine for Loue. Time. Hanger. A Halter.

ſo

so tender that you dare trust neither of them, then trust to your reason to turne your eyes away, or trust to your heeles as *Ioseph* did, to carrie all away.

 After you haue railed against women, you bring in a fable of a contempt betwixt the *Winde* and the *Sunne*; and you apply the morrall to women, when as it hath a farre other relation: for it euer hath been applyed to men, to instruct them in the gouernment of woman, for I pray you who is to gouerne, or who are to be gouerned? You should seeme to come from the *Sauromatians*, whose wiues were their Masters: but I will set you downe both the Fable and the Morrall, as it was written in English verse long sithence.

THe Sunne *and* Winde *at variance did fall,*
 Whose force was greatest in the open field:
A trauailer they chuse to deale withall;
Who makes him first vnto their force to yeeld
 To cast off Cloake, they that agreement make,
 The honour of the victory must take.

The Winde *began and did encrease, each blast*
With raging beate vpon the silly man;
The more it blew, the more he grasped fast
And kept his Cloake, let Winde *doe what it can:*
 When all in vaine the Winde *his worst had done,*
 It ceast, and left a tryall to the Sunne.

The Sunne *beginnes his beames for to display,*
And by degrees in heate for to encrease;

Ester hath hang'd Haman.

The Trauailer then warme, doth make a stay,
And by degrees his Cloake he doth release:
   At length is forc'd both Coate and Cloake to yeeld,
   So giues the Sunne the honour of the field.

Who by extreames doth seeke to worke his will,
By raging humors thinking so to gaine;
May like the Winde augment his tempest still,
But at the length he findes his furie vaine:
   For all he gets by playing franticke parts,
   He hard'neth more the milde and gentle hearts.

Like as all Plants, when at the first they spring,
Are tender, and soft bark'd on euery side;
But as they grow continuall stormes doe bring
Those are more hard which Northerne blasts abide:
   What's toward the Southerne tenderer we finde,
   And that more hard which feeles the Northern winde.

Nature his course most carefully doth bend,
From violence to seeke it selfe to arme;
Where raging blasts the trees would breake and rend,
There Nature striues to keepe her Plants from harme:
   Where violence is vnto Nature strange,
   Continuall custome there doth Nature change.

So 'tis with women, who by Nature milde,
If they on froward crabbed Husbands light;
Continuall rage by custome makes them wilde,
For crooked natures alter gentle quite;

Ester hath hang'd Haman.

Men euermore shall this in triall finde,
Like to her vsage so is womans minde.

As of themselues, let men of others iudge,
What man will yeeld to be compel'd by rage?
At crabbednesse and crustnesse hearts doe grudge,
And to resist, themselues they more engage:
Forbeare the Winde, *shine with the* Sunne *a while,*
Though she be angry, she will forthwith smile.

This is the true application of the Morrall. As for that crookednesse and frowardnesse with which you charge women, looke from whence they haue it; for of themselues and their owne disposition it doth not proceede, which is prooued directly by your owne testimonie: for in your 45. Page, Line 15. You say, *A young woman of tender yeares is flexible, obedient, and subiect to doe any thing, according to the will and pleasure of her Husband.* How commeth it then that this gentle and milde disposition is afterwards altered? your selfe doth giue the true reason, for you giue a great charge not to marrie a widdow. But why? because say you in the same Page, *A widdow is framed to the conditions of another man.* Why then, if a woman haue froward conditions, they be none of her owne, she was framed to them. Is not our aduersarie ashamed of himselfe, to raile against women for those faults which doe all come from men? Doth not hee most grieuously charge men to learne their wiues bad and corrupt behauiour? for hee saith plainely, *Thou must vnlearne a widdow, and make her forget and forgoe*

[margin:] Woman of her owne disposition gentle, and milde.

[margin:] Men infect.

Ester *hath hang'd* Haman.

forgoe her former corrupt & disordered behauiour. Thou must vnlearne her, *Ergo,* what fault shee hath, shee learned, her corruptnes commeth not from her own disposition, but from her Husbands destruction. Is it not a wonder, that your Pamphlets are so dispersed? Are they not wise men to cast away time and money vpon a Booke which cutteth their owne throates? 'Tis pittie but that men should reward you for your writing; if it bee but as the Romane *Sertorius* did the idle Poet, hee gaue him a reward, but not for his writing, but because he should neuer write more; as for women, they laugh that men haue no more able a champion. This author commeth to baite women, or as hee foolishly sayth, the *Beare bayting of Women*, and he bringeth but a mungrell Curre, who doth his kinde, to braule and barke, but cannot bite. The milde and flexible disposition of a woman is in philosophy proued in the composition of her body, for it is a Maxime, *Mores animi sequuntur temperaturam corporis,* The disposition of the minde is answerable to the temper of the body. A woman in the temperature of her body is tender, soft, and beautifull, so doth her disposition in minde corresponde accordingly; she is milde, yeelding, and vertuous; what disposition accidentally happeneth vnto her, is by the contagion of a froward husband, as *Ioseph Swetnam* affirmeth.

    And experience proueth. It is a shame for a man to complaine of a froward woman, in many respects all concerning himselfe. It is a shame he hath no more gouernment ouer the weaker vessell. It is a shame he

The disposition of the minde doth answere the composition of the body.

G 2   hath

Ester hath hang'd Haman.

hath hardned her tender sides, and gentle heart with his boistrous & Northren blasts. It is a shame for a man to publish and proclaime houshold secrets, which is a common practise amongst men, especially Drunkards, Leachers, and prodigall spend-thrifts: These when they come home drunke, or are called in question for their riotous misdemeanours, they presently shew themselues, the right children of *Adam*. They will excuse themselues by their wiues, and say that their vnquietnesse and frowardnesse at home, is the cause that they runne abroad. An excuse more fitter for a beast then a man. If thou wert a man thou wouldest take away the cause which vrgeth a woman to griefe and discontent, and not by thy frowardnesse encrease her distemperature: forbeare thy drinking, thy luxurious riot, thy gaming, and spending, and thou shalt haue thy wife giue thee as little cause at home, as thou giuest her great cause of disquiet abroad. Men which are men, if they chance to be matched with froward wiues, either of their own making, or others marring, they would make a benefit of the discommodity, either try his skill to make her milde, or exercise his patience to endure her curstnesse: for all crosses are inflicted either for punishment of sinnes, or for exercise of vertues; but humorous men will sooner marre a thousand women, then out of an hundred make one good.

Men are the Serpents

And this shall appeare in the imputation which our aduersarie chargeth vpon our sexe, to be laciuious, wanton and lustfull: He sayth, *Women tempt, alure, and prouoke men.* How rare a thing is it for women

May men complaine of women without cause?

women to proftitute and offer themfelues? how common a practife is it for men to feeke and folicite women to lewdnelfe? what charge doe they fpare? what trauell doe they beftow? what vowes, oathes and proteftations doe they fpend, to make them difhoneft? They hyer Pandors, they write letters, they feale them with damnations, and execrations, to aſſure them of loue, when the end proues but luft: They know the flexible difpofition of Women and the fooner to ouerreach them, fome will pretend they are fo plunged in loue that except they obtaine their defire they will feeme to drown'd, hang, ftab, poyfon, or banifh themfelues from friends and countrie. What motiues are thefe to tender difpofitions? Some will pretend marriage, another offer continuall maintenance, but when they haue obtained their purpofe, what fhall a woman finde, iuft that which is her euerlafting fhame and griefe, fhee hath made her felfe the vnhappie fubject to a luftfull bodie, and the fhamefull ftall of a lafciuious tongue. Men may with foule fhame charge women with this finne which they had neuer committed if fhee had not trufted, nor had euer trufted if fhee had not beene decciued with vowes, oathes, and proteftations. To bring a woman to offend in one finne, how many damnable finnes doe they commit? I appeale to their owne confciences. The lewd difpofition of fundry men doth appeare in this: If a woman or maide will yeeld vnto lewdneffe, what fhall they want? But if they would liue in honeftie, what helpe fhall they haue? How much will they make of the lewd? how bafe base account of the honest? how many pounds will they spend in bawdie houses? but when will they bestowe a penny vpon an honest maide or woman, except it be to corrupt them?

Shew a womans offence, but that man was the first beginner.

Our aduersary bringeth many examples of men which haue beene ouerthrowne by women. It is answered, before the fault is their owne. But I would haue him, or any one liuing, to shew any woman that offended in this sinne of lust, but that she was first sollicited by a man.

Helen was the cause of *Troyes* burning; first, *Paris* did sollicite her; next, how many knaues and fooles of the male kinde had *Troy*, which to maintaine whoredome would bring their Citie to confusion.

When you bring in examples of lewd women, and of men which haue beene stained by women, you shew your selfe both franticke, and a prophane irreligious foole to mention *Iudith* for cutting off *Holofernes* head, in that rancke.

You challenge women for vntamed and vnbrideled tongues; there was neuer woman was euer noted for so shamelesse, so brutish, so beastly a scold as you proue your selfe in this base and odious Pamphlet: You blaspheme God, you raile at his Creation, you abuse and slander his Creatures; and what immodest or impudent scurilitie is, which you doe not expresse in this lewd and lying Pamphlet?

Hitherto I haue so answered all your obiections against Women, that as I haue not defended the wickednesse of any; so I haue set downe the true state of the question. As *Eue* did not offend without the temptation

Ester *hath hang'd* Haman.

temptation of a Serpent; so women doe seldome offend, but it is by prouocation of men. Let not your impudencie, nor your consorts dishonestie, charge our sexe hereafter, with those sinnes of which you your selues were the first procurers. I haue in my discourse, touched you, and all yours, to the quick. I haue taxed you with bitter speaches; you will (perhaps) say I am a rayling scold. In this Obiection, *Ioseph Swetnam*, I will teach you both wit and honestie: The difference betwixt a railing scold, and an honest accuser, is this, the first rageth vpon passionate furie, without bringing cause or proofe; the other bringeth direct proofe for what she alleageth: you charge women with clamorous words, and bring no proofes; I charge you with blasphemie, with impudencie, scurilitie, foolery, and the like. I shew iust and direct proofe for what I say; it is not my desire to speake so much, it is your desert to prouoke me vpon iust cause so farre; it is no railing to call a Crow blacke, or a Wolfe a rauenour, or a drunkard a beast; the report of the truth is neuer to be blamed, the deseruer of such a report, deserueth the shame.

A difference betwixt accusing and slandering.

Now, for this time, to draw to an end; let me aske according to the question of *Cassius, Cui bono?* what haue you gotten by publishing your Pamphlet; good I know you can get none. You haue (perhaps) pleased the humors of some giddy, idle conceited persons: But you haue died your selfe in the colours of shame, lying, slandering, blasphemie, ignorance, and the like.

The

The shortnesse of time and the weight of businesse call me away, and vrge me to leaue off thus abruptly, but assure your selfe where I leaue now, I will by Gods grace supply the next Terme, to your small content. You haue exceeded in your furie against Widdowes, whose defence you shal heare of at the time aforesaide, in the meane space recollect your wits, write out of deliberation, not out of furie; write out of aduice, not out of idlenesse; forbeare to charge women with faults which come from the contagion of Masculine serpents.

Ester hath hang'd Haman.

A DEFENCE OF
Women, against the Author
of the *Arraignment of Women.*

Chap. VIII.

AN idle companion was raging of late,
Who in fury 'gainst Women expresseth his hate:
Hee writeth a Booke, an Arraignment he calleth,
In which against women he currishly bawleth.
He deserueth no answere but in Ballat or Ryme,
Vpon idle fantastickes who would cast away time:
Any answere may serue an impudent lyar,
Any mangie scab'd horse doth fit a scab'd Squire:
In the ruffe of his furie, for so himselfe saith,
The blasphemous companion he shamefully playeth.
The woman for an Helper, God did make he doth say,
But to Helpe to consume and spend all away.
Thus, at Gods creation to flout and to iest,
Who but an Atheist would so play the beast?
The Scriptures doe proue that when Adam did fall,
And to death and damnation was thereby a thrall.
Then woman was an Helper, for by her blessed seed,
From Hell and damnation all mankinde was freed.
He saith, women are froward, which the rib doth declare,
For like as the Rib, so they crooked are:
The Rib was her Subiect for body we finde,
But from God came her Soule, and dispose of her minde.
Let no man thinke much if women compare,
That in their creation they much better are:

H   More

More blessings therein to women doe fall,
Then vnto mankinde haue beene giuen at all.
Women were the last worke, and therefore the best,
For what was the end, excelleth the rest.
For womans more honour, it was so assign'd,
She was made of the rib of mettall refin'd:
The Countrey doth also the woman more grace,
For Paradice is farre the more excellent place.
Yet women are mischieuous, this Author doth say,
But Scriptures to that directly say nay:
God said, 'twixt the Woman and Serpent for euer,
Strong hatred he would put, to be qualified neuer.
The woman being hatefull to the Serpents condition,
How excellent is she in her disposition?
The Serpent with men in their workes may agree,
But the Serpent with women that neuer may be.
If you aske how it happens some women proue naught,
By men turn'd to Serpents they are ouer-wrought.
What the Serpent began, men follow that still,
They tempt what they may to make women doe ill.
They will tempt, and prouoke, and follow vs long:
They deceiue vs with oathes, and a flattering tongue,
To make a poore Maiden or woman a whore,
They care not how much they spend of their store.
But where is there a man that will any thing giue
That woman or maide may with honestie liue?
If they yeeld to lewd counsell they nothing shall want,
But for to be honest, then all things are scant.
It proues a bad nature in men doth remaine.
To make women lewd their purses they straine.
For a woman that's honest they care not a whit,
Theyle say she is honest because she lackes wit.

Theyle

Ester hath hang'd Haman.

Theyle call women whores, but their stakes they might saue,
There can be no Whore, but there must be a Knaue.
They say that our dressings, and that our attire
Are causes to moue them to lustfull fire.
Of all things which are we euermore finde,
Such thoughts doe arise as are like to the minde.
Mens thoughts being wicked they wracke on vs thus,
That scandall is taken, not giuen by vs.
If their sight be so weake, and their frailtie be such,
Why doe they then gaze at our beauty so much?
Plucke away those ill roots whence sinne doth arise,
Amend wicked thoughts, or plucke out the eyes.
The humors of men, see how froward they bee;
We know not to please them in any degree:
For if we goe plaine we are sluts they doe say,
They doubt of our honesty if we goe gay ;
If we be honest and merrie, for giglots they take vs,
If modest and sober, then proud they doe make vs:
Be we housewifly quicke, then a shrew he doth keepe,
If patient and milde, then be scorneth a sheepe.
What can we deuise to doe or to say,
But men doe wrest all things the contrary way.
'Tis not so vncertaine to follow the winde,
As to seeke to please men of so humerous minde.
Their humors are giddy, and neuer long lasting,
We know not to please them, neither full nor yet fasting.
Either we doe too little, or they doe too much :
They straine our poore wits, their humors are such.
They say, women are proud, wherein made they triall?
They moou'd some lewd suit, and had the deniall :
To be crost in such suites, men cannot abide,
And thereupon we are entitled with pride.

H 2   They

Ester hath hang'd Haman.

They say we are curst and froward by kinde,
Our mildnesse is changed, where raging we finde,
A good Iacke sayes the prouerbe, doth make a good Gill,
A curst froward Husband doth change womans will.
They vse vs (they say) as necessary euils,
We haue it from them, for they are our deuils.
When they are in their rages and humerous fits,
They put vs poore women halfe out of our wits.
Of all naughty women name one if you can,
If she proued bad, it came by a man.
Faire Helen forsooke her Husband of Greece,
A man called Paris, betrayed that peece.
Medea did rage, and did shamefully murther,
A Iason was cause, which her mischiefe did further.
A Cresside was false, and changed her loue,
Diomedes her heart by constraint did remoue.
In all like examples the world may see,
Where women proue bad, there men are not free.
But in those offences they haue the most share,
Women would be good, if Serpents would spare.
Let Women and Maides whatsoeuer they be,
Come follow my counsell, be warned by me.
Trust not mens suites, their loue proueth lust,
Both hearts, tongues, and pens, doe all proue vniust.
How faire they will speake and write in their loue,
But put them to tryall how false doe they proue?
They loue hot at first, when the loue is a stranger,
But they will not be tied to racke and to minger.
What loue call you that when men are a wooing,
And seeke nothing else but shame and vndoing.
As women in their faults I doe not commend,
So wish I all men their lewd suites they would end.

Let

Ester hath hang'd Haman.

Let women alone, and seeke not their shame,
You shall haue no cause then women to blame.
'Tis like that this Author against such doth bawle,
Who by his temptations haue gotten a fall.
For he who of women so wickedly deemeth,
Hath made them dishonest, it probably seemeth.
He hath beene a Traueller, it may be well so,
By his tales and reports as much we doe know.
He promiseth more poyson against women to thrust;
He doth it for phisicke, or else he would brust.
Thus I bid him farewell till next we doe meete,
And then as cause moueth, so shall we greete.

IOANE SHARP.

FINIS.

Faultes escaped.

Page 33. Line 1. for cary, read curry. p.36.l.30 for sincerity, r. scurility. p.38.l.28. for something, r. any thing. Ibid for countrey, r. counter. p.40. l.5. for contempt, r. contention.

THE WORMING of a mad Dogge:

OR,

A SOPPE FOR CERBERVS THE Iaylor of Hell.

NO CONFVTATION BVT A sharpe Redargution of the bayter of Women.

By CONSTANTIA MVNDA
—— *dux fœmina facti.*

Virg: Æn: 1.
Si genus humanum & mortalia temnitis arma,
At sperate Deos memores fandi atque nefandi.

LONDON
Printed for LAVRENCE HAYES, and are to be sold at his shop neere Fleet-bridge, ouer against S*t*. *Brides* Lane.
1617.

TO THE RIGHT WORSHIPFVL LADY
her most deare Mother, the Lady PRVDENTIA MVNDA, the true patterne of Pietie and Vertue, C. M. wisheth increase of happinesse.

AS first your paines in bearing me was such
A benefit beyond requitall, that t'were much
To thinke what pangs of sorrow you sustain'd
In child-birth, when mine infancy obtain'd
The vitall drawing in of ayre, so your loue
Mingled with care hath shewen it selfe, aboue
The ordinary course of Nature: seeing you still
Are in perpetuall Labour with me, euen vntill
The second birth of education perfect me,
You Trauaill still though Churched oft you be.
  In recompence whereof what can I giue,
But what I take, euen that I liue,
Next to the heauens 'tis yours. Thus I pay

My

*My debt by taking vp at interest, and lay
To p—vne that which I borrow of you : so
The more I giue I take, I pay, I owe.
Yet lest you thinke I forfait shall my bond
I here present you with my writing hand.
Some trifling minutes I vainely did bestow
In penning of these lines that all might know
The scandals of our aduersarie, and
I had gone forward had not* Hester *hang'd*
Haman *before : yet what here I wrote
Might serue to stop the curs wide throat,
Vntill the haltar came, since which I ceast
To prosecute what I intended, lest
I should be censur'd that I vndertooke
A worke that's done already : so his booke
Hath scapt my fingers, but in like case
As a malefactor changeth place
From* Newgate *vnto* Tiburne, *whose good hope
Is but to change his shackels for a rope.
  Although this be a toy scarce worth your view,
Yet deigne to reade it, and accept in lien
Of greater dutie, for your gracious looke
Is a sufficient Patrone to my booke.
  This is the worst disgrace that can be had,
A Ladies daughter worm'd a dog that's mad.*

Your louing Daughter
CONSTANTIA MVNDA.

To Joseph Swetnam.

WHat is thy shameles muse so fleg'd in sin
So cocker'd vp in mischiefe? or hast bin
Train'd vp by Furies in the schoole of vice,
Where the licentious Deuils hoyst the price
Of vncought mischiefe, & make a set reward,
For hell-hound slanderers that nought regard
Their reputation, or the wholesome Lawes
Of Vertues Common-wealth, but seek applause
By rayling and reuiling to depraue
The mirrour of Creation, to out-braue
Euen heauen it selfe with folly: could the straine
Of that your barren-idle-donghill braine,
As from a Chymick Limbeck so distill
Your poyson'd drops of hemlocke, and so fill
The itching eares of silly swaines, and rude
Truth-not-discerning rusticke multitude
With sottish lies, with bald and ribald lines,
Patcht out of English writers that combines
Their highest reach of emulation but to please

The

To Ioseph Swetnam.

The giddy-headed vulgar: whose disease
Like to a swelling dropsie, thirsts to drinke
And swill the puddles of this nasty sinke: (wit,
Whence through the channels of your muddy
Your hotch-potcht work is drawn and the slimy
Of your inuectiue pamphlet fild to th'brim (pit
With all defiled streames, yet many swimme
And bath themselues (oh madnes) in that floud
Of mischiefe, with delight, and deem that good
Which spoyls their reaso, being not vnderstood.
When people view not wel your diuellish book,
Like nibling fish they swallow bait and hooke
To their destruction, when they not descry
Your base and most vnreuerent blasphemy.
How in the ruffe of fury you disgrace
(As much as in you lies) and doe deface
Natures best ornament, and thinkst th'ast done
An act deseruing commendation;
Whereas thy merits being brought in sight,
Exclaime thus on thee, Gallows claime thy right.

 Woman the crowne, perfection, & the meanes
Of all mens being, and their well-being, whence
Is the propagation of all humane kinde,
Wherein the bodies frame, th'intellect and mind,
With all their operations doe first finde
Their Essence and beginning, where doth lie

The

To Ioseph Swetnam.

The mortall meanes of our eternity,
Whose vertues, worthinesse, resplendent rayes
Of perfect beauty haue alwaies had the praise
And admiration of such glorious wits,
Which Fame the worlds great Herauld fits,
Crowning with Lawrel wreaths & Mirtle bows,
The tribute and reward of learned browes,
And that this goodly peece of nature be   (thee.
Thus shamefully deteſted, and thus wrong'd by
How could your vild vntutour'd muse infold
And wrap it felfe in enuious, cruell, bold,
Nay impudent detraction, and then throw
And hurle without regard your venom'd darts
Of scandalous reuiling, at the hearts
Of all our female sexe promiscuously,
Of commons, gentry, and nobility?
Without exceptions hath your spungie pate
(Voyd in it selfe of all things but of hate)
Suckt vp the dregs of folly, and the lees
Of mercenary Pasquils, which doe squeefe
The slaunders of abuses in the face
Of them that are the cause that humane race
Keepes his continuance: could you be so mad
As to depraue, nay to call that bad
Which God calls good? can your filthy clawes
Scratch out the image that th' Almighty drawes

B   In

To Ioseph Swetnam.

In vs his pictures? no! things simply good,
Keep stil their essence, though they be withstood
By all the complices of hell: you cannot daunt
Not yet diminish, (how ere you basely vaunt,
With bitter termes) the glory of our Sex,
Nor, as you michingly surmize, you vexe
Vs with your dogged rayling, why! we know;
Vertue oppos'd is stronger, and the foe
That's queld and foyld, addeth but more
Triumph to th' conquest then there was before.
  Wherefore be aduised, cease to raile
    On them that with aduantage can you quaile.

THE

THE WORMING OF
a madde Dogge.

THE itching desire of oppressing the presse with many sottish and illiterate Libels, stuft with all manner of ribaldry, and sordid inuentions, when euery foule-mouthed male-content may disgorge his *Licambæan* poyson in the face of all the world, hath broken out into such a dismall contagion in these our dayes, that euery scandalous tongue and opprobrious witte, like the Italian Mountebankes will aduance their pedling wares of detracting virulence in the publique *Piazza* of euery Stationers shoppe. And Printing that was inuented to be the store-house of famous wits, the treasure of Diuine literature, the pandect and maintainer of all Sciences, is become the receptacle of euery dissolute Pamphlet. The nursery and hospitall of euery spurious and penurious brat, which proceeds from base phreneticall

ticall braine-sicke bablers. When *scribimus indocti* must be the motto of euery one that fooles himselfe in Print: tis ridiculous! but when *scribimus insani* should bee the signiture of euery page, tis lamentable our times so stupidly possest and benumd with folly, that wee shall verifie the Prouerbe, *peccata commune non è peccato*, sinnes custome-house hath *non sine priuilegio*, writ vpon his dores, as though community in offence could make an immanitie: No! vse of sinne is the soules extortion, a biting fænorie that eates out the principle. Yet wofull experience makes it too true, *consuetudo peccandi tollit sensum peccati*, as may bee seene by the workes of diuers men that make their pens their pensils to limne out vice that it may seeme delicious and amiable; so to detract from vertue and honesty, as though their essence were onely in outward appearance of goodnesse, as if mortality were onely circumscribed within the conditions of our sex, *cælum ipsum petimus stultitia*, foolish man will reprehend his Creator in the admirable worke of his generation and conseruation: Woman the second edition of the Epitome of the whole world, the second Tome of that goodly volume compiled by the great God of heauen and earth is most shamefully blurd, and derogatiuely rased by scribling penns of sauage & vncought monsters. To what an irregular straine is the daring impudence of bared-fold bayards aspired vnto? that they will presume to call in question euen the most absolute worke composed by the worlds great Architect?

The worming of a madde Dogge.

tect? A strange blasphemy to finde fault with that which the Privy Councell of the high and mighty Parliament of the inscrutable *Tri-vnitie* in Heauen determined to be very good. To call that imperfect, froward, crooked and peruerse to make an arraignment and Beare-baiting of that which the Pantocrator would in his omniscient wisedome haue to be the consummation of his blessed weekes worke, the end, crowne, and perfection of the neuer-sufficiently glorified creation. What is it but an exorbitant phrensie, and wofull taxation of the supreme deitie. Yet woman the greatest part of the *lesser world* is generally become the subiect of euery pedanticall goose-quill. Euery fantasticke Poetaster which thinkes he hath lickt the vomit of his *Coriphæus* and can but patch a hobling verse together, will striue to represent vnseemely ligments imputed to our sex, (as a pleasing theme to the vulgar) on the publique Theatre: teaching the worser sort that are more prone to luxurie, a compendious way to learne to be sinfull. These foule mouth'd taylers, *qui non vident vt corrigant, sed quærunt quid reprehendant*, that reprooue not that they might reforme, but pry into actions that they might carpe and cauill: so that in this infamous profession they farre exceed the vildest kinde of Pharisaicall ostentation, and so surmounting beyond all comparison railing *Anaxarchus*, who for his detracting and biting tongue was pestled to death in a brazen morter. Who as a learned *Tuscan* speaketh, *gli miseri vanno a tentone altreuolte*

The worming of a madde Dogge.

è carpone per facer mercatantia dell' altrui da lor inuentata è seminata vergogna, impudicamente cercano l'altrui deshonor erger la meretricia fronte & malzar la impudiche corna: these wretched miscreants goe groaping, and sometimes on all foure, to traffique with other folkes credits by their owne diuulged and disperfed ignominie. That impudently seeke by others dishonour to set a shamelesse face on the matter, and thus to put out their immodest hornes to butt at, and gore the name and reputation of the innocent, being so besotted with a base and miserable condition, and blinde in themselues, they blush not in their tongues to carry the gall of *Rabilius*, and in their chaps the poyson of *Colimachus* in their mouthes, the flame of mount *Ætna* in their eyes, *Iupiters* lightning which he darted at the *Centaures*, in their thoghts *Bellonaes* arrowes, in their serpentine words the bitternesse of *Sulmo* against *Orbecca*, blending and commixing all their discourse with epaticke aloes and vnsauourie simples, deriuing all their ingredients of their venomed Recipes from the Apothecaries shop of the Deuill. Notwithstanding, as the same learned man metaphorically speakes, *Cotesti vsci scangerati, città senza muro, naui senza gouerno, vasi senza coperto, caualli indomiti senza freno non considerano.* These wide open-dores, these vnwalled townes, these rudderlesse shippes, these vncouerd vessels, these vnbrideled horses doe not consider that the tongue being a very little member should neuer goe out of that same iuory gate, in which, (not without a great mysterie)

Plus aloes quam mellis habent.

The worming of a madde Dogge.

stery) diuine wisedome and nature together hath enclosed, it signifying that a man should giue him selfe eyther to vertuous speech, or prudent silence, and not let tongue and pen runne vp and downe like a weaponed madde-man, to strike and wound any without partiality, euery one without exception, to make such an vniuersall massacre (for so I may terme it, seeing words make worse wounds then swords) yet lest villanie domineere and triumph in furie, wee will manicle your dissolute fist, that you deale not your blowes so vnadusedly. Though feminine modesty hath confin'd our rarest and ripest wits to silence, wee acknowledge it our greatest ornament, but when necessity compels vs, tis as great a fault and folly *loquenda tacere, vt contra grauis est culpa tacenda loqui*, being too much prouoked by arrainments, baytings, and rancarous impeachments of the reputation of our whole sex, *stulta est clementia perituræ parcere cartæ*, opportunity of speaking slipt by silence, is as bad as importunity vpheld by babling λαλεῖν ἃ δεῖτω, κρατίων σωτᾶν. Know therefore that wee will cancell your accusations, trauers your bils, and come vpon you for a false indirement, and thinke not tis our waspishnesse that shall sting you; no sir, vntill we see your malepert sausinesse reformed, which will not be till you doe *make a long letter to vs*, we will continue Juno'es,

*Non sic abibunt odia vinaces. Aget violentus iras animus
Senusque dolor æterna bella pace sublata geret.*

Notwithstanding for all your iniuries as Gelo

6   *The Worming of a madde Dogge.*

Saracasmus answered *Syagrius the Spartane*, *You shall not induce mee though stird with anger, to demean my selfe irrevercently in the retribution of your iniuries.* Your idoll muse, and *musing being idle* (as your learned Epistle beginneth) shall bee no plea to make your viperous scandals seeme pleasing, *ipsa excusatio culpa est*. Where by the way I note your vntoward nature contrary to all men, for wheras in all others of your sex by your confession, idlenesse ingendreth loue, in you hate: you say in the dedication of your booke to your mistresses the common sort of women, that you had little ease to passe the time withall, but now seeing you haue lately wrong'd our wearied and warried Patience with your insolent inuectiue madnesse, you shall make a simple conuersion of your proposition, and take your *pastime* in *little* *ease*: why? if you delight to sow thornes, is it not fit you should goe on them bare-foot and barelegged. Your idle muse shall be frankt vp, for while it is at liberty, most impiously it throwes durt in the face of halfe humane kinde. *Coriolanus* when hee saw his mother and his wife weeping, naturall loue compeld him to leaue sacking the City for their sakes, *ab hoc exemplum cape*, but your barbarous hand will not cease to ruine the senses, and beleager the forces of *Gynæcia*, not sparing the mother that brought forth such an vntoward whelp into the world as thy selfe, playing at blindman-buffe with all, scattering thy dissolute language at whomsoeuer comes next: you neuer heard of a boy, an vnlucky gallowes that threw
                                         stones

The worming of a madde Dogge.

stones in the market-place he knew not whither: the wisely-cynicke Philosopher bade him take heed lest he hit his father. *Nomine mutato narratur fabula de te.* You might easily, if you had had the grace, perceiue what vse to make of it. But you goe forward, pretending you were in great *choller* against some women, and in the *ruffe* of your furie. Grant one absurditie, a thousand follow: Alas (good Sir) wee may easily gather you were mightily transported with passion. Anger and madnesse differ but in time. T were a pleasant sight to see you in your *great* standing *choller* and *furious ruffe* together. Your choller (no doubt) was too great for a Spanish *peccadillo*, and your shagge *ruffe* seemed so greesly to set forth your ill-looking visage, that none of your shee-aduersaries durst attempt to confront your follie. But now let vs talke with you in your cold bloud. Now the lees of your furie are settled to the bottome, and your turbulent minde is defæcated and clearer, lets haue a parle with you. What if you had cause to be offended with some (as I cannot excuse all) must you needs shoot your paper-pellets out of your potgun-pate at all women? Remember (sweet Sir) the counsell of *Nestor* to *Achilles*:

A little fiame.

— Σὺ δὲ μεγάλοις, θυμὸν
ἴσχειν ἐν στήθεσι· φιλοφροσύνη γὰρ ἀμείνων.

It had beene the part of humanitie to haue smothered your anger, hoping amends and reconcilement, and not presently to wrecke your spleene. *Architas* in *Tullie* would haue taught you another lesson: *Quo te inquit ñ odo accepissem nisi iratus*

*Animū tu pē- ē re sereniū ē tineas, sr ē q ē-
L ne temperat plurimus esto.*

Tusculi. 4.

C

The worming of a madde Dogge.

mata essem? But you, like a hare-brain'd scold, set your clawes in the face of the whole world. But this argues your leuitie ioyn'd with degenerate cowardize: for had you but considered with mature deliberation that (as *Virgil* speakes)

Aened. 2.

—— *nullum memorabile nomen*
Fœminea in pœna est, nec habet victoria laudem.

T'is a poore atchieuement to ouercome a woman, you would neuer haue beene so grieuously troubled with the ouer-flowing of the gall, neither would the relish of your furr'd palate haue beene so bitter, as what delicates soeuer you tasted should become vnpleasing. I read of a mad fellow, which had lost his goods by sea, that whatsoeuer ships had come into the port at *Athens*, he would take a catalogue of them, and very busie would he be in making an inuentorie of the goods they brought in and receiued, thinking all to bee his. So you hauing peraduenture had some curst wife that hath giuen you as good as you brought, whatsoeuer faults you espie in others, you take that to heart: you run a madding vp and downe to make a scrole of female frailties, and an inuentorie of meretriciall behauiours, ascribing them to those that are ioyned in the sacred bands of matrimonie. Because you haue beene guld with brasse money, will you thinke no coyne currant? Because you haue suffered shipwracke, will you disswade any from venturing to trafficke beyond Seas? Besides, you shew your selfe vniust in not obseruing a symmetrie and proportion of reuenge and the offence: for a pelting iniurie should not

not prouoke an opprobrious calumnie; a priuate abuse of your owne familiar doxies should not breake out into open slanders of the religious matron together with the prostitute strumpet; of the nobly-descended Ladies, as the obscure base vermine that haue bitten you; of the chaste and modest virgins, as well as the dissolute and impudent harlot. Because women are women, you will doe that in an houre, which you will repent you of all your life time after. Nay rather, if the ruffe of your fume would haue let you looke ouer it, you would haue diuerted the floud-gates of your poisoned streames that way where you perceiued the common shore to run, and not haue polluted and stained the cleere and crystalline waters. Because women are not women, rather might be a fit subiect of an ingenious Satyrist. *Cùm alterius sexus* Iuuen.Sat.6. *imitata figuram est*: the reason is,

Quàm præstare potest mulier galeata pudorem,
Quæ fugit à sexu?

But when women are women, when wee saile by the true compasse of honest and religious conuersation, why should you be so doggedly incensed to barke in generall? why should you imploy your inuention to lay open new fashions of lewdnesse, which the worst of women scarce euer were acquainted with? imitating the vice of that Pagan Poet, whose indignation made verses, whose filthy reprehension opened the doores of vnbridled luxurie, and gaue a president of all admired wickednesse, and brutish sensualitie, to succeeding ages; whom great *Scaliger* indeed censu- Scal.3.lib. reth P.lat.cap.9.

reth not worthy to be read of a pious and ingenuous man. That *Satyr* brands all his Countreywomen with the same marke:

Iamq; eadem summis pariter minimisq; libido est,
Nec melior pedibus silicem quæ conterit atrum,
Quàm quæ longorum vehitur ceruice Syrorum.

But he liued in a nation earthly, deuillish, sensuall, giuen ouer to a reprobate sense, that wrought all filthinesse with greedinesse. But you, sir, were whelpt in a better age, at least in a better climate, where the Gospell is preached, and *the voice of the Turtle is heard in our land*; where you might see (if you could perfectly distinguish) if you were not in the gall of bitternesse. Matchlesse beauties and glorious vertues shining together, you might behold (if outragious rage had not drawne a filme ouer your eye-light) the goodly habiliments of the minde combined with the perfection of outward comelinesse and ornaments of the body. Is there not as many monuments erected to the famous eternizing of charitable deeds of women renowned in their generations, as trophees to the most couragious Potentates? In the commemorations of founders and benefactors, how many women haue emulated your sex in bountifull exhibitions to religious vses and furtherance of pietie? I might produce infinite examples, if neede were: but bray a foole in a morter (said the wise man) yet he will not leaue his foolerie: Neither if whole volumes were compiled against your manifest calumnies, would you euer be brought to a palinodie and recantation. Wee haue your confession

The worming of a madde Dogge.

feffion vnder your owne hand, where you say you *might haue emploied your selfe to better ſe then in ſuch an idle buſineſſe.* True:

Πολλακι τοι ϰ μωρος ἀνηρ ϰαιριον ειπεν.

A foole ſpeakes ſometimes to the purpoſe. If you muſt needs be digiting your pen, the time had beene farre better ſpent if you had related to the world ſome ſtories of your trauels, with a Gentleman learneder and wiſer then your ſelfe: ſo you might haue beguiled the time, and expoſed your *ridiculous* wit to laughter: you might haue told how hardly ſuch an vnconſtant *bella cortizana de Venetys* entertained you, how your teeth watered, and after your affections were poiſoned with their hainous euils; how in the beginning of your thirty yeeres trauell and odde, your conſtitution inclined and you were addicted to prie into the various actions of looſe, ſtrange, lewd, idle, froward and inconſtant women; how you happened (in ſome Stewes or Brothelhouſes) to be acquainted with their cheats and euaſions; how you came to be ſo expert in their ſubtile qualities; how politikely you caught the daughter in the ouen, yet neuer was there your ſelfe; how in your voyages your ſtomacke was cloyd with theſe ſurfets, and therefore being a traueller, you had reaſon to cenſure hardly of women. Haue you traueld halfe as long againe as that famous Pilgrim, *which knew the faſhions of many men, and ſaw their Cities?* Haue you out-ſtript him in time, and come ſo ſhort of him in knowledge? Is this all the manners you haue learned abroad, theſe thirty

The morning of a madde Dogge.

thirty and odde yeeres? Is this the benefit of your obseruations? Is this all the profit your Country shall reape by your forraine endeuours? to bring home a company of idle humours of light huswiues which you haue noted, and divulge them in print to your owne disgrace and perpetuall obloquie? Haue you traueld three times as long as an Elephant, and is this the first fruit, nay all the fruit of your idle addle coxcombe? Certainly you mis-spent your time in your trauels: for it had beene more profitable for you, if you had brought dogges from *Iceland*; better for your Countrey, if you had kept a dogge there still. But tis easie to giue a reason of your exasperate virulence, from your being a traueller: for it is very likely when you first went abroad to see fashions, twas your fortune to light amongst ill company, who trying what metall you were made of, quickly matriculated you in the schoole of vice, where you proued a most apt *Non-proficient*, and being guld of your patrimonie, your purse was turned into a passe, and that by women. Like a dogge that bites the stone which had almost beat out his braines, you come home swaggering:

Prodiga non sentit pereuntem fœmina censum,
At velut exhausta rediuiuus pullulet arca
Nummus, & pleno semper tollatur aceruo,
Non vnquā reputant quantum sibi gaudia constant.

Which if you cannot vnderstand, is to this sense:

A lauish woman thinkes there is no flint
Vnto her purse: as though thou hadst a mint,

She

The worming of a madde Dogge. 13

She casts no count what money shee'l bestow,
As if her coine as fast as t'ebd, did flow.

Such it may be (I speake but on suspicion, were the conditions of those minions your minoritie had experience of in your voyages. Wherefore none either good or bad, faire or foule, of what estate soeuer, of what parentage or royall descent and lineage soeuer, how well soeuer nurtured and qualified, shall scape the conuicious violence of your preposterous procacitie. Why did you not snarle at them directly that wronged you? Why did not you collimate your infectious iauelins at the right marke? If a theefe take your purse from you, will you maligne and swagger with euery one you meet? If you be beaten in an Ale-house, will you set the whole Towne afire? If some curtezans that you haue met with in your trauels (or rather that haue met with you) haue ill intreated you, must honest and religious people be the scope of your malicious speeches and reprochfull tearmes? Yet it may be you haue a further drift, to make the world beleeue you haue an extraordinary gift of continencie; soothing your selfe with this supposition, that this open railing is some token and euidence you neuer were affected with delicate and effeminate sensualitie, thinking this pamphlet should assoile thee from all manner of leuie and taxation of a lasciuious life; as if, because you cynically raile at all both good and bad, you had beene hatcht vp without concupiscence; as if nature had bestowed on you all *sense. his.* and no *concupiscentia*. Twas spoken of *Euripides,* that he

hated

hated women in *choro*, but not in *thoro*, in *calamo*, but not in *thalamo*: and why cannot you be liable to the same obiection? I would make this excuse for you, but that the crabbednesse of your stile, the vnsauory periods of your broken-winded sentences perswade your body to be of the same temper as your minde. Your ill-fauoured countenance, your wayward conditions, your peeuish and pettish nature is such, that none of our sex with whom you haue obtained some partiall conference, could euer brooke your dogged frompard frowardnesse: vpon which male-contented desperation, you hanged out your flagge of defiance against the whole world, as a prodigious monstrous rebell against nature. Besides, if your currish disposition had dealt with men, you were afraid that *Lex talionis* would meet with you; wherefore you surmized, that inueighing against poore illiterate women, we might fret and bite the lip at you, wee might repine to see our selues baited and tost in a blanket, but neuer durst in open view of the vulgar either disclose your blasphemous and derogatiue slanders, or maintaine the vntainted puritie of our glorious sex: nay, you'l put gagges in our mouthes, and coniure vs all to silence: you will first abuse vs, then binde vs to the peace; wee must be tongue-tied, lest in starting vp to finde fault, wee proue our selues guiltie of those horrible accusations. The sinceritie of our liues, and quietnesse of conscience, is a wall of brasse to beat backe the bullets of your vituperious scandals in your owne face.

Like for like.

Tis

The worming of a madde Dogge.

Tis the resolued Aphorisme of a religious soule to answere, *ego sic viuam vt nemo tibi fidem adhibeat*: by our well-doings to put to silence the reports of foolish men, as the Poet speakes;

*Viuendum: recte tum, propter plurima, tum: de his
Præcipue causis vt linguas maxcipiorum contemnas.*

Liue well for many causes, chiefly this,
To scorne the tongue of slaues that speake amisse.

Indeed I write not in hope of reclaiming thee from thy profligate absurdities, for I see what a pitch of disgrace and shame thy selfe-pining enuie hath carried thee to, for thy greater vexation and more perplexed ruine. You see your blacke grinning mouth hath beene muzled by a modest and powerfull hand, who hath iudiciously bewrayed, and wisely layed open your singular ignorance, couched vnder incredible impudence, who hath most grauely (to speake in your owne language) *vnsoulded euery pleat, and shewed euery rinckle* of a prophane and brutish disposition, so that tis a doubt whether shee hath shewed more modesty or grauity, more learning or prudence in the religious confutation of your vndecent raylings. But as shee hath beene the first Champion of our sexe that would encounter with the barbarous bloudhound, and wisely dammed vp your mouth, and sealed vp your iawes lest your venomed teeth like madde dogges should damage the credit of many, nay all innocent damosels; so no doubt, if your scurrilous and deprauing tongue breake prison, and falls to licking vp your vomited

Vnde altior effet casus & impulsa præceps in maius ruine.

The worming of a madde Dogge.

ted poyson, to the end you may squirt out the same with more pernicious hurt, assure your selfe there shall not be wanting store of Helebore to scoure the sinke of your tumultuous gorge, at least we will cram you with Antidotes and Catapotions, that if you swell not till you burst, yet your digested poyson shall not be contagious. I heare you foame at mouth and groule against the Author with another head like the triple dog of hell, wherefore I haue prouided this sop for *Cerberus*, indifferent well steept in vineger. I know not how your pallat will bee pleased with it to make you secure hereafter. Ile take the paines to worme the tongue of your madnesse, and dash your rankling teeth downe your throat: tis not houlding vp a wispe, nor threatning a cucking-stoole shall charme vs out of the compasse of your chaine, our pens shall throttle you, or like *Archilochus* with our tart Iambikes make you *Lopez* his godson: we will thrust thee like *Phalaris* into thine owne brazen bull, and baite thee at thy owne stake, and beate thee at thine owne weapon, *Quippe minuti semper & infirmi est animi exiguique voluptas vltio: continuo sic collige quod vindicta nemo magis gaudet quam femina.* Tis your Poets owne assertion, that vltion being the delight of a weake and feeble minde belongs to vs. Thou that in thy selfe feelest the lash of folly, thou that confessest thy selfe to be in a fault, nay that thou hast offended beyond satisfaction, for tis hard to giue a recompence for a slander: thou that acknowledgest thy selfe to be madde, in a rough furie,

rie, your wits gon a woolgathering that you had forgot your selfe (as I think) Nero-like in ripping vp the bowels of thine owne Mother: for I haue learnt so much Logicke to know *quicquid dicitur de specie, dicitur de vnoquoq, indiuiduo eiusdem speciei*: whatsoeuer is spoken or predicated of the kinde is spoken of euery one in the same kinde: first therefore to bring you to an impious error or inconuenience. Is it not a comely thing to heare a Sonne speake thus of his mother: *My mother in her furie was worse than a Lion being bitten with hunger, than a beare being robbed of her yong ones, the viper being trod on. No spur would make my mother go, nor no bridle would hold her backe: tell her of her fault, she will not beleeue she is in any fault: giue her good counsell, but she will not take it: if my Father did but look after another woman, then she would be iealous: the more he loued her, the more shee would disdaine him: if he threatned her, shee would bee angry: when he flattered her, then she would be proud: if he forbore her, it made her bould: if hee chastened her, she would turne to a serpent: at a word, my mother would neuer forget an iniury, nor giue thankes for a good turne: what an asse then was my Father to exchange gould for drosse, pleasure for paine: tis a wonderfull thing to see the madde feates of my mother, for she would picke thy pocket, empty thy purse, laugh in thy face & cut thy throat, she is vngratefull, periurd, full of fraud, flouting, and deceit, vnconstant waspish, toyish, light, sullen, proud, discourteous and cruell: the breast of my mother was the harbourer of an enuious heart, her heart the storehouse of poisoned hatred,*

The worming of a madde Dogge.

hatred, her head deuised villany, and her hands were ready to put in practise what her heart desired, then who can but say but my mother a woman sprung from the Deuill? you from your mother, and so Swetnam is the Deuils Grand-child. Doe you not blush to see what a halter you haue purchased for your owne necke? You thought in your ruffe of furie like *Augustus Cæsar*, to make an edict that all the world should be taxed, when your selfe is tributary to the greatest infirmities: you blowed the fier of sedition with the bellowes of your anger and the coales are burning in your owne bosome, *Periculoso plenum opus aleæ, tractas & incedis per ignes suppositos cineri doloso.* Is there no reuerence to be giuen to your mother because you are weaned from her teat, and neuer more shall be fedde with her pappe? You are like the rogue in the Fable which was going to the gallowes for burglarie, that bit off his mothers nose, because shee chastised him not in his infancy for his pettie-Larcenies: is this the requitall of all her cost, charge, care, and vnspeakeable paines she suffered in the producing of such a monster into the light? if she had cram'd grauell downe thy throat when shee gaue thee sucke, or expofed thee to the mercy of the wilde beasts in the wildernesse when she fed thee with the pap, thou couldst not haue showen thy selfe more vngratefull then thou hast in belching out thy nefarious contempt of thy mothers sexe. Wherefore mee thinkes it is a pleasing reuenge that thy soule arraines thee at the barre of conscience, and thy distracted mind cannot chuse but

The worming of a madde Dogge.

but hant thee like a bumbaylie to serue a *subp.ena* on thee, the stile and penning of your pamphlet hath brought you within the compasse of a *Præmunire*, and euery sentence beeing stolne out of other bookes, accuseth you of robbery. So that thou carriest in thy selfe a walking Newgate vp & downe with thee, thy owne perplexed suspicions like *Promotheus* vulture is alwaies gnawing on thy liuer. Besides, these books which are of late come out (the latter whereof hath preuented me in the designes I purposed in running ouer your wicked handi-worke) are like so many red-hot irons to stigmatize thy name with the brand of a hideous blasphemer and incarnate Deuill. Although thou art not apprehended and attached for thy villany I might say fellonie, before a corporall iudge, yet thine owne conscience if it be not seared vp, tortures thee, and wracks thy tempestuous minde with a dissolution and whurring too and fro of thy scandalous name, which without blemish my penne can scarce deigne to write, you finde it true which the Poet speakes;

Exemplo quodcunque malo committitur, ipsi
Displicet authori, prima est hæc vltio quod se
Iudice nemo nocens absoluitur, improba quamuis
Gratia fallacis prætoris vicerit vrnam.   Iuuen: Sat: 13.

What sin is wrought by ill example, soone
The displeased Author wisheth it vndone.
And tis reuenge when if the nocent wight,
Vmpires his cause himselfe: in his owne sight,
He findes no absolution, though the eyes
Of iudgement wink, his soule still guilty cries.

D 2   Tis

20 *The worming of a madde Dogge.*

Tis often obserued, that the affections of auditors (and readers too) are more offended with the foule mouthed reproofe of the brawling accuser, than with the fault of the delinquent. If you had kept your selfe within your pretended limits, and not medled with the blamelesse and innocent, yet your preiudicate rayling would rather argue an vnreuerent and lasciuious inclination of a depraued nature, then any loue or zeale to vertue and honesty: you ought to haue considered that in the vituperation of the misdemeanors and disorders in others liues; this cautelous *Prouiso* should direct you that in seeking to reforme others, you deforme not your selfe; especially by mouing a suspition that your minde is troubled and feltered with the impostume of inbred malice, and corrupt hatred: for tis alwaies the badge and cognisance of a degenerous and illiberall disposition to bee ambitious of that base and ignoble applause, proceeding from the giddy-headed Plebeians, that is acquired by the miserable oppressing and pilling of vertue. But euery wrongfull contumely & reproach hath such a sharpe sting in it, that if it fasten once on the minde of a good and ingenuous nature, tis neuer drawen forth without anxiety & perpetuall recordation of dolour, which if you had known, your hornet-braines would not haue buzd abroad with a resolution to sting some tho you lost your sting and died for it: you would not like the cuttle fish spew'd out your inkie gall with hope to turne the purest waters to your owne sable hew; *vt non odio inimicitiarum ad vituperandū*

sed

The worming of a madde Dogge.   21

sed studio calumniandi ad inimicitias descēderes, that you would arme your selfe, not with the hate of enmity to dispraise vice, but with the study of calumny to make enmity with vertue: yet tis remarkable that ignorance & impudence were partners in your worke, for as you haue of all things vnder the sunne, selected the bayting, or as you make a silly solæcisme the bearebayting of Women, to be the tenterhookes whereon to stretch your shallow inuentions on the triuiall subiect of euery shackragge that can but set penne to paper: so in the handling of your base discourse, you lay open your imperfections, *arripiendo maledicta ex triuio*, by heaping together the scraps, fragments, and reuersions of diuers english phrases, by scraping together the glaunders and offals of abusiue termes, and the refuse of idle headed Authors, and making a mingle-mangle gallimauphrie of them. Lord! how you haue cudgeld your braines in gleaning multitudes of similies as twere in the field of many writers, and thrasht them together in the floure of your owne deuizor; and all to make a poore confused misceline, whereas thine owne barren soyled soyle is not able to yeeld the least cōgruity of speech. Tis worthy laughter what paines you haue taken in turning ouer *Parismus*, what vse you make of the *Knight of the Sunne*, what collections out of *Euphues, Amadis a Gaule*, and the rest of *Don Quixotes* Library, sometimes exact tracing of *Æsopicall Fables*, and *Valerius Maximus*, with the like schooleboyes bookes, so that if these Pamphleters would seuerally plucke a crow with you. *Furtiuis nudata coloribus moueat cornicula rifum*, let euery bird take his owne feather, and you would be as naked as *Æsops* iay. Indeed you haue shewen as much foolery as robberie in feathering your neast, which is a cage of vncleane birds, and a storehouse for the off-scowrings of other writers. Your indiscretion is as gre..e in the laying together, & compiling of your stolne ware, as your blockishnesse in stealing, for your sentences hang together like sand without lime: you bring a great heape of stony rubbish comparisons one vpon the necke of another, but they concurre no more to sense, then a company of stones to a building without morter, and tis a familiar Italian Prouerb, *duro e duro non fa muro*, hard and hard makes no wall, so your hard dull pate hath collected nothing that can stand together with common sense, or be pleasing to any refined disposition, rough and vnhewen morsells digd out of others quarries, potsherds pickt out of sundry dunghills: your mouth indeed is full of stones, *lapides loqueris*, but not so wisely nor so warily cramd in as the geese that flie ouer the mountaines in Silicia, which carry stones in their beakes lest their cackling should make them a pray to the Eagles, where you might learne witte of a goose.

ἃ λίγε αἴγες κρίνει ἡ ἀγρη ἔχει.

Either speake peace, or hold your peace. Is it not irksome to a wise and discreet iudgement, to heare a booke stuft with such like sense as this, *The world is not made of oatmeale?* I haue heard of some that haue thought the world to haue beene
composed

The worming of a madde Dogge.

compofed of atomes, neuer any that thought it made of oatmeale: Nor all is not gold that glifters, nor the way to heauen is ftrewd with rufhes, for a dramme of pleafure an ounce of paine, for a pint of hony a gallon of gall, for an inch of mirth an ell of mo*a*ne, &c. None aboue the fcumme of the world could endure with patience to reade fuch a medly compofed of difcords. Sometimes your dogrill rhymes make mee fmile, as when you come,

> Man muft be at all the coft,
> And yet liue by the loffe:
> A man muft take all the paines,
> And women fpend all the gaines:
> Their catching in ieft,
> And keeping in earneft.
> And yet fhe thinkes fhe keepes her felfe blamelesse,
> And in all ill vices fhe would goe namelesse.
> But if fhe carry it neuer fo cleane,
> Yet in the end fhe will be counted for a cunny-catching queane.
> And yet fhe will fweare that fhe will thriue,
> As long as fhe can finde one man aliue.

I ftand not to defcant on your plaine fong; but furely if you can make ballads no better, you muft be faine to giue ouer that profeffion: for your Mufe is wonderfully defectiue in the bandileeres, and you may fafely fweare with the Poet,

> Nec fonte labra prolui caballino,
> Nec in bicipiti fomniaffe Parnaffo
> Memini.——

Sometimes you make me burft out with laughter, when I fee your contradictions of your felfe;

24 *The worming of a madde Dogge.*

I will not speake of those which others haue espied, although I had a fling at them, lest I should *aliam agere.* Meethinkes, when you wrote your second Epistle, neither to the wisest Clerke, nor yet to the Markett foole, the giddinesse of your head bewrayes you to be both a sillie Clerke, and a starke foole: or else the young men you write to must be much troubled with the megrim and the dizzinesse of the braine: for you beginne as if you were wont to runne vp and downe the Countrey with Beares at your taile. If you meane to see the Beare-baiting of women, then trudge to this Beare-garden apace, and get in betimes, and view euery roome where thou maist best sit, &c.

Now you suppose to your selfe the giddy-headed young men are flockt together, and placed to their owne pleasure, profit, and hearts ease. Let but your second cogitations obserue the method you take in your supposed sport: In stead of bringing your Beares to the stake, you say, I thinke it were not amisse to driue all women out of my hearing, for doubt lest this little sparke kindle into such a flame, and raise so many stinging hornets humming about mine eares, that all the wit I haue (which is but little) will not quench the one, nor quiet the other. Doe yee not see your apparant contradiction? *Spectatum admissi risum teneatis amici?* You promise your spectators the Bearebaiting of women, and yet you thinke it not amisse to driue all women out of your hearing; so that none but your selfe the ill-fauoured Hunckes is left in the Beare-garden to make your

inuited

inuited guests merry: whereupon it may very likely be, the eager young men being not willing to be guld and cheated of their money they paid for their roome, set their dogges at you, amongst whom *Cerberus* that hell-hound appeared, and you bit off one of his heads; for presently after you call him the two-headed dogge, whom all the Poets would faine to haue three heads: You therefore hauing snapt off that same head, were by the secret operation of that infernal substance, conuerted into the same essence: and that may serue as one reason that I tearme you *Cerberus* the Iaylor of hell; for certainly *Quicquid dicitur de toto, dicitur de singulis partibus*: That which is spoke of the whole, is spoken of euery part; and euery limbe of the deuill is an homogeneall part. Doe yee not see (goodman woodcocke) what a springe you make for your owne selfe? Whereas you say tis a great discredit for a man to bee accounted a scold, and that you deale after the manner of a shrew, which cannot ease her curst heart but by her vnhappy tongue; obserue but what conclusion demonstratiuely followes these premises:

   A man that is accounted a scold, hath great discredit:

   Ioseph Swetnam *is accounted a scold:*

   Ergo, Ioseph *hath great discredit.*

If you denie the *Minor*, tis proued out of your owne assertion, because you deale after the manner of a shrew, &c. where wee may note first a corrupt fountaine, whence the polluted puddles of your accustomed actions are deriued, *A curst heart*; then the cursednesse of your booke (which if you might be your owne Iudge, deserues no more the name of a booke, then a Colliers Iade to be a Kings Steed) to bee the fruit of an vnhappie tongue: thirdly, your commoditie you reape by it, discredit. Nay if you were but a masculine scold, twere tolerable; but to be a prophane railing *Rabshekeh*, tis odious. Neither is this all your contrarietie you haue included: for presently after you professe you wrote this booke with your hand, but not with your heart; whereas but iust now you confest your selfe to deale after the manner of a shrew, which cannot otherwise ease your curst heart, but by your vnhappy tongue: so your hand hath proued your vnhappy tongue a lier. This vnsauorie non-sense argueth you to be at that time possest with the fault you say commonly is in men, to wit, drunkennesse, when you wrote these iarring and incongruous speeches, whose absurdities accrew to such a tedious and infinite summe, that if any would exactly trace them out, they should finde them like a Mathematicall line, *Diuisibilis in semper diuisibila*. Twould put downe the most absolute Arithmetician to make a catalogue of them: wherefore I could wish thee to make a petition, that you might haue your bookes called in and burnt; for were it not better that the fire should befriend thee in purifying the trash, and eating out the canker of thy defamation, then thy execrable designes and inexcusable impudence should blazon abroad thy drunken temeritie.

The worming of a madde Dogge.

ritie and temulent foole-hardinesse to future ages, then thy booke should peremptorily witnesse thy open and Atheisticall blasphemy against thy Creator euen in the very threshold and entrance? but aboue all, where thou doest put a lie on God himselfe, with this supposition, *if God had not made them only to be a plague to man, he would neuer haue called them necessary euils*: Which I thus anticipate; But God neuer called them necessary euils, Therefore God made them not to be a plague to man. Or else turning the conclusion to the meane thus: But God did not make them to be a plague, but a helper and procurer of all felicitie; therefore God neuer called them necessary euils. Were it not (I say) farre better for you that your laborious idle worke should be abolished in the flames, then it should publikely set forth the apert violation of holy writ in sundry places? one in the beginning (as I remember) where you falsly auerre, that the blessed Patriarke *Dauid* exclaimed bitterly against women, and like the tempting deuill you alledge halfe Scripture, whereas the whole makes against your selfe: for thus you affirme he saith; *It is better to be a doore-keeper, than to be in the house with a froward woman*. In the whole volume of the booke of God, much lesse in the Psalmes, is there any such bitter exclamation? But this is the dittie of the sweet finger of *israel*, whereby he did intimate his loue vnto the house of God, and his detestation of the pauilions of the vnrighteous by this Antithesis: *It is better to be a doore-keeper in the house of the Lord, than to dwell in the Taberna-*

cles of the vngodly. Now if you haue a priuate spirit that may interpret by enthusiasmes, you may confine the Tabernacles of the vngodly onely to froward women; which how absurd and grosse it is, let the reader iudge. Doest thou not blush (gracelesse) to peruert (with *Elemas*) the strait wayes of God, by prophaning the Scriptures, and wreathing their proper and genuine interpretations to by-senses, for the boulstering and vpholding of your damnable opinion? besides thy pittifully wronging of the Philosophers, as *Socrates, Plato,* and *Aristotle,* &c. whom your illiterate and clownish Muse neuer was so happy to know whether they wrote any thing or no. Your ethnicke histories, although they rather make against men than women, yet in your relation you most palpably mistake, and tell one thing for another, as of *Holophernes, Antiochus, Hannibal, Socrates,* and the rest which the poore deluded *Corydons* and sillie swaines account for oracles, and maintaine as axiomes. The quirkes and crotchets of your owne pragmaticall pate, you father on those ancient Philosophers that most extremely oppose your conceit of mariage: for *Plato* made this one of his lawes, that whosoeuer was not maried at thirty fiue yeeres of age, should be punished with a fine. Further he implies a necessitie of mariage, euen in regard of the adoration of God himselfe:

χρὴ δὴ ζηεῖν χρωντας κ̀ ἐκτρέφοντας παιδας αυτω λαμπαδα τὸν βίον παρεκδιδοντας ἀν̀ οὐκ ἐξ ἀλλων θεραπενειν τὸν θεὸν χ⁷ νόμον : Tis necessary that there should be a lawfull generation and education of children, that life as a lampe may continu∍

The worming of a madde Dogge. 29

continue to posteritie, that so there might alwaies be some to worship God. What more diuinely or religiously could be spoken by a Paynim? How then durst you say that the Philosophers that liued in the old time had so hard an opinion of mariage, that they tooke no delight therein, seeing the chiefe of them were maried themselues? I could be infinite to produce examples and symboles to make you a lier in print: *ἐλὶ νόμω ἀγαθῆς γναικὸς* *Theognis*. *ἐντὸς ἰσχύουσιν,* Nothing is more sweet than a good wife. *οὐδὲν γυναικὸς ἐστι τιμιώτερον ἀνδρὶ δέοντι διανοίας,* He that *Protagoras.* hath a good wife, hath a merry life. Most famous is that retortion of *Pittachus*, one of the seuen wise men of *Greece*, when he demanded a fellow wherfore he would not take to him a wife, and the fellow answered, *ἂν καλὴν γήμω, ἕξω κοινὴν, ἂν δ' αἰσχρὰν, ἕξω ποινὴν.* If I take a faire wife, I shall haue her common; if a foule, a torment. The wise man replied, *ἂν καλὴν γήμης, ἐξ ἴσης ποινὴν, ἂν δ' αἰσχρὰν, ἐξ ἴσης κοινὴν,* If thou getst a foule wife, thou shalt not haue her common; if a faire, no torments. There is as much reason for the one as the other: but tis but wasting paper to reckon vp these obuious sayings. Let that same acclamation of *Horace* stand for a thousand others:

> *Fœlices ter & amplius,*
> *Quos irrupta tenet copula, nec malis*
> *Divulsus querimonys,*
> *Suprema citius soluet amor die.*
>
> Thrise and more times are they blest,
> That in wedlockes bands doe rest,

Whose

Whose faithfull loues are knit so sure,
That blamelesse endlesse they endure.

But you that will traduce the holie Scriptures, what hope is there but you will depraue humane authors. You take *Plato* and *Aristotle* of a lasciuious life that by the light of naturall reason were chiefest establishers of Matrimony, both in regard of *œconomicke*, and *politicke* affaires. doe these things deserue commendations of any, but rather the scorne and reproofe of all: what a silly thing it is, let Monsieur *Swetnam* iudge, when *Valerius Maximus* relates in his 4. booke, a history of one *Tiberius Gracchus*, that found two serpents in his bed-chamber and killed the male, which by the prediction of Southsayers designed himselfe to death, because he dearely loued his wife *Cornelia*, and you like an Asse tel this tale of *Valerius Maximus*, as if because *Ioseph* tells a tale of one *Bias* that bought the best and worst meate which was tongues, in the market: hee that reades it should say that one lying Asse *Swetnam* bought the best and worst tongues; but certainely if that *Bias* had met with your tongue in the Market, hee would haue taken it for the worst and most vnprofitable meat, because from nothing can come worse venome then from it: What should I speake of the figments of your dull pate, how absurdly you tell of one *Theodora* a Strumpet in *Socrates* time, that could intise away all the Philosophers Schollers from him: is not the vaine and inconstant nature of men more culpable by this ensample than of women, when they should be so luxuriously bent

that

that one silly light woman should draw a multitude of learned Schollers from the right way: yet neyther *Laertius*, nor any that writte the liues of Philosophers make mention of this *Theodora*, but I haue read of a glorious Martyr of this name, a Virgin of Antiochia, in the time of *Dioclesian* the Emperor, who being in prison, a certaine barbarous Souldier moued with lust in himselfe, and the lustre of her beauty, would haue rauished her by violence, whom she not onely deterred from this cursed act by her perswasiue oratory, but by her powerfull intreaties by changing vestments wrought her deliuery by him. I would runne through all your silly discourse, and anatomize your basery, but as some haue partly beene boulted out already, and are promised to be prosecuted, so I leaue them as not worthy rehearsall or refutation. I would giue a *supersedeas* to my quill: but there is a most pregnant place in your booke which is worthy laughter that comes to my mind where you most graphically describe the difference and antipathie of man and woman, which being considered, you thinke it strange there should be any reciprocation of loue, for a man say you delights in armes, and hearing the ratling drum, but a woman loues to heare sweet musicke on the Lute, Cittern, or Bandora: I prethee who but the long-eard animall had rather heare the Cuckoe than the Nightingale? Whose eares are not more delighted with the melodious tunes of sweete musicke, then with the harsh sounding drum? Did not *Achilles* delight himselfe with his harpe

harpe as well as with the trumpet? Nay, is there not more men that rather affect the laudable vse of the Citterne, and Bandore, and Lute for the recreation of their mindes, than the clamourous noyse of drums? Whether is it more agreeable to humane nature to march amongst murthered carkasses, which you say man reioyceth in, than to enioy the fruition of peace and plenty, euen to dance on silken Carpets, as you say, is our pleasure? What man soeuer maketh warres, is it not to this ende, that hee might enioy peace? Who marcheth among murdered carkasses, but to this end, that his enemies being subdued and slaine, he may securely enioy peace? Man loues to heare the threatning of his Princes enemies, but woman weepes when shee heares of warres, What man that s a true and loyall subiect loues to heare his Prin es enemies threaten: is not this a sweet commendation thinke you? is it not more humane to bewaile the wars and losse of our countrimen, then to reioyce in the threats of an aduersary? but you goe forward in your paralelling a mans loue to lie on the cold graffe, but a woman must bee wrapped in warme manties. I neuer heard of any that had rather lie in the could graffe then in a feather-bed, if he might haue his choyce; yet you make it a proper attribute to all your sexe. Thus you see your cheefest elegancie to bee but miserable patches and botches: this Antithesis you haue found in some Author betwixt a warrier and a louer; and you stretch it to shew the difference betwixt a man and a woman; *sed nos has a scabie*

The worming of a madde Dogge.

a scabie teneamus vngues: I loue not to scratch a mangie rascall, there is neither credit nor pleasure in it. You threaten your second volly of pouder and shot, wherein you will make vs snakes, venemous adders, and scorpions, & I know not what: are these termes beseeming the mouth of a Christian or a man, which is *ovo prognatus eodem*, did not your mother hatch the same Cockatrice egge to make you in the number of the generation of Vipers? and I take you to be of that brood which *Homer* calls γλωσσων, alwaies lolling out the tongue, and all the Historiographers terme *Scopes* that giue a most vnpleasing and harsh note, *quasi* γλωσσονα, cauilling and taunting, and as *Cælius* wittily notes them to be so called, *quasi Sciopies*, ὁ σκια ἔχοντε τῆς ὄπω hauing their face obscur'd in darknesse, so this your booke being but the howling of a night-bird shall circumscribe thy name in the dungeon of perpetuall infamy. Thou that art extold amongst clownes and fooles, shalt be a hissing, and a by-word to the learned and iudicious: in so much as thine vnlucky shrieking shall affect thee with gastly terrors and amazements: neuer thinke to set forth more larums of your brutishnesse, but as *Labienus*, who was sirnamed *Rabies* madnesse, because hee vsed such liberty of his detracting tongue, that he would without regard or discretion, rayle vpon all men in his exasperate mood; When all his bookes and writings were made a bonfire of (which in those dayes was a new-found way of punishing vntoward wits) *Eam contumeliam* (saith mine Author) *La-*

F 2 *bienus*

Second Reply

bienus non tulit neque superstes ingenio suo esse voluit. Labienus tooke snuffe at this contumelious destruction of his despised labours, he was vnwilling to be the suruiuing executor of his owne wit, whereupon in a melancholy and desperate mood he caused himselfe to be coffin'd vp, and carried into the vault where his ancestors were entombed (thinking (it may be) that the fier which had burned his fame should be denied him) hee died and buried himselfe together. I doe not wish you the same death, though you haue the same conditions and surname as hee had, but liue still to barke at Vertue, yet these our writings shall be worse then fiers to torture both thy booke and thee: Wherefore transcribing some verses that a Gentleman wrote to such an one as your selfe, in this manner I conclude.

   Thy death I wish not, but would haue thee liue,
To rayle at vertues acts, and so to giue
Good vertues lust e. Seeing enuy still
Waites on the best deserts to her owne ill.
But for your selfe learne this, let not your hand
Strike at the flint againe which can withstand
Your malice without harme, and to your face
Returne contempt, the brand of your disgrace;
Whilst women sit vnmou'd, whose constant mindes
(Arm'd against obloquy) with those weake windes
Cannot be shaken: for who doth not marke
That Dogs for custome, not for fiercenesse barke.
These any foot-boy kicks, and therefore we
Passing them by, with scorne doe pitty thee.

Fo;

The worming of a madde Dogge.

For being of their nature mute at noone,
Thou darst at midnight barke against the moone;
Where mayest thou euer barke that none shall heare,
But to returne the like: and mayst thou beare
With greefe more slanders then thou canst inuent,
Or ere did practise yet, or canst preuent,
Mayst thou be matcht with enuy, and defend
Scorne toward that which all besides commend.
And may that scorne so worke vpon thy sense,
That neither suffering nor impudence
May teach thee cure: or being ouerworne
With hope of cure may merit greater scorne.
If not too late, let all thy labours be
Contemn'd by vpright iudgements, and thy fee
So hardly earn'd, not pay'd: may thy rude quill
Be alwaies mercenary, and write still,
That which no man will read, vnlesse to see
Thine ignorance, and then to laugh at thee;
And mayst thou liue to feele this, and then groane,
Because tis so, yet cannot helpe, and none
May rescue thee, till your check't conscience cry,
This this I haue deseru'd, then pine and die.

 Et cum fateri furia iusserit verum,
 Prodente clames conscientia; scripsi.

FINIS.

SWETNAM,
THE
VVoman-hater,
ARRAIGNED BY
WOMEN.

A new Comedie,
Acted at the *Red Bull*, by the late
Queenes Seruants.

LONDON,
Printed for *Richard Meighen*, and are to be sold at his Shops
at Saint *Clements* Church, ouer-against *Essex* House, and
at *Westminster* Hall. 1 6 2 0.

Enter LORETTA,
PROLOGVS.

The Women are all welcome; for the men,
They will be welcome: our care's not for them.
'Tis we poore women, that must stand the brunt
Of this dayes tryall: we are all accused.
How wee shall cleere our selues, there lyes the doubt.
The men, I know, will laugh, when they shall heare
Vs rayl'd at, and abused; and say, 'Tis well,
We all deserue asmuch. Let vms laugh on,
Lend but your kind assistance; you shall see
We will not be ore-come with Infamie,
And slanders that we neuer merited.
Be but you patient, I dare boldly say,
(If euer women pleased) weele please to day.

    Vouchsafe to reade, I dare presume to say,
    Yee shall be pleased; and thinke 'tis a good play.

ACTORVM NOMINA.

Atticus, *King of Sicilie.*
Lorenzo *his Sonne.*
Lisandro, *Prince of Naples.*
Iago, ⎫
Sforza, ⎬ *three Noblemen of Sicilie.*
Nicanor, ⎭
Scanfardo, *Seruant to Nicanor.*
Two Gentlemen.
A Captaine.
Swetnam, *alias,* Misogynos, *The Woman-hater.*

Swash, *his Man.*
Two Iudges.
Notarie.
Cryer.

Womens Parts.

Aurelia, *Queene,*
Leonida, *the Princesse.*
Loretta, *her Maid.*
Three or foure other Women.

Act. I. Scen. I.

Enter IAGO *and* NICANOR, *two Noblemen of* Sicilia, *in priuate conference.*

NICANOR.

Ee was a vertuous and a hopefull Prince,
And we haue iuſt cauſe to lament his death,
For had he liu'd, and Spaine made war agen,
He would ha' prou'd a Terror to his Foe.
  Iag. A greater cauſe of griefe was neuer knowne,
Not onely in his death, but for the loſſe
Of Prince *Lorenzo* too, his yonger brother;
Who hath beene miſſing almoſt eighteene moneths,
And none can tell whether aliue or dead.
  Nic. How do's the King beare theſe afflictions?
  Enter another Lord.
  Iag. Now you ſhall heare how fares his Maieſtie.
  Lord. Oh my good Lords, our ſorrowes ſtill increaſe,
A greater tide of woe is to be fear'd,
The Kings decay, with griefe for his two ſonnes.
  Iag. The gods forbid, let's in and comfort him.
  3. Lord. Alas, his ſorrow's ſuch
He will not ſuffer vs to ſpeake to him,
But turnes away in rage, and ſeemes to tread
The pace of one (if liuing) liuing dead.
  Iag. See where he comes,

A   Lords.

SWETNAM,

Lords, let vs all attend, *Enter King in black, reading.*
Vntill his grace be pleas'd to speake to vs.
        Dead March.
  Attic. Death is the case of paine, and end of sorrow,
How can that be? Death gaue my sorrowes life,
For by his death my paine and griefe begun,
And in beginning, neuer will haue end : for though I die,
My losse will liue in future memorie,
I and (perhaps) will be lamented too,
And regiftred by some, when all shall heare
Sicilia had two sonnes, yet had no heire.
Ha! What are you?
Who dares presume to interrupt vs thus?
What meanes this sorrow? Wherefore are these signes?
Or vnto whom are these obseruances?
  Nic. Vnto our King.
  3. *Lords.* To you my Soueraigne.
  Iag. Your Subiects all lament to see you sad.
  Attic. You all are Traytors then, and by my life
I will account you so :
Can you not be content with State and rule,
But you muft come to take away my Crowne?
For solitude is sorrowes chiefeft Crowne.
Griefe hath resign'd ouer his right to mee,
And I am King of all woes Monarchie.
You powers that grant Regeneration,
What meant yon firft to giue him vitall breath?
And make large Kingdomes proud of such a Prince
As my *Lusyppus* was, so good, so vertuous :
Then, in his prime of yeares,
To take him from mee by vntimely death?
Oh! had my spirit wings, I would ascend
And fetch his soule againe from——
Oh my sad sorrowes! Whither am I driuen?
Into what maze of errors will you lead mee?
This Monfter (Griefe) hath so diftracted mee,

                                      I had

Arraigned by Women.

I had almost forgot mortalitie.   (are pleas'd
　Iag. Deare Lord haue patience, though the heauens
To punish Princes for their Subiects faults,
In taking from vs such a hopefull Prince,
No doubt they will restore your yonger sonne,
Who cannot be but stay'd, and will, I hope
Be quickly heard of, to recall your ioyes.
　Attic. No, I shall neuer see *Lorenzo* more,
This eighteene moneths I haue not heard of him,
I feare some Traytors hand had seyz'd his life:
If hee were liuing, as that cannot bee;
I sooner looke to see the dead then hee:
For I am almost spent; This heape of age,
Mixt with my sorrow, soone will end my dayes.
　Nic. My Liege, take comfort, I (your Subiect) vow
To goe my selfe to seeke *Lorenzo* forth,
And ne'r returne vntill I find him out,
Or bring some newes what is become of him.
　3. *Lord.* The like will I, or ne'r come backe agen.
　Iag. Old as I am, I'le not be last behind,
And if my Soueraigne please to let mee goe.
　Attic. I thanke your loues, but I'le restrain your wils:
If I should part from you, my dayes were done,
For I should neuer liue till your returne,
　　　　　　Enter Nicano.
Nicanor my deare friend, *Iago*, *Sforza*,
One of you three, if I die issueless,
Must after mee be King of Sicilie.
Doe not forsake mee then.
　Omnes. Long liue your grace:
And may your issue raigne eternally.
　Attic. As for our daughter fayre *Leonida*,   *Shout*
Her female Sexe cannot inherit here,   *within.*
One must inioy both her and Sicilie.
What sudden shout was that? Some know the cause;
Can there be so much ioy left in our Land,

A 2　　　　　　　　　To

To raise mens voyces to so high a sound?
    Enter Nicanor.
Or wast a shreeke of some new miserie?
For comfort cannot be expected here.
The newes, *Nicanor*.   *Trumpets.*
 Nic. Happie, Sir, I hope,
There is a Souldier new arriu'd at Court,
Can tell some tidings of the long lost Prince:
 Sfor. Sir, shall he haue accesse?
 Iag. Oh ioyfull newes!
 Attic. Is it a question, *Sforza*? Bring him in,
As you would doe some great Ambassadour;
He is no lesse. Comes he not from a Prince?
He do's, if from *Lorenzo* hee be sent.
 A flourish, with Trumpets. Enter a Captaine,
  brought in by the Lord Scaufardoe.
Thou Man of Warre, once play the Orator,
Proue Griefe a guiltie Thiefe, condemne my feares,
And let my sorrowes suffer in these teares:
Haue I a sonne or no? Good Souldier speake.
 Capt. Sir, I arriu'd by chance vpon your coast,
Yet hearing of the Proclamation
Which promis'd thousands vnto any man
That could bring newes to the Sicilian King,
Whether *Lorenzo* were aliue or dead.
 Attic. We'le double our reward what-e'r it be,
If hee be liuing: Dead, we'le keepe our word:
Then prethee say, What is become of him?
 Capt. Not for reward, but loue to that braue Prince,
Whose memorie deserues to out-liue time,
Come I to tell what I too truely know;
In the Lepanthean battel not long since,
Where he was made Commander of a Fleet,
Vnder Don *Iohn* the Spanish Generall,
He did demeane himselfe so manfully,
That he perform'd wonders aboue beliefe;

          For

Arraigned by Women.

For when the the Nauies ioyn'd, the Cannons plaid,
And thundring clamors rang the dying knels
Of many thousand soules; He, void of feare,
Dalli'd with danger, and pursu'd the Foe
Thorow a bloudy Sea of Victorie:
Whether there slaine, or taken prisoner
By the too mercilesse misbeleeuing Turkes,
No man can tell:
That when Victorie fell to the Christians,
The conquest, and the glorie of the day
Was soone eclipst, in braue *Lorenzo's* losse;
That when the battel and the fight was done,
They knew not well whether they lost or wonne.

  Attic. This newes is worse then death; Happy were I
If any now could tell me he were dead;
Death is farre sweeter then captiuitie:
My deare *Lorenzo*! Was it thy desire
To goe to Warre, made thee forsake thy Father,
Countrie, Friends, Life, Libertie? and vndergoe
Death, or Captiuitie, or some disaster
That exceeds 'em both? Yet, howso'er,
Captaine, We thanke thy loue; giue the reward
Was promis'd in the Proclamation.

  Capt. I'le not be nice in the refusall, Sir,
It is no wonder t'see a Souldier want:
All good wait on yee; may the Heauens be pleas'd
To make you happy in your long lost sonne.

  Attic. My comfort is, whether aliue or dead,
He brauely fought for Heauen and Christendome;
Such battels martyr men: their death's a life
Suruiuing all this worlds felicitie.
Lords, Where's *Leonida*, Our beautious child,
She's all the comfort we haue left Vs now;
She must not haue her libertie to match,
The Girle is wanton, coy, and fickle too:
How many Princes hath the froward Else

A 3

SWITNAM,

Set at debate, desiring but her loue?
What dangers may insue? But to preuent,
Nicanor, wee make you her Gardian:
Let her be Princely vs'd; but no accesse
By any to her presence, but by such
As wee shall send, or giue commandment for:
'Tis death to any other dares attempt it.
I heare, the Prince of Naples seekes her loue:
Shee shall not wed with that presumptuous Boy,
His father and Our selfe were still at oddes,
Nor shall He thinke Wee will submit to Him.
Certaine he knowes not of *Lisandro's* sute,
For if he had, he would a come himselfe,
Or sent Ambassadors to speake for him.
We'le giue his answer ere to morrows Sunne
Shall retch to his Meridian, wretched state of Kings,
What end will follow where such woes begins?

Nic. Scanfardoe?   *Exeunt omnes,*
Scan. My good Lord?   *Manet Nic.*
Nic. How lik'st thou this?   *& Scanfardoe.*
I am made Gardian of my owne harts blisse,
The Princesse is my Prisoner, I her Slaue,
I keepe her Body, but shee holds my Heart
Inuiron'd in a Chest of Adamant.

Scan. Is your Heart Iron?

Nic. Steele, I thinke it is;
And liue an Anuile hammerd by her words,
It sparkles fire that neuer can bee quencht,
But by the dew of her cœlestiall breath.
Oft haue I courted, bin reiected too,
Yet what of that? I'le trye her once agen.
What many Princes haue attempting fail'd,
I by accesse may purchase, that's my hope;
The King I'me sure affects mee, nothing then
Is wanting but her loue, that once obtain'd
Sicill is ours: *Scanfardee?* if we win,
Thou shalt be Lord *Nicanor*, I the King. *Exeunt.* SCEN.

Arraigned by Women.

SCEN. II.
Enter MYSOGENOS *solus.*

Mis. By this, my thundering Booke is prest abroad,
I long to heare what a report it beares,
I know't will startle all our Citie Dames,
Worse then the roring Lyons, or the sound
Of a huge double Canon, *Swetnams* name,
Will be more terrible in womens eares,
Then euer yet in *Misogenysts* hath beene.
Enter Clowne.
Clow. Puffe, giue me some ayre,
I am almost stifled, puffe, Oh, my sides! (heate?
Mis. From whence comm'st thou in such a puffing
Hast thou been running for a wager, *Swash*?
Thou art horribly imbost. Where hast thou beene?
My life, he was haunted with some Spirit.
Clow. A Spirit? I thinke all the Deuils in Hell,
Haue had a pinch at my hanches,
I haue beene among the Furies, the Furies:
A Pox on your Booke: I haue beene paid ifaith,
You haue set all the women in the Towne in an vprore.
Mis. Why, what's the matter, *Swash*?
Clow. Ne'r was poore *Swash*, so lasht, and pasht,
And crasht and dasht, as I haue beene,
Looke to your selfe, they're vp in armes for you.
Mis. Why, Haue they weapons, *Swash*?
Clow. Weapons, Sir, I, Ile be sworne they haue.
And cutting ones, I felt the smart of 'em,
From the loines to the legs, from the head to th' hams,
From the Front to the foot, I haue not one free spot.
Oh, I can shew you, Sir, such Characters.
Mis. What dost thou mean, man, wilt shame thy selfe?
Clow. Why, here's none but you and I, Sir, is there?
Mis. Good, good, ifaith. This was a braue Reuenge.
Clow.

Clow. If 'tbe so good, would you had had't for me.
Mis. And if I liue, I will make all the World
To hate, as I doe, this affliction, Woman.
Clow. But we shall be afflicted in th' meane time.
Pray let's leaue this Land: if we stay heere,
We shall be torne a-pieces: would we had kept
In our owne Countrey, there w'are safe enough:
You might haue writ and raild your bellifull,
And few, or none would contradict you, Sir.
Mis. Oh, but for one that writ against me, *Swash*,
Ide had a glorious Conquest in that Ile,
How my Bookes tooke effect! how greedily
The credulous people swallowed downe my hookes
How rife debate sprang betwixt man and wife!
The little Infant that could hardly speake,
Would call his Mother Whore. O, it was rare!
Clow. Oh, damn'd Rogue!
I stay but here, in hope, to see him hang'd,
And carrie newes to *England*, then I know,
The women there will neuer see me want,
For God he knowes, I loue vm with my heart,
But dare not shew it for my very eares.
What course, Sir, shall we take to hide our selues?
Mis. The same we did at *Bristow*, Fencing Boy;
Oh 'tis a fearefull name to Females, *Swash*,
I haue bought Foiles alreadie, set vp Bils,
Hung vp my two-hand Sword, and chang'd my name:
Call me *Mysogenos*.
         Enter Scanfardo.
Clow. A sodden Nose.
Mis. Mysogenos, I say. Remember, *Swash*, heere
comes a Gentleman.
I know him well, he serues a Noble Lord.
Seignior *Scanfardo*, happily encountred.
Scan. Thanks, my noble Gladiator, Doctor of Defence.
Mis. A Master, Sir, of the most magnanimous Method
of Cudgell-cracking.   *Scan.*

Arraigned by Women.

Scan. Ime glad I met with you,
I was now comming to be entred, Sir.
  Mif. That you shall presently. My Rapier, *Swash.*
Come, Sir, I'll enter you.
  Scan. What meane you, Sir?
  Mif. You say you would be entred, if you will,
Ile put you to the *Puncto* presently.
  Scan. Your Scholler, Sir, I meane.   (Fees?
  Mif. O welcome, Sir, What, haue you brought your
  Scan. Yes, Sir : what is't?
  Mif. Twentie *Piaftros*, your admittance Sir,
And fiue, your quarteridge.
  Clow. Besides Vshers Fees.
There goes a garnish and a breake-faft too.
  Scan. Well, I'm content, there 'tis.
  Clow. Come when you will, find you *Piaftros*, Sir,
And we'll find you crackt crownes.
  Mif. Booke him, my bold Vsher.
  Clow. That I will, you denomination, Seignior.
  Scan. Seignior *Scanfardo, Della Sancta Cabrado.*
  Clow. Seig. *Scan. Della Sancta Cabrado*? a terrible name.
  Mif. Giue me your hand, Scholer, so Ile cal you now.
Ile make you one of the Sonnes of Art.
Swash, giue my Scholer the Foyle.
  Clow. Doe not take it in scorne,
I haue gi'n many a good Gentleman the Foyle, Sir.
  Mif. I was going this morning to practise a young
That shortly goes to fight at *Callis Sands.*   (Duellift,
Come, Sir, to your guard.
  Scan. Not here in publike, I am a young beginner.
Come to my Chamber, Sir, Ile practise there.
  Mif. Doe, and Ile teach you the very myfterie of Fencing, that in a fortnight, you shall be able to challenge any Scholer vnder the degree of a Prouoft, and in a quarter of a yeere, beat all the Fencers in *Germany*. Our English Mafters of this Noble Science would ha' gi'n fortie pound to haue knowne that tricke.

              B   *Scan.*

Scan. Say you so, Sir? By this hand, I shall thinke my money well bestowed then: but to tell you the truth, Sir, the reason I would learne, is, because I am to bee married shortly: and they say, Then or neuer, is the time for a man to get the mastery.

Mis. How, marry, Scholer? thou art not mad, I hope. Doe you know what you doe?

Scan. I know what I shall doe, Master, that's as good.

Mis. Doe you know what she is you are to marrie?

Scan. A woman, I am sure a that.

Mis. No, she's a Deuill, Harpie, Cockatrice.

Scan. And you were not my Master.

Mis. Scholer, be aduised, they are all Most vile and wicked.

Scan. How, Sir?

Mis. Dissemblers, the very curse of man, Monsters (indeed.

Clow. That Ile be sworne they are, for I haue knowne some of vm, that ha' deuoured you three Lordships, in Cullices and Caudles before Break-fast.

Mis. And creatures the most imperfect: for looke yee, Th'are nothing of themselues, (Sir, Onely patcht vp to coozen and gull men, Borrowing their haire from one, complexions from another, Nothing their own that's pleasing, all dissembled, Not so much, but their very breath Is sophisticated with Amber-pellets, and kissing causes. Marry a woman, Scholer? thou vndergo'st an harder task, Then those bold Spirits, that did vndertake To steale the great *Turke* into Christendome. A woman! she's an Angell at ten, a Saint at fifteene, A Deuill at fortie, and a Witch at fourescore. If you will marry, marry none of these: Neither the faire, nor the foule; the rich, nor the poore; The good, nor the bad.

Scan. Who should I marry then, Sir?

Mis. Marry none at all.

Scan.

Arraigned by Women.

Scan. Proceeds this from Experience?

Mis. From Reason, Sir, the Mistris of Experience.
Happy were man, had woman neuer bin.
Why did not Nature infuse the gift of Procreation
In man alone, without the helpe of woman,
Euen as we see one seed, produce another?

Clow. Or as you see one Knaue make twentie, Master.

Mis. Thou saist true, *Swash*: or why might not a man
Reuiue againe, like to the Elme and Oake?

Clow. Many Logger-heads doe, Sir.

Mis. When they are cut downe to the very roote,
Yet in short time you see young branches spring againe.

Clow. If 'twere so at Tyburne, what a fine companie
of Crack-ropes would spring vp then?

Mis. Then we should ne'r be acquainted with the deceitfull deuices of a womans crooked conditions, which
are so many, that if all the World were Paper, the Sea,
Inke, Trees and Plants, Pens, and euery man Clarkes,
Scribes, and Notaries: yet would all that Paper be scribled ouer, the Inke wasted, Pens worne to the stumps, and
all the Scriueners wearie, before they could describe the
hundreth part of a womans wickednesse.

Scan. Me thinks you are too generall: some, no doubt,
As many men, are bad: condemne not all for some.
What thinke you, Sir, of those that haue good wiues?
I hope, you will confesse a difference.

Mis. And Reason too: and here's the difference,
Those that haue good wiues, ride to Hell
Vpon ambling Hackneyes, and all the rest.
Vpon trotting Iades to the Deuill.

Scan. Is that the difference? Ile not marrie sure,
Ile rather turne Whore-master,
And gee a-foot to the Deuill.

Clow. You'l hardly doe that, if you loue whoring, Sir,
For many lose a Legge in such seruice.

Scan. But doe you heare, Sir? how long is 't since you

B 2 be-

SWETNAM,

became such a bitter Enemie to women?

Mis. Since I had wisdome: When I was a Foole, I doted on such Follies, but now I haue left vm, and doe vow to be the euerlasting scourge to all their Sex: What the reason is, Ile tell you, Sir, hereafter: reade but that, I haue arraign'd vm all, and painted forth Those Furies to the life, That all the World may know that doth it read, I was a true Mysogenist indeed. *Exeunt.*

SCEN. III.

Enter IAGO, *and* LORENZO *disguised.*

Iag. You haue not seene the Court then?
Lor. Not as yet.
But I desire to obserue the Fashions there.
How doe you stile your King of Sicilie?
Iag. Men call him, Sir, The iust King *Atticus;*
And truly too: for with an equall Scale
He waighes the offences betwixt man and man,
He is not sooth'd with adulation,
Nor mou'd with teares, to wrest the course of Iustice
Into an vniust current, to oppresse the Innocent,
Nor do's he make the Lawes
Punish the man, but in the man the cause.
Shall I in briefe giue you his Character?
Lor. A thing I couet much.
Iag. Attend mee then.
His state is full of maiestie and grace,
Whose basis is true Pietie and Vertue,
Where, vnderneath a rich triumphant Arch,
That does resemble the Tribunall Seat,
Garded with Angels, borne vpon two Columnes,
Iustice and Clemencie, he sits inthron'd,
His subiects serue him freely, not perforce,
And doe obey him more for loue, then feare;

Being

Arraigned by Women.

Being a King not of themselues alone,
And their estates, but their affections:
A soueraigntie that farre more safetie brings,
Then do's an Armie to the guard of Kings.

Lor. You haue describ'd, Sir, such a worthy Prince,
That well I cannot say, who is most happie;
Either the King for hauing so good subiects,
Or else the subiects for so good a King.
But pray proceed.

Iag. The Heauens to crowne his ioy,
With Immortalitie in his happie Issue
Sent him two Royall sonnes, of whom the eldest
Was the sweet Prince *Lysippus.* Was! oh me,
That euer I should liue to say, he was:
He was, but is not now, for he is dead.
The yongest was *Lorenzo,* for his yeeres,
The pride and glory of Sicilians,
And miracle of Nature, whose aspect,
Euen like a Comet, did attract all eyes
With admiration, wonder and amazement,
And he good Prince, is lost, or worse, I feare:
But for his Daughter faire *Leonida,*
Her Fame not able to be circumscrib'd
Within the bounds of Sicilie, hath gone
Beyond the Pirean Mountaines, and brought backe
The chiefe Italian Princes, but their Loues
Were quitted with contempt and crueltie:
And many of our braue Sicilian Youths
Haue sacrific'd their liues to her disdaine.
Now to preuent the like euent hereafter,
'Twas thought fit her libertie should be awhile restraind,
For which intent, his Highnesse hath elected
The Lord *Nicanor* for her Guardian,
Who, 'tis thought, shall after his decease,
Espouse the Princesse, and be heire of Sicill.

Lor. You told me of a Prince, you said was lost,

B 3   Which

SWETNAM,

Which you pronounc'd so feelingly, as if
It had beene your losse in particular.

Iag. Oh, it was mine, and euery good mans else,
That is oblig'd to vertue and desert.

Lor. See how Report is subiect to abuse.
I knew the Prince *Lorenzo*.

Iag. Did you, Sir?

Lor. But neuer knew in him any one sparke
Of worth or merit, that might thus inflame
The zeale of your affection.

Iag. Traytor, thou lyest.
Which I will proue eu'n to thy heart, thou ly'ft,
I tell thee, thou hast committed such a sinne
Against his deare Report, that thy base life
Is farre too poore to expiate that wrong.
Sir, will you draw?

Lor. Forbeare, incensed man. I doe applaud
Thy noble courage, and I tell you, Sir,
The Prince *Lorenzo* was a man I lou'd
As dearely as my selfe: but pray resolue me;
Does he liue or not?

Iag. He liues,
In our eternall memorie he liues: but otherwise,
It's the generall feare of Sicily,
That he is dead, or in Captiuitie.
For when *Don Iohn*, the Spanish Generall,
Went with an Armie 'gainst the cruell Turkes,
In that still memorable Battell of Lepanto,
Our braue *Lorenzo*, too too vent'rous,
There lost his life, or worse, his libertie.

Lor. Hath not Time with his rude hand
Defac'd the Impression of his Effigies
In your memories yet?

Iag. No, nor will euer be, so long
As worth shall be admir'd, and vertue loued.

Lor. You know him, if you see him.

Iag.

Arraigned by Women.

Iag. My Lord *Lorenzo*!
Lor. Rise, my worthy Friend,
I haue made proofe of thy vnfayned loue.
 Iag. Th'exceeding happinesse to see you well,
Is more then ioy can vtter: On my knees
I beg your pardon for th'vnciuill speech
My ignorant tongue committed.
 Lor. No, thus I'le be reueng'd. *Imbraces him.*
I know thou louest mee, and I must inioyne
Thy loue vnto an act of secresie,
Which you must not denie.
 Iag. Sir, I obey.
 Lor. Then thus it is, I must coniure your faith,
And priuacie in my arriuall yet,
For I intend a while in some disguise
To obserue the times and humors of the Court.
 Iag. How meanes your Grace? can you indure to see
The Court eclipst with clouds of discontent,
Your father mourne your absence, and all hearts
Ore-whelm'd with sorrow, and you present, Sir?
 Lor. Iago, I'me resolu'd:
Therefore what shape or humor I assume,
Take you no notice that I am the Prince.
 Iag. Sir, I consent,
And vow to your concealement.
 Lor. It is enough, my brother's dead, thou saist,
I haue some teares to spend vpon his Tombe,
We are the next vnto the Diadem,
That's the occasion I obscure my selfe.
Happie's that Prince, that ere he rules, shall know,
VVhere the chiefe errors of his State doe grow.

Exeunt.

Act. II.

Act. II.

Enter Lisandro, *and* Loretta, *seuerall.*

Lor. My Lord *Lisandro*, y'are met happily.
Lis. *Loretta*! welcome, welcome as my life.
How fares my dearest Saint?
  Lor. Like a distressed Prisoner, whose hard fate
Hath bard her from all ioy in losing you,
A torment which she counts insufferable.
  Lis. This separation, like the stroke of death,
Makes a diuorce betwixt my soule and mee;
For how can I liue without her
In whom my life subsists?
For neuer did the Load-stone more respect
The Northerne Pole, by natures kind instinct,
Then my affections truly sympathize
With her, the Starre of my felicitie.
  Lor. Therefore shee prayes you, henceforth to desist,
Respecting your owne safetie: VVorthie Prince,
The times are troublesome and dangerous:
As for her selfe, she's arm'd to vndergoe
All malice that for you they can inflict.
  Lis. Oh my *Loretta*! thou appli'st a balme
VVorse then the wound it selfe: It is impossible
For me to liue at all but in her sight.
But was this all shee said,
That I should leaue her? Death could not ha' spoke
A word more fatall to my soule and mee:
Let her inioyne mee to some other taske,
Tho it were greater then the sonne of Ioue
Did for his Step-dame *Iuno* euer act:
Let it be any thing, so I may not leaue
Her sweet societie.

Lor.

Arraigned by Women.

Lor. Then, here my Lord, read this.
Lif. I kisse thee for her sake, whose beauteous hand
Hath here inclos'd so mild and sweet a doome.
See what a negatiue command shee hath
Impos'd vpon my sloth to visit her,
As if she taxed my neglect so long:
But pardon, deare *Leonida*, I come
To intimate thy fauor for my stay,
Tho thou wert garded with an host of men.
But how?
I must disguise me in some other shape,
For this is noted, and too full of danger.
Loretta, Who's admitted best accesse
Vnto thy Lady?
  Lor. Frier *Anthonie*,
Her Graces Confessor.
  Lif. As I could wish: I know the Frier well;
I must assume that shape; It is the best:
Loretta, weare this Iewell for my sake;
Nay, prethee take it, not as recompence,
But as a token of that future good
Shall crowne thy merits, with such height and honour,
Fortune shall be asham'd, and held a Foole,
To suffer poore desert to ouer-match her. *Exit Lif.*
  Lor. I humbly thanke your Grace: Why, here's a gift
Able to make a Saint turne Oratrix,
And pleade 'gainst Chastitie: I must confesse,
Lisandro is a Noble Gentleman, and ha's good gifts,
And is, indeed, gracious with my Ladie: Yet for all
that, wee poore Gentlewomen, that haue no other for-
tunes but our attendance, must now and then make the
best vse of our places: wee haue president, and very lately
too. But who comes here? my Lord *Nicanor*?
      Enter Nicanor.
Here's another Client---- I must deuise some quaint de-
uice for him, to delude his frostie apprehension-----
Oh I ha't.   G   *Nic.*

Nic. *Loretta*, how is't, wench? How thriues my suit, ha? Haſt broke with thy Lady yet?
Lor. He takes me for a Shee-Broker, but I'le fit him:
I haue my Lord, but find her ſo obdure,
That when I ſpeake, ſhe turnes away her eare;
As if her mind were fixt on ſomething elſe.
The other day, finding her Grace alone,
I came and mou'd your ſuit; told her how deare
She ſtood in your affection; and proteſted,
You lou'd her more then all the World beſide.
    Nic. Good, good: proceed.
    Lor. At this ſhe anſwer'd not a word,
But kept her eye ſtill fixt vpon me;
Then I begun agen, and told her Grace
(As from my ſelfe) how much your Honour
Had merited her fauour by deſert;
How great you ſtood ith' generall eye of all,
And one ſelected by the King her Father,
(Since Prince *Lorenzo's* death) to perſonate
The King of Sicill after his deceaſe.
    Nic. Excellent good i'faith. Then what ſaid ſhee?
    Lor. At this, I might perceiue her colour change
From red to pale, and then to red againe,
As if difdaine and rage had faintly ſtroue
In her confuſed breſt for victorie.
At length, hauing recal'd her ſpirits,
She broke forth into theſe words; What, wilt thou
Conſpire with youth and frailtie, to inforce
The rule of my affection 'gainſt my will?
Tho' my body be confin'd his priſoner,
Yet my mind is free. With that, ſhee charg'd mee
That I neuer ſhould hereafter vrge your ſuit;
And this was all the comfort that I could
From her with all my diligence attaine.
    Nic. Cold comfort, Wench, but 'tis the generall fault
Of women all, to make ſhew of diſlike

To

Arraigned by Women.

To thofe they moft affect: and in that hope
Thou fhalt to her againe: No Citie
Euer yeelded at firft skirmifh. Before,
You came but to a parley, thou fhalt now
Giue an affault: There's nothing batters more
A womans refolution, then rich gifts;
Then goe, *Loretta*.
    Lor. 'Las, my Lord, you know------   (pearle,
    Nic. Feare nothing, Wench, giue her this chaine of
With it my felfe.
    Lor. My Lord, I'le fee what I can doe with her,
But---
    Nic. What, *Loretta*? Oh, you looke for a fee:
Here, take this Gold: And if thou canft preuaile,
(Harke in thine eare) When I am King----
    Lor. I thanke your Lordfhip: Ha, ha, ha--- *Exit Lor.*
    Nic. This womans weakneffe was wel wrought vpon,
Her words may take effect: 'Tis often feene
That women are like Diamonds; nothing cuts fo foone
As their owne powder: yet there is one more
Will make a happy fecond,
Frier *Anthonie* her Confeffor; fuch men as hee
Can preuaile much with credulous Penitents
In caufes of perfwafion. Hoe, within?
           Enter Seruant.
    Scan. Your Lordfhip call?
    Nic. Bid Frier *Anthonie*
Come vifit mee with all fpeed poffible,
I could not thinke vpon a better Agent.
Their feeming fanctitie makes all their acts
Sauour of Truth, Religion, Pietie,
And proue that loue's a heauenly Charitie,
Without which there's no fafetie. Here he comes.
        Enter Lifandro *like a Frier.*
    Lif. The benediction of the bleffed Saints
Attend your honour.
    Nic. Welcome, holy Frier.   C 2   And

SWETNAM,

Lis. And crowne your wishes to your hearts desire.
Nic. Amen, *Anthonio*,
I'le say Amen to that; but yet the meanes
To make mee happy, lies within thy power.
  Lis. Your Honour may command mee.
  Nic. Then 'tis thus;
Thou know'st with what a generall consent
Of all Sicilia I was prelected
By my dread Soueraigne, to espouse the faire
Yet fond *Leonida*; granting me for dower
The Crowne of Sicil, after his decease.
  Lis. I hope, my Lord, there's none dares question that.
  Nic. To which intent, how many hopefull Princes
Haue beene non-suted, onely for my sake?
And to preuent all meanes of their accesse,
Establish'd mee her Guardian: Now, the Princesse,
Although I haue her Person, yet her Heart
I find estrang'd from mee, and all my loue
Is quitted with contempt.
  Lis. The Heauens forbid.
  Nic. It is forbidden both by Heauen and Earth,
And yet Shee do's it; and thou know'st then, Frier,
My hopes are frustrate. Therefore (holy Man)
Thou art her Counsel-Closet, her Confessor,
Of reuerend opinion with the Princesse.
  Lis. I doe conceiue your Honour.
  Nic. Be my Orator.
  Lis. In what I may, my Lord.
  Nic. If thou preuail'st,
I'le make thee Metropolitane of Sicil.
  Lis. It shall be all my care.
  Nic. Then farewell, Father.   *Exit Nic.*
  Lis. All my Prayers attend yee.
So, here's the fence throwne open; now my way
Is made before mee: Godamercy Cowle;
It is no maruell tho' the credulous World

                                    Thought

Arraigned by Women.

Thought themselues safe from danger, when they were
Inuested with this habit, 'tis the best,
To couer, or to gaine a free accesse,
That can be possible in any proiect.
How finely I haue guld my Politician,
That couets Loue, onely to gaine a Crowne?
But if my Loue proue constant, Ile withstand
All his desires with a more powerfull hand. *Exit.*

Enter LEONIDA *and* LORETTA.

Le. Tell me, *Loretta*, Art thou sure 'twas he?
Lor. Madame, I liue not else.
Le. Thou do'st delude
My feares with fond impossibilities:
Prethee resolue me truly, I do long
Most infinitely.
Lor. Not a syllable more now,
And 'twould saue your life: not be-beleeu'd?
Le. Nay, sweet *Loretta.*
Troth, I doe beleeue thee.
Lor. Discredited?
I could fight with any liuing creature,
In this quarrell 'tis so iust.
Le. Haue I deseru'd
No more respect, then to be trifled thus?
Come, prethee tell me.
Lor. Yes? to delude
Your feares with fond impossibilities?
Le. Nay, now thou tortur'st me.
Lor. Well, I haue done.
But leaue your sighes, your heigh-ho's, and ay-me's:
For I haue newes will warme you like the Sunne,
And make you open like the Marigold.
Le. Why, now thou rauish'st me.
Lor. I heard you not cry out yet.
Le. Thou takest such a delight in crossing me.

Lor.

Lor. 'Faith, now you talke of Crosses, Ile tell you,
You haue chosen a Husband, so handsome, so complete,
As if he had beene pickt
Out of the Christ-Crosse row.

Le. As how, I prethee?

Lor. Why, Madame, thus:
Ile begin with A. and so proceed to the latter end of the Alphabet, comparing his good parts as thus: for A. hee is Amiable, Bountifull, Courteous, Diligent, Eloquent, Faithfull, Gracious, Humble, Iouiall, Kind, Louing, Magnanimous, Noble, Patient, Quiet, Royall, Secret, Trustie, Vigilant, Wittie, and Xceeding Youthfull. Now for Z, he's zealous: so I conclude, pray God hee bee not Iealous.

Le. An excellent obseruation.

Lor. Who doe you think's in loue with you?
The old Dragon *Nicanor*, that watches the fruit of your Hesperides.

Le. Oh, that newes is stale.

Lor. He met but iust now, and would needs know,
What returne I had made of his Aduenture.
But I deuised such a Tale for my old Marchant,
Able to make a Bankrout at report,
But he notwithstanding fraughts me agen,
With that he was not able, but with this,
This Chaine of Pearle.

Le. Prethee, away with it, Ile not be chain'd to him.

Lor. Faith, and 'tis true, a Chaine is the worst Gift
A Louer can send his Mistris, 'tis such an Embleme
Of bondage hereafter. Who's that?

Enter LISANDRO.

Le. Father.

Lis. How fares my worthy Daughter?

Le. Eu'n as one

Deuo-

Arraigned by Women.

Deuoted vnto sorrow, griefe and mone.
  Lis. Then I must blame you, Ladie, you doe ill,
To blast those Rosiall blossomes. Will you kill
This gift of Nature, Beautie in the prime?
  Le. Father, I vnderstand not what you say:
The other day you talkt of Penitence,
Commended Patience, Sorrow and Contrition,
As Antidotes against the soules decay:
And now, me thinkes, you speake of no such thing.
  Lis. Mistake me not, deare Daughter, I spake then,
Onely to mortifie the sinfull minde,
But now I come with comfort, to restore
Your fainting spirits that were grieu'd before:
But Daughter, I must chide you.
  Le. Father, why?
  Lis. For your neglect, and too much crueltie
To one that dearely loues you.
  Le. Whom in the name of wonder?
  Lor. On my life,
This Frier's made an agent in my suit.
  Lis. The hope of Sicill, Map of true Nobilitie,
Patterne of Wisdome, Grace and Grauitie.
  Le. You prayse him highly, ha's he ne'r a name?
  Lis. Yes, is't my Lord *Nicanor*.
  Le. Oh, is't he?
His gray head shewes his wisdomes grauities
And are you made his Agent,
His Aduocate, to play the spokesman? Fie.
  Lis. Daughter, this is a worke of Charitie,
A holy action to combine in one:
Two different hearts in holy Vnion.
  Le. Frier, no more.
I doe not like of these perswasions,
Either ya're not the same you seeme to be,
Or all your Actions are Hypocrisie,
My Faith is past alreadie, and my heart:

In-

SWETNAM,

Ingag'd vnto a farre more worthy man:
Lisandro is the Prince my loue hath wonne.
   Lis. Then here the Frier concludes: my taske is done.
   Le. Lisandro, my deare Loue!
   Lis. The same, sweet Princesse.
   Le. Oh, you were too aduentrous, dearest Loue,
What made you vndertake this hard attempt?
   Lis. Your loue, sweet Lady,
That makes all things easie.
   Le. Oh, I am made immortall with thy sight:
Here let me euer liue: I feare not now
The worst that Fate or Malice can afflict:
I haue enough, hauing thy companie.
   Lis. And when I leaue to loue you, vertuous Madame,
Vpon that minute, let me leaue to liue,
That loue and life may both expire together.
   Lor. Come, leaue your prating and protesting,
And get you both in, and be naught awhile,
'Tis dangerous talking here in publike,
Good Frier, look my Ladie dye no Nun. *Exit Le. & Lis.*
Heigho! now could I wish my Sweet-heart
Heere too, I feele such a tickling, somewhere
About me: if he were here now, I would
Neuer cast such an vnwilling deniall vpon him
As I haue done, hauing so good a president as I haue.
But stay, who's this?
As true as I liue, 'tis he.
Oh, sweet Rogue, thou art come
In the happiest minute.

Enter SCANFARDO.

   Scan. Am I, *Loretta*? Masse, I like that well.
What, all alone? I like that better too.
But where's the Princesse?
   Lor. Oh, she's safe enough!

Scan.

Arraigned by Women.

Scan. Is she indeed? I like that best of all.
Lor. And so do's shee, I warrant yee,
Or any woman else, that's in her Case: ha, ha, ha!
  Scan. There's something in the wind now, that you laugh at.
  Lor. Nothing indeed, sweet Loue: but ha, ha! I laugh at an odde Iest.
  Scan. Come, I must know't.
  Lor. 'Deed but you must not.
  Scan. Why? Dare you not trust me?
  Lor. Yes, I dare: but
As you are a ma.., reueale it not.
  Scan. In troth, Ime angry, that you should mistrust me.
  Lor. The Frier, the Frier: ha, ha, ha!
He that the Lord imploy'd to be his Agent,
Who doe you thinke it was?
  Scan. Father *Anthonie*, wast not?
  Lor. The Deuill it was: no faith,
It was, ha, ha, ha!
It was no other, then *Lisandro* Prince of *Naples*,
That stole to my Lady in that Habit,
And guld your Lord most palpably.
  Scan. Is't possible?
And where are they now?
  Lor. Why ?faith th'are eu'n at,
Ha, ha, ha, ha!
But good Sweet-heart, be silent.
  Scan. Not a syllable I: it was a bold attempt,
Knowing 'twas death, if but discouered once.
But come, Sweet-heart, weele eu'n doe,
As our betters haue done before vs,
The example is easly followed,
Hauing so good a Schoole-mistris.
Shall we to bed?
  Lor. Fye, seruant, how you talke?
Troth you are to blame, to offer to assault

D   The

The chastitie of any Gentlewoman,
Vpon aduantage.

Scan. Pox, leaue this forc'd modesty: for by this hand,
I must enioy you now before we part.

Lor. I haue so farre ingag'd my selfe, you know,
'Tis now vaine to resist.

Scan. Why, now I like thee well.
Where shall we meet?

Lor. In the with-drawing Chamber, there I lye.

Scan. Goe then, Ile follow.

Lor. Ile put out the light.

Scan. No matter, I shall find the way i'the darke.
Here was a strange discouerie but indeed,
What will not women blab to those they loue?
I am very loth to leaue my sport to night,
And yet more loth to lose that rich reward
My Lord will giue for this discouerie,
Chiefly to be reueng'd vpon his riuall:
Ile not forsake it, Venerie is sweet.
But he that has good store of gold and wealth,
May haue it at command, and not by stealth.

Enter Lisandro *and* Leonida.

Lis. 'Tis late, deare Loue.

Le. You shall not part from me,
Good sooth, you shall not. Frier *Anthonie*,
You say, is faithfull: for *Loretta's* truth
I dare ingage my life.

Lis. Why, so you doe;
Should she proue false, both yours and mine, you know,
Are forfeit to the Law.

Le. You are secure.
Mistrust not then: true loue is void of feare.
No danger can afflict a constant mind.
This is no durance, no imprisonment,
Rather a Paradise in ioying thee:
My libertie alone consists in thee.

Lis.

Arraigned by Women.

Lif. That is the reaſon, Ime ſo iealous, Sweet,
Since in my freedome both our liues remaine.
As for my ſelfe, what perill could be thought,
I would not vndergoe to gaine your loue?
Were it to ſcale the flaming Ætna's top:
Whoſe ſulphurous ſmoke kils with infection,
Cut through the Northerne Seas, or ſhoote the Gulfe?
Or——

Le. I doe beleeue thee, Sweet.

Lif. But yet this houre
Is not frequented by your Confeſſor, there lyes the danger.

Le. I ha' confeſt to thee, from morne till night,
From night till morne againe, all my tranſgreſſion.

Enter Nicanor.

Lif. Were I your Confeſſor, I know you would
Both ſinne, and be confeſt.

Nic. Breake ope the doore.

Lif. By Heauen, we are betrai'd.

Le. Oh my deare Loue.

Lif. My thoughts preſag'd as much.   *Enter* Nicanor
What ſhall we doe?   *and a Guard.*

Le. Do not reſiſt, *Liſandro*, ſtand: the worſt,
We can but dye.
Oh, this *Loretta*, falſe, inhumane wretch!

Nic. Lay hands vpon them both. Is't ſo Indeed?
Is this the zeale of your Confeſſion?
I feare, death giues the abſolution.

Le. Hence, doting Foole, more welcome far is death,
Then to bee linkt to Ages Leproſie.   *Exeunt.*

Nic. Beare vm away into their ſeuerall Wards.
Let them be guarded ſtrongly, till ſuch time
I ſhall acquaint my Soueraigne with this Plot.
Rather then loſe the Royall Dignitie,
Ile ſtriue to ruine a whole Progenie.   *Exit.*

D 2   Act.

SWETNAM,

Act. III.

Enter ATTICVS, IAGO, NICANOR, *two Iudges, Notarie, and Attendants.*

Att. How full of troubles is the state of Kings,
Abroad with Foes, at home, with faithlesse Friends,
Within with cares, without, a thousand feares?
Yet all summ'd vp together, doth not make
Such an impression in our troubled thoughts,
As this one Act of disobedience
In our owne Issue.

Iag. Gracious Soueraigne, yet for that high respect,
Be fauourable: she is your Daughter.

1. *Iud.* And the onely hope
Of all Sicilie, since *Lorenzo's* losse.

Att. Bring to the Barre the Prisoners: this offence
Hath lost in vs a Father and a Friend,
And cals for Iustice from vs, as a King:
Yet thinke not, Lords, but 'tis with griefe of mind,
Nor can a Father easly forget a Daughter,
Whom hee once so dearely lou'd:
Yet we had rather become Issuelesse,
Then leaue it noted to Posteritie,
An Act of such Iniustice.

2. *Iud.* Yet, dread Liege,
Oh, doe not too much aggrauate the crime,
Rather impute it to their childish loue.

Att. To loue my Lords? if that were lowable,
What Act so vile, but might be so excus'd?
The Murderer, that sheddeth guiltlesse bloud,
Might plead, it was for loue of his Reuenge,
The Felon likewise might excuse his theft,
With loue of money, and the Traytor too
Might say, It was for loue of Soueraigntie.
And indeed, all offenders so might plead. *A Barre.*

There-

Arraigned by Women.

Therefore, my Lords, you that sit here to Iudge,
Let all respect of persons be forgot,
And deale vprightly, that you may resemble
The highest Iudge, whose seat on Earth you hold:
And for you know, the Lawes of Sicilie
Forbid to punish two, for one offence,
Let your care be to find the principall,
The *Primus Motor* that begun the cause;
For the effect (you see) is but the issue
That one of them may worthily receiue
Deserued death; the other, may be sent
(As lesse offending) into banishment.   *Exit* King.
  The Prisoners brought to   *Enter* Lisandro,
  the Barre by a Gard.   *and* Leonida.
  1. *Iudg.* Th'offence wherewith you both stand tax'd
Appeares so manifest in gro sse, that now   (withall,
We need not question all particulars
In publique here: yet your triall shall
Be honourable, as your Persons were
Before this blacke Impression. Therefore say,
Which of you two begun th'occasion,
By any meanes, direct or indirect?
And answer truely, as you looke for grace.
  Lis. 'Twas I, my honour'd Lords.
  Leo. My Lords, 'twas I.
  Lis. Let not this honourable Court be swaid
By false suggestions; that the fault was mine,
Appeares as manifest as mid-dayes Sunne,
'Twas I that first attempted, su'd, and prai'd,
Vs'd all the subtile engins Art could inuent,
Or Nature yeeld, to force affection,
Onely to gaine the royall Princesse loue;
For what can Women aboue weakenesse act?
Or, what Fort's so strong, but yeelds at length
To a continued siege?
Th'attempt, I knew, was hard and dangerous:

D 3   There-

Therefore more honourable in the conquest;
Which ere I would haue left, I would ha' past
More dangers then ere *Iason* vnder-went.
Then, since you see (my Lords) the guilt was mine,
Pardon the Princesse, Mee to death resigne.

   Leo. Pardon (my Lords) *Lisandro*, let me dye:
If euer you'le performe an act of iustice
Shall make you truely famous, doe it here,
Here vpon me; the guilt alone is mine:
'Twas this alluring face, and tempting smiles,
That drew on his affections. Say that Hee
Did first commence the suit; the fault was mine
In yeelding to it: 'Tis a greater shame
For women to consent, then men to aske:
And yet, before he spoke, I had ingag'd
My heart and loue to him, vnask'd, vnpraid;
And then (you know) how soone our eyes discouers
The true affection that we beare our Louers:
Then since the guilt alone remaines in Mee,
Let me be iudg'd, and set *Lisandro* free.

   2. *Iudg.* This knot is intricate.

   Lis. 'Tis fallacie.
Who can alledge one Article 'gainst her?
Th'offence was, breaking of the Kings command,
That none, on paine of death, should visit her,
Vnlesse appoynted by the King himselfe;
And that alone was mine: 'Twas my deuice;
I tooke the borrowed shape; I broke the Law,
And I must suffer for't: Then doe not wrong
Her spotlesse Chastitie.

   4. *Iudg.* How, Chastitie?

   Lis. If any here conceiue her otherwise,
That very thought will damne him:
She's as chaste
As ere your Mothers in their cradles were,
For any act committed.

                                       2. *Iudg.*

Arraigned by Women.

2. *Iudg.* Harder still.
1. *Iudg.* A confused Labyrinth: we shal ne'r wind out.
Leo. My Lords, beleeue him not; the guilt lies here:
'Twas I that sent him that deluding shape,
In which he got admittance; The offence
Rests onely here: And therefore (good my Lords)
Let the condemning sentence passe on mee;
Or else, I will protest to all the world,
You are vniust;
And take my death vpon't.
  Lis. Fie, Madam, how you wrong your innocence!
And seeming (Lady) to be pittifull
To mee, you are most cruell; for my life
Should be a willing sacrifice to death,
To expiate the guilt of my offence.
Remember what continuall paines I tooke,
By messages, intreaties, gifts, and prayers,
To win your fauour, deare *Leonida*.
Iustice in this will be Impietie,
Vnlesse it here be shew'd. I beg it may.
  Leo. I beg against him: He is innocent;
The fact alone was mine: I was the first,
The middle, and the end;
And Iustice here must end,
Or 'tis iniustice.
                    Enter King.
  Attic. Is the sentence giuen?
  2. *Iudg.* Not yet, my Lord: We are as far to seeke,
In the true knowledge of the prime Offender,
As at the first; for they plead guilty both;
Both striue to aggrauate their owne offence,
And Both excuse each other. On our liues,
We cannot yet determine where's the cause.
  Attic. It is impossible
That sacred Iustice should be hudwink't still,
Though she be falsly painted so; Her eyes

SWETNAM,
Are cleare, and so perspicuous, that no cryme
Can maske it selfe in any borrowed shape,
But shee'le discouer it. Let vm be returnd
Backe to their seuerall Wards, till we deuise
Some better course for the discouery.
  Nic. Dread Soueraigne, I know no better way,
Then to assay by torture, to inforce
A free confession, seuerall, one from other:
For though they now, out of affection,
Plead their owne guilt, as if they feard not death;
Yet, when they feele him sting once, then the care
Of life, and safetie, will discouer all.
  Iag. My Lord *Nicanor*, this is ill aduis'd,
Sauoring too much of force and tyrannie.
Is't fit that Princes should subiect themselues
To any tortures, such as are prepared
For base Offendors? 'Tis ignobly done,
So to incense the King.
  Nic. How, Sir!
  Iag. Eu'n so:
You shew a proud aspiring mind, my Lord,
After a Kingdome, that would ruinate
Two royall Louers for so small a fact:
But, Marke my words, *Nicanor*; Ere the Crowne
Impale thy Temples by Her timelesse end,
Mine and fiue thousand liues shall all expire.
  Nic. I wey thy words not this.
  Iag. Nor I thy frowne;
I'le incense one, shall quickly pull you downe   *Exit.*
  Attic. How's your opinion then,
To search it out?
  1. *Iudg.* My Liege, we know no better way then this,
Let there be publique Proclamation made
Throughout the Kingdome, that there may be found
Two Aduocates, to plead this difference
In publique disputation, Man and Woman,
                                            The

Arraigned by Women.

The wisest, and the best experienc'd
That can be found, or heard of in the Land:
Or any such will proffer of themselues
To vndertake the plea; For, questionlesse,
None are so impudent to vndergoe
So great a controuersie, except those
That know themselues sufficient.
   Attic. Wee are pleas'd.
See it effected with all the speed you can: *Exeunt*
The charge be yours,my Lord.Dissolue the Court. *Om.*
     Enter Iago *and* Lorenzo, *disguised like*
           an Amazon.
   Lor. Has my poore Sister then withstood a triall?
   Iag. I, and behau'd her selfe
Most royall, and discreetly: Insomuch,
Shee put the Iudges to a non-plus, Sir;
Defending and excusing eythers cause,
Vntill *Nicanor*, with his kind aduice,
Desir'd the King they might be tortured,
To see if that would force confession.
   Lor. Was he the onely Tyrant? Well, ere long
It may be in Our power to quittance him.
I'me glad I know the Serpents subtiltie.
But how concluded they?
   Iag. I was so vext,
I could not stay a full conclusion.
The Prisoners were dismist before I ctme:
But how they did determine afterwards,
I long to heare. But what intends your Grace
In this disguise?
   Lor. To visit the sicke Court,
And free my Sister from captiuitie,
With that good Prince *Lisandro*.
      Enter Misogynos *and* Scanfardo.
   Mis. A Woman!
Why the more I thinke,of their wickednesse,
             E   The

SWETNAM,
The more incomprehensible I find it;
For they are, coozening, cologuing, vngrateful, deceitful,
Wauering, waspish, light, toyish, proud, sullen,
Discourteous, cruell, vnconstant; and what not.
Yet, they were created, and by nature formed,
And therefore of all men to be auoyded.
 Lor. Oh impious conclusion! What is hee?
 Iag. I ne'r had conuersation with him yet;
But (by report) I'le tell you, He's a man,
Who's breeding has beene like the Scarrabee,
Altogether vpon the excrement of the time;
And being swolne with poysonous vapors,
He breakes wind in publique, to blast the
Reputation of all Women; His acquaintance
Has bin altogether amongst Whores and Bawds,
And therefore speakes but in's owne element.
His owne vnworthie foule deformitie,
Because no Female can affect the same,
Begets in him despaire; and despaire, enuie.
He cares not to defame their very soules,
But that he's of the Turkes opinion: They haue none.
He is the Viper, that not onely gnawes
Vpon his Mothers fame, but seekes to eat
Thorow all Womens reputations.
 Lor. Is't possible! that Sicilie should breed
Such a degenerate Monster, shame of men?
 Iag. Blame not your Countrie, he's an Englishman.
 Lor. I will not see the glories of that Sexe
Be-spawld by such a dogged Humorist,
And passe vnpunisht.
 Iag. What intends your Grace?
 Lor. To vndertake this iust and honest quarrell,
In the defence of Vertue, till I haue
Seuerely punisht his opprobrious word,
Committed against Women, who's iust fame
Merits an Angels Pen to register.
          Scan.

Arraigned by Women.

Scan. Sir, you haue alter'd me, I thanke you for't.
Mif. Oh! they are all the very pits of Sin,
Which men, for want of wifdome, fall into.
   Scan. I fee it, Sir, and will proclaime as much. *Exit Scan.*
   Lor. Leaue me, *Iago*.
   Iag. I'me gone, fweet Prince.
   Lor. Tell me, thou iangling Maftiffe, with what feare
Dar'ft thou behold that too much wronged Sex,
Whofe Vertues thou haft bafely flander'd?
   Mif. Ha, ha, ha.
   Lor. Laugh'ft thou, inhumane wretch? By my beft (hope,
But that thy malice hath deferu'd reuenge
More infamous, and publique, then to fall
By me in priuate, I would hew thy flefh
Smaller then Attomes.
   Mif. What, haue we here?
A Woman rampant? ha!
Tempt me not, Syren, left thou doft inuoke
A Furie worfe then Woman.
   Lor. Hellifh Fiend,
How dar'ft thou ytter fuch blafphemous words,
In the contempt of Women, whofe deferts
Thy dunghill bafeneffe neuer could difcerne?
Affure thy felfe, thy malice fhall be plagu'd
Seuerely, as in iuftice thou deferu'ft. (fons,
   Mif. I wey not your threats this; fpit out your poy-
Till your gals doe burft. I will oppofe you all;
I cannot flatter, I: nor will I fawne
To gaine a fauor; Prayfe the hand and foot,
And fweare your face is Angel-like, and lye
Moft grofly. No, I will not do't.
But when I come, it fhall be in a ftorme,
To terrifie you all, that you fhall quake
To heare my name refounding in your eares:
And Fortune, if thou be'ft a deitie,
Giue me but opportunitie, that I

E 2   May

SWETNAM,
May all the follies of your Sex declare,
That henceforth Men of Women may beware.

Enter a Herald with a Proclamation, a Trumpet before him, a great rabble of men following him.

Heral. *Atticus,* King of Sicilia, to all his louing Subiects sendeth greeting : Whereas there is a doubtfull question to be decided in publique disputation, which concernes the honour of all men in generall, that is to say, Whether the Man or the Woman in loue, stand guilty of the greatest offence: Know therefore, if that any man, of what estate or condition soeuer, will vndertake to defend the equitie of men, against the false imputations of women, let vm repayre to the Court, they shall be honourably entertayned, graciously admitted, and well rewarded.

God saue the King.

Omnes. Heauen preserue his Grace.

Mis. Fortune, I doe adore thee for this newes:
Why, here's the thing I lookt for; 'tis a prize
Will make me euer famous. *Herald,* stay;
I will maintaine the Challenge, and approue
That women are first tempters vnto loue.
I'le blazon forth their colours in such sort,
Shall make their painted cheekes looke red, for vm
To haue them noted theirs, that all may know
That women onely are the cause of woe.

Omnes. A Champion, a Champion! *Exeunt.*

Enter a Woman with a Proclamation, and as many Women as may be, with a Trumpet afore them.

I.or. *Aurelia,* Queene, by the especiall priuiledge of the Maiestie of Sicilia, to all Ladies, gentle and others, of the Female Sex, sends greeting: Whereas there is a question

Arraigned by Women.

tion to be decided in publike disputation before, an Honourable Assembly of both parts, that is, whether the man or the woman in loue comit the greatest offence, by giuing the first and principall occasion of sinning: therefore know, that if any woman will vndertake to defend the innocency of women, against the false imputations of detracting men, let her repaire to the Court, shee shall bee honourably entertayned, graciously admitted, and well rewarded. *God saue the Queene.*

Omnes. Heauens preserue her.
Lor. I doe accept it, tis a cause so iust,
In equitie and vertue, in defence
Of wronged women, whose distressed fames
Lye buried in contempt, whose Champion
I doe professe my selfe, and doe desire
No greater glorie, then to haue that name.
What woman can indure to heare the Wrongs,
Slanders, Reproches, and base Forgeries,
That base men vaunt forth, to dimme the rayes
Of our weake tender Sex? But they shall know,
Themselues, not women, are the cause of woe.
A Champion, a Champion. *Exeunt Omnes.*

Enter Atticus, Misogynos, *two Iudges, Notarie, Cryer, and Attendants——And then* Lisandro, *and* Hortensia *guarded.*

Att. That Equitie and Iustice both may meet,
In paralels, like to *Apollo's* Twinnes,
We haue ordayn'd this Session. In the which
Let all vnequall and impartiall thoughts
Be laid aside, with such regard of truth,
As not the name of Daughter, or the Bloud
Which we call ours, running in her veines,
May any way diuert vs. Therefore goe on,
And take your seat, stout Champion, and preuaile,
As is the truth you deale for, in this doubtfull,

And

SWETNAM,

And much ambiguous businesse.
 Miſ. So I wiſh――   *Paſſe to his ſeat with Trumpets.*

Enter to them Aurelia, *leading* Atlanta, Loretta, *and two or three more women.*

 Aur. Braue Amazonian beautie, learned *Atlanta*,
Now is it time your intellectuall powers,
Of wit and iudgement ſhou'd aduance themſelues
Againſt the forked tongues of Slanderers,
That pierce the ſpotleſſe innocence of women,
And poyſon ſweetneſſe with the breath of Malice.
So on, and take thy ſeat! It is our truſt,
Th'euent will proſper, for our cauſe is iuſt.
 Atlan. That makes me confident―― *Paſſe to the ſeat.*
 Att. Prepare the Court.
 Cry. O yes! O yes! O yes! If there be any man, or woman―― in this Honourable Court,―― that can produce―― any lawfull cauſe,―― againſt either of the Aduocates―― why they ſhould not bee admitted―― Let them now ſpeake, or for euer hereafter hold their peace――
 Att. 'Tis well. Now ſweare the Iudges.
 Not. Yee ſhall ſweare by the ſacred hand of *Atticus*, not to reſpect the perſon of either of the Offendors: but iuſtly and truly to waigh and ballance the Reaſons and Arguments of the deputed Aduocates, and thereupon to determine and proceed in iudgement, according to the Lawes of this Iland, as you tender the pleaſure of Royall *Atticus*.
 Both Iudg. To this we freely ſweare.
 Att. Now then, to your Arguments.
 Aur. Atlanta, for poore innocent women.
 Att. Miſogynos for the men.
 Atlan. It is an honour farre beyond my weakneſſe,
(Moſt equall Iudges) that I am accepted,
I but a woman, before men to plead,
Dumbe feare and baſhfulneſſe to ſpeake before

           Bold

Arraigned by Women.

Bold Orators of State, men graue and wise,
That can at euery breathing pause, correct
The slipp'ry passages of a womans speech:
But yet withall my hopes are doubly arm'd.
   1. *Iudg.* How doubly arm'd?
   2. *Iudg.* Presume not more then Reason.
   Atlan. First, that my bashfull weaknesse claymes excuse,
And is to speake before such temp'rate Iudges,
Who in their wisdome will, no doubt, conniue
At small defects in me a silly woman.
   1. *Law.* Smoothly put on.
   2. *Law.* A quaint insinuation.
   Atlan. Next, that the cause I handle, is so iust,
And full of truth, as were corruption seated
Vpon your hearts (as who can euer doubt
Wisdome shou'd so decline) I wou'd not feare,
But that my pregnant Reasons soone shou'd purge,
And clense your secret bosomes from vntruth.
   1. *Law.* A promising *Exordium.*
   2. *Law.* The successe is all.
   Atlan. I need not tell you what I come to prooue:
That rayling Woman-hater hath alreadie
With his foule breath belcht forth into the Ayre,
The shamelesse cause in question, and doth charge
The supple wax, the courteous natur'd woman,
As blamefull for receiuing the impression
Of Iron-hearted man, in whom is grauen,
With curious and decciuing Art, foule shapes
And stamps of much abhord impietie.
Wou'd any man, once hauing fixt his Seale
To any Deed, though after he repent
The Fact so done, rayle at the supple Wax,
As though that were the cause of his vndoing?
O idle leuitie! Wax hath's vse,
And woman easly beares the mans abuse.
   1. *Law.* Here's a by-blow.
                                          2. *Law.*

2. *Law.* How can my Fencer ward it?
Stay: he comes on.
　Mis. Hum. Doe you wax vpon me? as if man
Once hauing fixt the Seale of Armes of loue,
On waxen-harted woman, though another
Came after him, and did adulterate
The stampe imprinted on her, she, forsooth,
Must still be held excus'd. 'Tis weake, and fond,
And woman-like: you flye on waxen wings,
That melt against the Sunne. Therefore attend,
And I will proue vnto this honour'd Court,
In all their passions women are impetuous,
And beyond men, ten times more violent.
　Atlan. I grant you that. But who begins the motion,
And is first agent? for as I conceiue,
That's the cause in question.
　Mis. Deluding woman.
　Atlan. Flattring and periur'd man.
　Mis. Did not th'inticing beautie of a woman,
Set Troy on fire?
　Atlan. Did not man first begin
To tempt that beautie with the fire of lust?
　Mis. Beautie first tempts to lust.
　Atlan. Lust tempteth Beautie:
Witnesse the vowes, the oaths, the protestations,
And Crocadile teares of base dissembling men,
To winne their shamelesse purpose: Whereof missing,
Then but obserue their Gifts, their Messages,
Their wanton Letters, and their amorous Sonnets,
Whereby they vent the smoke of their affections,
Readie to blind poore women, and put out
The Eye of Reason. But if still they faile,
Then come they on with vndermining cunning,
And with our Maides, our Pages and Attendants,
Corruptly worke and make insinuation,
Whilst they at hand with fained languishment,

Make

Arraigned by Women.

Make shew as if they meant to dye for loue,
When they but swelter in the reeke of Lust.
But heere's not all: for if this all preuaile not,
Then are they vp againe, and with pale cheekes,
Like some poore Starueling, or some Mimick Ghost,
They stalke into the presence of their Mistris,
Fold vp their armes, hang downe their wanton heads,
Cast loue-sicke glances, and as wofull Comma's,
In this dumbe Oratorie, now and then they breathe
A passionate sigh, whereat the gentle nature
Of milde compassionate woman once relenting,
Straight they fall out into such sweet complaints
Of their sad suffrings, tuning words of Art,
Able to melt a gentle Eye in teares,
As they doe speake. Then with officious dutie,
They licke a Moat off from her vpper garment,
Dust her curl'd Ruffe with their too busie fingers,
As if some dust were there: and many toyes
They vse to please, till side by side they ioyne,
And palme with palme supplies the amorous heart,
To pay a wanton kisse on Loues faire lips,
And then the Prize is wonne. Iudge therefore, Lords,
Whether the guilt doth lye on vs or them,
And as your Wisdomes find, saue or condemne.

A Plaudite by the women with shouts, crying, Atlanta,
Atlanta, Atlanta!
Lisan. Truth hath she said in all.
Hort. O, but the Art of Woman――
1. *Iud.* Silence! you haue no voice in Court. (speake
2. *Iud.* You haue your Aduocates, therefore must not
1. *Law.* These Allegations are vnanswerable.
2. *Law.* The Court must needs allow them.
Mis. Bragge not too fast! for all this glorious speech,
Is but a painted Pageant, made to vsher
Some homely Scauenger, and is borne vp,

F   Vpon

SWETNAM,

Vpon the backes of Porters. It wants true worth,
To carrie State, and vsher learned Iudgement
Into this Court. For what a foolish reason,
Is it to say, Lust tempteth garish Beautie,
Because men court their wanton Mistresses,
In sundry formes of Complement? There's not
A Citie Tradesman throughout all the Streets,
From the East Chappell, to the Westerne Palace,
But knowes full well the garish setting out
Of Beautie in their shops, will call in Customers
To cheapen ware: Beautie set forth to sale,
Wantons the bloud, and is mans tempting Stale.
 1. *Law.* How boldly he comes on?
 2. *Law.* But marke his reasons.   (strength,
 Mis. And this is woman, who well knowes her
And trimmes her Beautie forth in blushing Pride,
To draw as doth the wanton Morning Sunne,
The eyes of men to gaze. But marke their natures,
And from their Cradles you shall see them take
Delight in making Babies, deuising Christnings,
Bidding of Gossips, calling to Vp-sittings,
And then to Festiuals, and solemne Churchings,
In imitation of the wanton ends,
Their riper yeeres will ayme at. But goe further,
And looke vpon the very Mother of Mischiefe,
Who as her Daughters ripen, and doe bud
Their youthfull Spring, straight she instructs them how
To set a glosse on Beautie, adde a lustro
To the defects of Nature, how to vse
The mysterie of Painting, Curling, Powdring,
And with strange Periwigs, pin knots, Bordrings,
To deck them vp like to a Vintners Bush,
For men to gaze at on a Midsummer Night.
 1. *Law.* The tyde begins to turne.
 2. *Law.* Women goe downe.
 Mis. This done, they are instructed by like Art,
               How

Arraigned by Women.

How to giue entertainment, and keepe diftance
With all their Sutors, Friends, and Fauourites,
When to deny, and when to feed their hopes,
Now to draw on, and then againe put off,
To frowne and fmile, to weepe and laugh out-right,
All in a breath, and all to trayne poore man
Into his ruine : Nay, by Art they know
How to forme all their gefture, how to adde
A *Venus* Mole on euery wanton cheeke,
To make a gracefull dimple when fhe laughes :
And (if her teeth be bad) to lifpe and fimper,
Thereby to hide that imperfection:
And thefe once learn'd, what wants the Tempter now,
To fnare the ftouteft Champion of men ?
Therefore, graue Iudges, let me thus conclude :
Man tempts not weman, woman doth him delude.

A Plaudite by the Men with fhouts , crying,
Mifogynos, Mifogynos, Mi-
fogynos !

1. *Law.* Women, looke to't, the Fencer giues you a veney.
2. *Law.* Beleeue it, he hits home.

Mif. Nay, I wou'd fpeake.
What Tyrannies, Oppreffions, Maffacres,
Women ftand guiltie of : and which is more,
What Cities haue beene fackt and ruinate,
Kingdomes fubuerted, Lands depopulated,
Monarchies ended? and all thefe by women. (tongue,

Atlan. Bafe fnarling Dogge, bite out thy flandrous
And fpit it in the face of Innocence,
That at once all thy rancour may haue end:
And doe not ftill opprobrioufly condemne
Woman that bred thee, who in nothing more
Is guiltie of difhonour to her Sex :
But that fhe hath brought forth fo bafe a Viper,

To teare her reputation in his teeth,
As thou hast done.
    Mis. O doe not scold, good woman!
    1.*Iud.* Goe to the purpose.
    Atlan. I forgot my selfe:
Therefore, graue Iudges, let this base Impostor,
Tell me one man that euer gaue his life,
To keepe his vow safe and inuiolate,
Against the assaults of Lust: and for that one,
Ile find a thousand women, that to keepe
Their Chastities and Honours vndefil'd,
Haue laid their liues downe at base Tyrants feet.

    A Plaudit: by Women, crying, Atlanta, At-
    lanta, Atlanta!

    1.*Law.* This is but a flourish.
    2.*Law.* The Fencers Schoole-play beares it.
    Mis. What hath beene is not now: The Kalender
Of Women-Saints is fild vp long agoe:
For now a vniuersall leprosie,
Like to an Inundation, ouer-flowes,
And breakes vpon you all: scarce one is free
From wanton lightnesse and vaine leuitie.
    Atlan. None like to *Nero*, and *Heliogabulus*.
    Mis. Yes, wanton *Hellen* and *Cleopatra*.
    Atlan. I cou'd name more.
    Mis. I, ten for one, of Women.
    Atlan. Sense-pleasing *Sardanapalus* is beyond
All Women that can be nam'd.
    Mis. Ile name you one
Beyond all Men, th'insatiate *Messalina*:
Who when she had to satisfie her lust,
Imbrac'd the change of Louers, and was weakened
So farre, she cou'd no longer hold it out:
And being askt if then she were satisfied,
She answered, No: for though she then were tyr'd,

Arraigned by Women.

No change could satisfie her appetite.

A Plaudite by the Men, crying, Misogynos, Misogynos, Misogynos.

Atlan. O monstrous impietie!
Aur. Stop the Detractors mouth: Away with him.
Women. Teare him in pieces.
Not. Silence in the Court.
Attic. It is enough: my Lords, proceed to iudgement; And lead away *Misogynos* to his Chamber.

The two Lawyers lead Misogynos *away.*

1. *Iudge.* Read the decree.
Not. We the sworne Iudges of this present Court, In equall ballance hauing weigh'd the reasons, And allegations of both Aduocates, In their late Declamations, doe adiudge, And here conclude that----
Attic. Read out.
Not. That women are the first and worst temptations To loue and lustfull folly: and to this We are here present, ready to subscribe.
Atlan. You are impartiall, and we doe appeale From you to Iudges more indifferent: You are all men, and in this weightie businesse, Graue Women should haue sate as Iudges with you.
Aur. 'Tis true, 'tis true: Let vs haue iustice.
Attic. It is decreed already; atter'd the iudgement.
Aur. Yet at the last let your *Aurelia* kneele, And for the Offspring of your loynes and mine, Begge fauour.
Attic. Peace.
Aur. You alwayes haue bin iust In other causes; Will you in your owne Be so vniust, seuere, nay tyrannous? The very Beasts, by naturall instinct,

F 3 Pre-

Preserue their issue; and will you be then,
More cruell and vnnaturall then they?
  Attic. Arise; and know, A King is like a Starre,
By which each Subiect, as a Mariner,
Must steere his course. Iustice in Vs is ample,
From whom Inferiors will deriue example.
  Aur. Oh, be not so obdurate!
  Attic. I'le heare no more.
  Atlan. Yet, gracious Sir, for my indeuouring paines,
(Though fruitlesse now) let mee (a Stranger) beg
One boone----
  Attic. But not the the freedome of *Leonida.*
  Atlan. Since she must die; I beg she may not basely
Be hurried forth amongst vnciuill men;
But that your Queene, and I, and some few others,
With any one of your attendant Lords,
May see her execution.
  Attic. Take your desire.
  Leo. The blessed Heauens be thankfull to *Atlanta.*
  Lis. And crowne her with all blessings.   (ceed,
  Attic. Take my thanks too. And now, my Lords, pro-
And giue your finall censure.
                                              Exit Attic.
        Cornets, a flourish.
  Au. Come, *Atlanta,* come;
Teares fill mine eyes, and Griefe doth strike me dumbe.
              Exit Aur. Atlan. and all the Women.
  1. *Iudge. Leonida,* By the iudgement of this Court,
You are found guiltie as the Principall,
In the offence committed; for which, we doome you
(According to the Lawes of this our Iland)
To lose your Head.
  2. *Iudge.* And you withall, *Lisandro,*
By the like Law, must within fifteene daies,
Betake you to perpetuall banishment.
  Leo. Welcome, sweet death.

                                                   Lis.

Arraigned by Women.

Lis. Nothing can expiate
The Kings seuere Decree, and Her hard fate. *Exeunt.*

Act. IIII.

Enter Iago *and* Sforza, *seuerall.*

Sfor. Health to your Honour.
Iag. Noble *Sforza*, thankes.
Sfor. Haue you not heard the newes?
Iag. Of what, my Lord?
Sfor. Lisandro, and the Princesse.
Iag. Not as yet.
Sfor. Then I'le resolue you.
Iag. Pray you doe, my Lord.
Sfor. The Aduocates both vsed their vtmost skill,
To iustifie and quit the Sex they stood for,
With arguments, and reasons so profound
On eyther side, that it was hard to say,
Which way the scale of Iustice would incline.
   Iag. I ioy to heare it; And to say the truth,
Both Sexes equally should beare the blame;
For both offend alike. But pray' proceed.
   Sfor. At length, the Aduocate that stood for vs,
Preuail'd so farre, with his forc'd Oratorie,
The Lord *Nicanor* too, abetting him,
That maugre all the Amazonians wit,
Which was (indeed) beyond expression,
The sentence past against the female Sex;
And the poore Princesse is adiudg'd to death.
   Iag. The Heauens forbid! The Princesse doom'd to die?
Sfor. Too true, my Lord: I heard the words pronounc'd.
   Iag. A sentence most vniust, and tyrannous.
Where's the Detractor?
   Sfor. Crown'd with Victorie,
And intertain'd with Triumph.

Iag.

SWETNAM.

Iag. That iust Heauen
Should suffer such an impious wretch to liue!
I must goe looke the Princesse; when must she dye?
  Sfor. To morrow's Sun beholds a daughters fall.
  Iag. A Sunne must rise to night, to dimme that Sunne,
From the beholding such a horrid deed.
'Twas cruell in a King, for such a fact;
But in a Father, it is tyrannie.
Enter Misogynos.
  Sfor. Forbeare, my Lord, the times are dangerous.
See! here's the Champion.
  Iag. Looke how the Slaue glories in his conquest,
How insolent he stalkes!
Shall we indure such saucie impudence?
  Sfor. Put vp, put vp, my Lord,
He is not worth our indignation:
Let vs a-while obserue him for some sport.
Enter Scanfardoe.
  Scan. My noble Fencer, I congratulate
Your braue atchieuements in the last dayes triumph.
  Mis. I thanke you, Scholler. Was't not brauely done?
  Scanf. Done like thy selfe: the spirits of *Mantua*
And old *Diogenes* doubled in thee.
  Mis. I thinke, I haue giuen
The Female reputation such a wound,
Will not be cured in haste.
Enter two Gentlemen.
  Iag. Ha, ha, ha, ha; Pernicious slaue.
  1. *Gent.* Worthie *Misogynos.*
  2. *Gent.* Noble Champion,
We doe applaud
Your merit, in the report
Of your late conquest.
  Mis. Thanke you, Gentlemen;
Truth will preuaile, you see.
I speake not for my selfe, in my owne quarrell;
But the generall good of all men in the world.   1. *Gent.*

Arraigned by Women.

1. Gent. We know it, Sir.

Iag. Degenerate Monster, how he iustifies
His slandrous forgeries?

Mis. But, Gentlemen,
How goes the rumour?
What do's the Multitude report of mee?

1. Gent. Oh Sir, the Men applaud you infinitely;
But the Women----

Mis. I respect not them:
Their curses are my prayers.

Iag. Oh damn'd Rogue!

1. Gent. If you'le be rul'd by me, go shew your selfe
Amongst them all in publique: O 'twill fret
Their very galls in pieces.

Iag. That was well.
Some body second that, and we shall see
Excellent pastime; for they'le ne'r indure
His sight with any patience.

Scanf. Doe i'faith,
That they may see you haue conquer'd.

Mis. And I will.
But should they grow outragious--

2. Gent. Feare not that: we'le all along with ye.

Mis. Will you conduct me safe vnto my Schoole?

Scan. I, I, we'le be your Gard. *Exeunt.*

Sfor. Oh what a Coward 'tis?

Iag. You doe him wrong:
He fights not with his hands, but with his tongue.
Why doe I trifle time? I'le to the Court;
This crueltie afflicts my very soule.
Good my Lord, ioyne with me; we'le to the King,
And see if wee can alter this decree.
Oh 'tis a royall Princesse, faire, and chaste!

Sfor. But her disdaine, my Lord, hath bin the cause
Of many hopefull Youths vntimely end;
'Tis that has harden'd both the Commons hearts,

G   And

SWETNAM,
And many a noble Peeres.
  Iag. Why, what of that?
It is not fit affection should be forc'd:
Let's kneele vnto his Grace for her releafe.
Iustice (like Lightning) euer should appeare
To few mens ruine, but to all mens feare.

SCEN. II.
Enter NICANOR, *and a Gentleman.*

  Nic. The Princesse suffers then?
  Gent. This Morning, Sir,
Vnlesse the mercie of the King be found
More then is yet expected.
  Nic. Oh my heart,
Canst thou indure to heare that heauie sound,
And wilt not burst with griefe?
  Gent. Nay, good my Lord:
  Nic. Oh, worthie Sir, you did not know the ioyes
That we all lost in her. She was the hope,
And onely comfort of Sicilia;
And the last Branch was left of that faire stocke;
Which (if she dye) is wither'd, quite decay'd.
But I haue such a losse.
  Gent. You haue indeed:
Yours is the greatest of a particular:
For you haue lost a beautious Spouse, my Lord;
And yet the rich hopes of a royall Crowne
Might mitigate your sorrow. You are next.
  Nic. Doe not renew my griefe with naming that.
Oh that it were to morrow! happie day,
Bestow'd on some more meritorious,
That might continue long, for I am old.
I should be well content.
  Gent. Say not so:
There's no one merits that more then your selfe:
You are elected by the Kings owne house,   And

Arraigned by Women.

And generall consent of all the Realme,
For the Successour after his decease:
Whose life pray Heauen defend.

Nic. Amen, Amen,
And send him long to raigne; but not on earth.
Sir, you are neere the King; Pray, if you heare
His Highnesse aske for me, excuse me, Sir:
You see my sorrow's such, I am vnfit
To come into the presence of a King.

Gent. I see it, Sir, and will report as much.

Nic. You will report a lye then; ha, ha, ha.
My Lungs will not afford me wind enough
To laugh my passions out. To gaine a Crowne,
Who would not at a funerall laugh and sing?
All men of wisedome would, and so will I:
Yet to the worlds eye, I am drown'd in teares,
And held most carefull of the King and State,
When I meane nothing lesse. *Lorenzo's* dead:
The scornefull Princesse, that refus'd my loue,
Is going to her death. The King, I know,
Cannot continue long: Then may I say,
As our Italian heires at fathers deaths,
Quid Inde, Reine ta soll.
The King alone made mee the King:
Me thinkes I feele the royall Diadem
Vpon my head already; ha, ha, ha. *Exit.*

A dumbe shew.
Enter two Mourners, Atlanta *with the Axe,* Leonida
all in white, her haire loose, hung with ribans; supported on eyther side by two Ladies, Aurelia
*following as chiefe Mourner. Passe
softly ouer the stage.*

A Song in parts.
Whilst wee sing the dolefull knell
Of this Princesse passing-bell,

G 2   Lie.

SWETNAM,

Let the Woods and Valleys ring
Eechoes to our sorrowing;
And the Tenor of their Song,
Be ding dong, ding, dong, dong,
   ding, dong, dong,
    ding, dong.

Nature now shall boast no more,
Of the riches of her Store,
Since in this her chiefest prize,
All the Stocke of beautie dies;
Then, what cruell heart can long
Forbeare to sing this sad ding dong?
   This sad ding dong,
    ding dong.

Fawnes and Siluans of the Woods,
Nimphes that haunt the Cristall flouds,
Sauage Beasts more milder then
The vnrelenting hearts of men,
Be partakers of our mone,
And with vs sing ding dong, ding dong,
   ding dong, dong,
    ding dong.

Exeunt Omnes.

Enter Misogynos, *and* Swash.

Mis. Swash.
Swa. At your Buckler, Sir?
Mis. Perceiu'st thou nothing, *Swash*?
Swa. How meane you, Sir?
Mis. No strange signe of alteration; hum.
Swa. Beyond imagination.
Mis. How, good *Swash*?
Swa. Why, from a Fencer, you're turn'd Orator.
Mis. Oh! *Cedunt arma Togæ*; that's no wonder.
Perceiu'st thou nothing else? Looke I not pale?

Are

Arraigned by Women.

Are not my armes infolded? my eyes fixt,
My head deiected, my words paſſionate,
And yet perceiu'ſt thou nothing?

Swaſh. Let me ſee, me thinkes, you looke Sir, like ſome
Deſperate Gameſter, that had loſt all his eſtate
In a dicing Houſe: you met not
With thoſe Money-changers, did you?
Or haue you falne amongſt the female Sex,
And they haue paid you for your laſt dayes worke?

Miſ. No, no, thou art as wide, as ſhort in my diſeaſe:
Thou neuer canſt imagine what it is,
Vnleſſe, I tell thee. *Swaſh*, I am in loue.

Swaſh. Ha, ha, ha, in loue?

Miſ. Nay, 'tis ſuch a wonder, *Swaſh*, I ſcarce beleeue,
It can be ſo, my ſelfe, and yet it is.

Swaſh. The Deuill it is as ſoone, and ſooner too:
You loue the Deuill, better then a woman.

Miſ. Oh, doe not ſay ſo, *Swaſh*, I doe recant.

Swaſh. In loue? not poſſible:
This is ſome tempting Syren has bewitcht you.

Miſ. Oh! peace, good *Swaſh.*

Swaſh. Some Cockatrice, the very Curſe of man?

Miſ. No more, if thou doſt loue me.

Swaſh. Your owne words.
I know not how to pleaſe you better, Sir.
Will you from Oratour, turne Heretike,
And ſinne againſt your owne Conſcience?

Miſ. Oh, *Swaſh, Swaſh*!
Cupid, the little Fencer playd his Prize,
At ſeuerall weapons in *Atlanta's* eyes,
He challeng'd me, we met and both did try
His vtmoſt skill, to get the Victorie.
Lookes were oppos'd 'gainſt lookes, and ſtead of words,
Were banded frowne 'gainſt frowne, and words 'gainſt
But cunning *Cupid* forecaſt me to recoile: (words
For when he plaid at ſharpe, I had the foyle.

G 3 *Swaſh.*

SWETNAM,

Swash. Nay, now he is in loue, I see it plaine:
I was infpir'd with this Poeticall vaine,
When I fell firſt in loue; God bo'y yee, Sir:
I muſt goe looke another Maſter.
　Miſ. Swaſh.
　Swaſh. Y'are a dead man: beleeue it, Sir,
I would not giue two-pence for a Leaſe
Of a hundred pound a yeere made for your life.
Can you that haue bin at defiance with vm all,
Abuſed, arraigned vm, hang'd vm, if you could;
You hang'd vm more then halfe, you tooke away
All their good names, I'me ſure, can you then hope,
That any will loue you? A Ladie, Sir,
Will ſooner meet a Tinker in the ſtreet,
And try what Metall lyes within his Budget,
A Counteſſe lye with me, an Emperour
Take a poore Milke-maide, Sir, to be his Wife,
Before a Kitchen-Wench will fancie you.
　Miſ. Doe not torment me, misbeleeuing Dolt,
I tell thee, I doe loue, and muſt enioy.
　Swaſh. Who, in the name of women, ſhould this bee?
　Miſ. What an obtuſe Conception do'ſt thou beare?
Did not I tell thee, 'twas *Atlanta*, Swaſh?
　Swaſh. Who, ſhe the Amazonian Dame, your Aduocate,
A Maſculine Feminine?
　Miſ. I, Swaſh,
She muſt be more then Female, has the power
To mollifie the temper of my Loue.
　Swaſh. Why, ſhe's the greateſt enemie you haue.
　Miſ. The greater is my glorie, Swaſh, in that
That hauing vanquiſht all, I attaine her.
The Prize conſiſts alone
In my eternall credit and renowne.
Oh, what a Race of wittie Oratours
Shall we beget betwixt vs: Come, good Swaſh,
Ile write a Letter to her preſently.

Which

Arraigned by Women.

Which thou shalt carry: if thou speed'st, I sweare,
Thou shalt be *Swetnams* Heire.
  Swash. The Deuill I feare,
Will dispossesse me of that Heritage.

Enter two Gentlemen.

  1.*Gent.* But are you sure she is beheaded, Sir?
  2.*Gent.* Most certaine, Sir, both by the Kings Decree,
And generall voyce of all, for instance see.
  1. *Gent.* The wofull'st sight,
That ere mine eyes beheld.
  2. *Gent.* A sight of griefe and horrour.
  1.*Gent.* It is a piece of the extremest Iustice
That euer Memory can Register.
  2.*Gent.* I, in a Father.
  1.*Gent.* Oh, I pray forbeare,
The time is full of danger euery-where.   *Exeunt.*

Enter Lisander, *and the Guard.*

  Lis. Good gentle friends, before I leaue the Land,
Suffer me to take my last fare-well
Of my owne dearest deare *Leonida*.
Accept this poore reward: would time permit,
I would more largely recompence your loues. (briefe.
  1.*Gua.* You haue preuail'd, my Lord, but pray bee
We are inioyn'd by strict Commission,
To see you shipt away this present tyde.
  Lis. Indeed, I will.
  1.*Gua.* Then here you may behold,
All that is left of faire *Leonida*.
  Lis. Oh ———
  2. *Gua.* How fare you, Sir.
  Lis. Oh, Gentlemen,
Can you behold this sacred Cabinet,
Which Nature once had made her Treasurie?
But now broke ope by sacrilegious hands,
                                    And

And not let fall a teare : you are vnkind,
Not Marble but would wet at such a sight,
And cannot you, strange stupiditie !
Thou meere Relike of my dearest Saint.
Vpon this Altar I will sacrifice
This Offering to appeaze thy murd'red Ghost.
  1.*Gua.* Restraine, my Lord, this Passion, we lament
As much as you, and grieue vnfaynedly
For her vntimely losse.
  Lis. As much as I? Oh, 'tis not possible,
You temporize with sorrow: mine's sincere,
Which I will manifest to all the World.
See what a beauteous forme she yet retaynes,
In the despight of Fate, that men may see,
Death could not seize but on her mortall parts :
Her beautie was diuine and heauenly.   (short.
  1.*Gua.* Nay, good my Lord, dispatch, the time's but
  Lis. Indeed, I will, to make an end of time:
For I can liue no longer, since that she,
For whose sake onely, I held truce with time,
Hath left me desolate : no, diuinest loue,
What liuing was deny'd vs, weele enioy
In Immortalitie, where no Crueltie,
Vnder the forme of Iustice, dare appeare.
Sweet sacred Spirit, make not too much haste
To the Elizian Fields, stay but awhile,
And I will follow thee with swifter speed,
Then meditation : thus I seale my vow.   *Kisse.*
Me thinkes, I feele fresh heat, as if her soule
Had resum'd her former seate agen,
To solemnize this blessed Vnion,
In our last consummation, or else it stayes,
Awayting onely for my companie:
It does, indeed, and I haue done thee wrong,
To let thy heauenly eyes want me so long,
But now I come, deare Loue, Oh, oh!
               2.*Gua.*

Arraigned by Women.

1. *Gua.* What found was that?
2. *Gua.* Oh, we are all vndone,
The Prince has flaine himfelfe: what fhall we doe?
   1. *Gua.* There is no way but one, let's leaue the Land:
If we ftay heere, we fhall be fure to dye,
And fuffer for our too much lenitie,
Though we are innocent.
   2. *Gua.* Then hafte away:
The doome weele execute vpon our felues,
And fhip with fpeed for Holland, there, no doubt,
We fhall haue entertaynment,
There are warres threatned betwixt Spaine and them.
   1. *Gua.* Then let vs hoyfe vp fayle, mercy recciue
Thy foule to Heauen, Earth to Earth we leaue.   *Exeunt.*

Enter Atlanta.

Atlan. What fpectacle is this? A man new flaine,
Clofe by the Princes Herfe! Who is't? Oh, me,
The Noble Prince *Lifandro.* Cruell Fate,
Is there no hope of life? See, he looks vp,
Ile beare him out of the ayre, and ftop his wound:
f there be any hope, I haue a Balme
Of knowne experience, in effecting cures
Almoft impoffible, and if the wound
Be not too deadly, will recouer him.   *Exit Lorenzo.*

Enter Aurelia *and* Iago.

Iag. Deare Queene, haue patience.
Aur. How, *Iago,* patience?
Tis fuch a finne, that were I guiltie of,
I fhould defpayre of mercie. Can a Mother
Haue all the bleffings both of Heauen and Earth,
The hopefull iffue of a thoufand foules
Extinct in one, and yet haue patience?
I wonder patient Heauen beares fo long,
And not fend thunder to deftroy the Land.

H   The

SWETNAM,
The Earth, me thinkes, should vomit sulph'rous Damps,
To stifle and annoy both man and beast,
Seditious Hell should send blacke Furies forth,
To terrifie the hearts of tyrant Kings.
What say the people? doe they not exclaime,
And curse the seruile yoke, in which th'are bound
Vnder so mercilesse a Gouernour?
 Iag. Madame, in euery mouth is heard to sound,
Nothing but murmurings and priuate whispers,
Tending to seuerall ends: but all conclude,
The King was too seuere for such a Fact.

   Enter Atlanta.

 Aur. *Atlanta*, welcome, Oh my child, my child,
There lies the summe of all my miserie!
 Atl. Gracious Madame, doe but heare me speake.
 Aur. *Atlanta*, I should wrong thy merit else,
What wouldst thou say?
Something I know, to mitigate my griefe.
 Atl. Rather to adde to your afflictions.
I am the Messenger of heauie Newes.
Leander, Prince of Naples,
 Aur. What of him?
 Atl. Beholding the sad object of his loue,
His violent passion draue him to despayre,
And he hath slaine himselfe.
 Iag. Disastrous chance!
 Atl. I found him gasping for his latest breath,
And bore him to my Lord *Iago's* house,
I vs'd my best of skill to saue his life:
But all, I feare, in vaine: the mortall wound
I find incurable: yet I prolong'd
His life a little, that he yet drawes breath:
Goe you and visit him with vtmost speed:
The Queene and I will follow.
 Iag. Goe? Ile runne.   *Exit Iago.*
             Aur.

Arraigned by Women.

Aur. Was euer Father so vnmercifull,
But for that Monster that was cause of this,
That bloudie, cruell, and inhumane wretch,
That slanderous Detractor of our Sex:
That *Misogynos*, that blasphemous Slaue?
I will be so reueng'd.

Enter Clowne.

Atlan. Madame, no more,
He is not worth your wrath:
Let me alone with him.
 Clow. Whist, doe you heare?
 Atlan. How now, what art thou?
 Clow. Not your Seruant, and yet a Messenger,
No Seruingman, and yet an Vsher too.
 Atlan. What are you then, Sir? speake.
 Clow. That can resolue you, and yet cannot speake,
I am no Foole, I am a Fencer, Sir.
 Aur. A Fencer, sirrah? ha, what Countrey-man?
 Clow. This Countrey-man, forsooth, but yet borne in England.
 Aur. How? borne in England, & this Countrey-man?
 Clow. I haue bin borne in many Countreyes, Madame,
But I thinke I am best be this Countrey-man,
For many take me for a silly one.
 Aur. For a silly one?
 Clow. I, a silly one.
 Atlan. Oh, Madame, I haue such welcomenesse!
 Aur. For me, what is't?
 Atlan. The baytes of women haue preuented vs,
And hee has intrapt himselfe.
 Aur. How, by what accident?
 Atlan. Loue, Madame, loue, read that.
 Aur. How's this?
To the most wise and vertuous Amazon,
Chiefe pride and glorie of the Female Sex.

H 2

A promising induction : what's within?
Magnanimous Ladie, maruell not,
That your once Aduersary do's submit himselfe
To your vnconquer'd beautie.
  Atlan. Cunning Slaue.
  Aur. Rather impute it to the power of loue,
Whose heauenly influence hath wrought in me,
So strange a Metamorphosis.
  Atlan. The very quinteßence of flatterie. (*aßdes.*)
  Aur. In so much, I vow hereafter, to spend all my
Deuoted to your seruice, it shall be
To expiate my former blasphemies:
My desire is shortly to visit you.
  Atlan. It shall be to your cost then.
  Aur. To make testimony of my hearty contrition,
Till when and euer I will protest my selfe,
To be the conuerted *Misogynist.*
  Atlan. Ha, ha, ha, why, this is excellent !
Beyond imagination.
  Aur. You must not slip this oportunitie.
  Atlan. Ile not let passe a minute : his owne man
Ile make an instrument to feed his
Follies with a kind acceptance, and when he comes,
Let me alone to plot his punishment.
  Aur. Excellent *Atlanta*, I applaud thy wit.
  Atlan. Ile make him an example to all men,
That dares calumniate a womans fame.
Attend an answere, Ile reward thee well.
  Clow. I thanke your Madame-ship, Ime glad o' this.
Tis the best hit that euer Fencer gaue. *Exeunt.*

  Enter Atticus, Iago, Sforza, *and* Nicanor.
  Att. How tooke the Girle her death? did she not raue?
Exclaime vpon me for the Iustice done
By a iust Father? how tooke Naples sonne
His Exile from our Land? What, no man speake?

             My

Arraigned by Women.

My Lords, whence springs this alteration?
Why stand you thus amaz'd? Methinks your eyes
Are fixt in Meditation; and all here
Seeme like so many senceleffe Statues,
As if your soules had suffer'd an eclipse,
Betwixt your iudgements and affections:
Is it not so? 'Sdeath, no man answers?
Iago, you can tell: I'me sure you saw
The execution of *Leonida*.
Not yet a sillable? If once agen
We doe but aske the question, Death ty'es vp
Your soules for euer. Call a Headf-man there.
If for our daughter this dumbe griefe proceed,
Why should not We lament as well as you?
I was her father; whose deare life I priz'd
Aboue mine owne, before she did transgresse:
And, could the Law haue so bin satisfi'd,
Mine should ha' paid the ransome of her cryme.
But, that the World should know our equitie,
Were she a thousand daughters she should die.

Iag. I can forbeare no longer. Then (Sir) know,
It was about that time, when as the Sunne
Had newly climb'd ouer the Easterne hils,
To glad the world with his diurnall heat,
When the sad ministers of Iustice tooke
Your daughter from the bosome of the Queene.
Whom now she had instructed to receiue
Deaths cold imbraces with alacritie:
Which she so well had learn'd, that shee did striue,
Like a too forward Scholler, to exceed
Her Teachers doctrine;
So cheerefully she went vnto the Block,
As if shee'd past vnto her nuptiall bed:
And as the trembling Bride when she espies
The Bridegroome hastily vncloathe himselfe,
And now beginning to approch the bed,

Then

Then she began to quake and shrinke away,
To shun the separation of that head,
Which is imaginary onely, and not reall.
So, when she saw her Executioner
Stand readie to strike out that fatall blow,
Nature, her frailtie, and the alluring world,
Did then begin to oppose her constancie:
But she, whose mind was of a nobler frame,
Vanquish'd all oppositions, and imbrac'd
The stroke with courage beyond Womans strength;
And the last words she spoke, said, I reioyce
That I am free'd of Fathers tyrannie.
   Attic. Forbeare to vtter more. We are not pleas'd
With these vnpleasing accents: Leaue the world
So cheerefully, and speake of tyrannie:
She was not guiltie sure. We'le heare no more.
   Iag. Sir, but you shall: since you inforc'd me speake,
I will not leaue a sillable vntold.
You ask'd if Naples sonne were banish'd too?
Yes, he is banish'd euer from the sight
Of mortall eyes againe: for he is dead.
   Nic. Lisandro dead! By what occasion?
   Iag. I scorne to answer thee. The King shall know,
It was his chance vpon that haplesse houre,
To passe that way, conducted by his gard,
Towards his banishment; where he beheld
The wofull obiect of the Princesse head:
There might you see loue, pittie, rage, despaire,
Acting together in their seuerall shapes;
That it was hard to iudge, which of all those
Were most predominant. At last, despaire
Became sole Monarke of his passions,
Which drew him to this error: Hauing got
Leaue of his gard to celebrate his vowes,
Vnto that precious relique of his Saint,
Where hauing breath'd a mournfull Elegie,
After a thousand sighs, ten thousand grones,

Arraigned by Women.

Still crying out, *Leonida*, my loue!
Then, as his death were limited by hers,
He facrifiz'd his life vnto her loue:
For there (vnluckily) he flew himfelfe.
  Sfor. The King's difpleas'd, my Lord.
  Iag. No matter: I'me glad I touch'd his confcience
To the quicke. Did you not fee
How my relation chang'd his countenance,
As if my words ingendred in his breft
Some new-bred paffions?
  Sfor. Yes, and did obferue
How fearefully he gaz'd vpon vs all: *Enter Queene.*
Pray heauen it proue not ominous. *Iag.* The Queene!
  Quee. Where is this King? this King? this tyrant? He
That would be cald The iuft and righteous King,
When in his actions he is moft vniuft;
Beyond example, cruell, tyrannous?
Where is my daughter? Where's *Leonida?*
Where is *Lufippus* too, my firft borne hope?
And where is deare *Lorenzo?* dead? all dead?
And would to God I were intomb'd with them,
Emptie of fubftance. Curfe of Soueraigntie,
That feed'ft thy fancie with deluding hopes
Of fickle fhadowes; promifing to one,
Eternitie of fame; and vnto all,
To be accounted wife and vertuous,
Obferuing but your Lawes and iuft decrees;
That vnder fhew of being mercifull,
Art moft vnkind, and cruell: nay, 'tis true.
Goe, where thou wilt, ftill will I follow thee,
And with my fad laments ftill beat thy eares, *Ex. King,*
Till all the world of thy iuftice heares. *and Qu.*
  Nic. This Phyfick works too ftrongly, and may proue a
deadly potion. *Sforza*, good my Lord, if any anger be
'twixt you and I, let it lye buried now; and let's deuife
fome paftime to fuppreffe this heauineffe. A melancholy
King makes a fad Court. *Iag.*

SWETNAM,

I neuer heard him speake so carefully
Of the Kings welfare. I, with all my heart.
 Sfor. Who'le vndertake this charge?
 Nic. I will, my Lord : Let the deuice be mine.
 Iag. I'le get the Amazon to ioyne with you:
Her rare inuention, and experience too,
In forraine Countries may auaile you much,
In some new quaint conceit.
 Nic. Doe, good my Lord :
I'de ha't assoone presented as I could.
 Iag. To night, if it be possible : farewell.
I must goe looke her out.
 Nic. Ha, ha, ha, ha.
So by this meanes, I shall expresse my selfe
Studious and carefull.

Scen. II.

Enter ATLANTA *and* AVRELIA.

 Aur. But dost thou thinke hee'le come?
 Att. He cannot chuse.
I sent him such a louing answer backe
By his Solliciter, able to make
An Eunuch to come with the conceit.
The houre's almost at hand. Madam, command
A banquet be set forth : My charge shall be
 Enter with a Banquet, Women.
To giue him intertainement : whilst your Grace,
Loretta, and the Ladies of your traine,
Or any others you shall please to appoint,
Be ready to surprise him. So 'tis well.
Now leaue the rest to mee.
 Aur. My deare *Atlanta*, I commend thy care.
 Att. Call it my dutie, Madam, and the loue
I owe to sacred vertue, to defend

The

Arraigned by Women.

The fame of women. All withdraw awhile, *Ex. Women*
I thinke I heare him comming. I, 'tis he.
     Enter Misogynos *and* Swash.
 Swash. This is the place, Sir, she appoynted you.
 Mis. Is this the Orchard then,
Where I must pluck the fruit from that faire tree?
 Swash. I would it might proue Stone-fruit,
And so choke him.
 Mis. Ha! what's here? a banquet?
 Swa. Banquet? Where?
 Mis. Readie prepar'd? why, this is excellent!
What a kind creature 'tis?
 Swa. Did not I say
How monstrously she lou'd you? Come, fall to.
 Mis. Before my Mistresse come?
 Swa. I'faith Sir, I;
This is but onely a prouocatiue,
To make you strong and lustie for the incounter.
 Mis. And here's Wine too;
Nothing but Bloud and Spirit.
Fall to, *Swash.*
 Swa. A sweet thing is loue,
That fills both heart and mind:
There is no comfort in the world,
To women that are kind. Here, Sir, I'le drinke to you.
 Mis. I would she would come away once: Now, me-
I could performe. And see! but wish and haue. (thinks,
     Enter Atlanta.
 Atlan. Oh, are you come? I see you keep your houre.
 Mis. I should be sorry else.
 Atl. Nay, keepe your place.
 Mis. Will you sit downe then? Sirrah? Walke aloofe.
 Atl. Let him be doing something. Here, take this.
 Mis. I haue made bold to taste your Wine and Cates.
And when you please, we'le try the operation.
 Atl. How?

     I   *Mi*

Mif. You know my mind.
Atlan. You men are all so fickle, that poore we
Doe not know whom to trust.
But doe you loue me truely?
Mif. By this kisse.
Atl. No, saue that labour, Sir: I'le take your word.
Yet, how should I beleeue you, when so late
You rail'd against our Sex, and slander'd vs?
Mif. Oh doe not thinke of that, that's done and gone.
Doe not recall what's past. I now recant:
And (by this hand) I loue thee truly, Loue.
Atl. May I beleeue all this?
Mif. Come hither, *Swash*.
How often haue I sworne to thee alone,
I lou'd this Lady; neuer none but shee?
Swa. Yes truely, that he has.
Mif. You may be proud, I tell you, of my loue,
There is a thousand Women in this Towne,
To imbrace me, would clap their hands for ioy,
And run like so many wild Cats.
Swa. That they would,
I dare be sworne for vm,
And hang about him like so many Catch-poles,
He would ne'r get from vm,
And yet this happinesse is profer'd you.
Atl. Which I cannot refuse,
You haue, you know, such a preuayling tongue,
No woman can deny you any thing. (meet?
Mif. Why, that was kindly spoke. Where shall wee
Atl. Hearke in your eare, I'le tell you.
Mif. Best of all.
Atl. But—
Mif. Doe you thinke me such a foole?
Atl. Till then farewell: I'le speedily returne. *Ex. Atl.*
Mif. Why law now, *Swash*, I told thee she would yeeld,
No woman in the world can hold out long.

Oh

Arraigned by Women.

Oh beware when a man of Art courts a woman.

Swa. I, or a Fencer, Sir: We lay vm flat before vs.
But, pray you tell me, Master, Doe you loue
This Lasse sincerely?

Mif. Ha, ha, ha. Loue? that were a iest indeed,
To passe away the time for sport, or so;
Th'are made for nothing else:
And he that loues vm longer, is a foole.

Swa. Me thinkes 'tis pittie to delude her, Sir:
I'faith she's a handsome wench.

Mif. Away, you Asse.
Delude? what are they good for else?

Enter Atlanta.

She comes againe. Out of the Orchard, *Swash*.
Welcome, Sweet heart.

Atl. Are you in priuate, Sir?

Mif. There's not an eye vnder the Horizon
That can behold vs; If Suspicion tell,
I'le beat her blind as euer Fencer was.

Atl. Sir, now you talke of Fencing, I heare you
Professe that noble Science.

Mif. 'Tis most true.

Atl. I loue you, Sir, the better; 'tis a thing
I honour with my heart. If any one
Should scandalize or twit me with your loue,
You can defend my fame, and make such men—

Mif. Creepe on their knees, aske thee forgiuenesse,
Or any other base submission.

Atl. Oh, what a happinesse shall I inioy?
But can can you doe this if occasion serue?

Mif. Would some were here to make experience,
That thou mightst see my skill.

Atl. Sir, that will I.   *Strike him.*

Mif. How's this?

Atl. Impudent slaue,
How dar'st thou looke a woman in the face,

I 2   Or

SWETNAM,

Or commence loue to any: Specially to'mee?
Thou know'st I'me vow'd thy publique enemie,
Which this, and this, and this shall testifie.

Mis. Oh that I had a weapon, thou shouldst know,
A thousand women could not stand one blow,
From my vnconquerd arme.

Atl. That shall be tride.
I'le fit you, Sir, in your owne element.
I thinke thou darest not looke vpon a sword.
See, there's a foyle: I will but thumpe you, Sir.
Thy life's reseru'd vnto a worse reuenge. *Play.*

Mis. Oh. Some Deuil's enterd in this Idol sure,
To make mee misbelieue. Oh.

Atl. Cowardly slaue. A Fencer? you a Fidler.
He cannot hold his weapon,
Gard his brest; no, nor defend a thrust. Art not asham'd
Thus to disgrace that noble exercise?

Mis. Oh: Hold, hold; I yeeld, I yeeld.

Atl. Has our Countrie meats fed you so high,
You needs must haue a stale for your base lust?
I'le satiate your fences ere I haue done:
And so much for your feeling: For your taste,
You haue had sufficient in your sweet-meats, Sir:
Your drinke too was perfum'd to please your smell.

Mis. I, but I haue had but sowre sauce to vm. *(fight.*

Atl. Why then the Prouerbe holds. Now for your.
Madam, Come forth, and bring your followers.

Enter all the Women.

Mis. I'de rather see so many Cockatrices.
Oh that my eyes might be for euer shut,
So that I might ne'r behold these Crocadils.

Aur. Where's this bawling Bandog.

Omnes. Here, here, here, here.

Mis. Murder, murder, murder. I'me betraid.
I shall be torne in pieces. Murder, ho.

Aur.

Arraigned by Women.

Aur. Is this the dogged Humorist that cals
Himfelfe the woman-hater?
 Mif. On my knees.
Aur. Doft thou reply, vile Monfter? Binde him, come.
Old W. Let me come to him, Ile fo mumble him.
 Aur. Remember faire *Leonida* my child,
Whofe innocence was made a Sacrifice
To thy bafe Forgeries and Sophiftrie.
 Omnes. Out, you abominable Rafcall.
 Aur. This for your hearing, Sir: now all is full.
 Mif. Ladies, Gentlewomen, fweet *Atlanta*, all,
Heare me but fpeake.
 Lor. No, not a fyllable.
You haue fpoke to match alreadie, you damn'd Rogue.
But weele reward you for't. Skrew his iawes.
 Mif. Oh, oh, oh.
 Aur. Now, thou inhumane wretch, what punifhment
Shall we inuent fufficient to inflict,
According to the height of our reuenge?
 Omnes. Let's teare his limmes in pieces, ioynt from
 Mif. Oh, oh. (ioynt.
 Scold. Three or foure paire of Pincers, now red hot,
Were excellent.
 Lor. Will not our Bodkings ferue?
 Aur. Hang him, Slaue, fhall he dye as noble a death
As *Cæfar* did? No, no: pinch him, pricke him.
 A Boy. I haue fmall Pins enow to ferue vs all.
 Scold. We cannot wifh for better: take him vp,
And bind him to this Poft.
 Lor. Faith, Poft and Paire,
As good a Game as can be.
 Aur. Come, let's to't,
Shuffle the Cards, and leaue out all the Knaues.
 Atl. No, the Knaues in at Poft, and out at Paire.
 Aur. Shall it be fo? Agreed?
Deale round.

I 3 *Scold.*

SWETNAM,

Scold. First, stake.
Mis. Oh, oh, oh, oh.
Atl. Passe.
Aur. Passe.
Lor. Nay, Ile not passe it so. *Mis.* Oh, oh.
A Boy. Faith, Ile be in too.
Mis. Oh!

Enter two Old Women and Swash.

Aur. Againe, for me too, I will vye it. *Mis.* Oh.
Atl. And for me, Ile not deny it. *Mis.* Oh.
Lor. Ile see you, and revy't agen. *Mis.* Oh, oh.
Scold. For your two, Ile put in ten. *Mis.* Oh, oh, oh,
Aur. How now? stay, who's this? (oh, oh.
Swash. I could not find the way out of the Orchard,
If I should ha' beene hang'd, but fell into these
Old Womens mouthes: but the best is,
They had no teeth to bite me; but my Grandame heere
Scratches most deuillishly.
Atl. Here's a Whelpe of the same Litter too.
Come hither Sirrah, doe you know this man?
Swash. Yes, forsooth, I know him,
He was my Master once, want of a better.
Lor. Then you were one of his Confederates, Sir.
Swash. I his Confederate? I defye him,
He knowes I alwayes gaue him good counsell,
If he had had the grace to follow it:
Here he is himselfe, let him deny't if he can.
Mis. Oh, oh, oh,
Swash. Did not I euer say, Master, take heed,
Wrong not kind Gentlewomen,
Honest louing women? Many a time
Haue I beene beaten by him blacke and blue,
For looking on a woman, is't not true?
Mis. Oh, oh.
Swash. You see his bringing vp,

To

Arraigned by Women.

To make a mouth at all this companie.
  Aur. This is an honest fellow; he shall escape.
Sirrah, thou lou'st a woman?
  Swash. I, with all my heart.
  Scold, He lookes as if he did.
  Atl. Well, stand aside, weele imploy you anon:
Forbeare your tortors yet, something is hid,
That we must haue reueal'd, and he himselfe
Shall be his owne accuser: you all know,
He hath arraign'd vs for inconstancie:
But now weele arraigne him, and iudge him too,
This is womans counsell: Madame, we make you
Ladie Chiefe Iustice of this Female Court,
Mistris Recorder, I. *Loretta*, you,
Sit for the Notarie: *Crier*, she:
The rest shall beare inferior Offices,
As Keepers, Seriants, Executioners.
  Swash. Ide rather be a Hangman then a Seriant:
Yet there's no great difference, if one will not,
T'other must.
  Atl. Mother, goe you and call a Iurie full,
Of which y'are the fore-woman.
  1. *Old W.* Thanke you forsooth, Ile fetch one presently:
'Tis fit he should be scratcht, and please your Grace:
Sure, he is no man.
  Atl. We want a Barre. O, these two foyles shall serue:
One stucke i'the Earth, and crosse it from this Tree.
Now take your places, bring him to the Barre,
Sirrah, vngag him.
  Swash. Let him be gag'd still:
Then you are sure what e'r you say to him,
He cannot contradict you.
  Atl. Pull it out.
  Swash. Doe not bite y'are best.
  M.J. Oh that I were a Serpent for your sakes,
Bearing a thousand stings.
                                Aur.

Aur. Worse then thou art,
Thou canst not wish to be, abortiue wretch,
Bring him to the Barre.
  Swash. You'ld not be rul'd by me: I told you o'this,
And now you see what followes,
Hanging's the least, what-eu'r followes that.
  Aur. Clarke of the Peace,
Reade the Indictment.
  Scold. Silence in the Court.
  Swash. Silence? & none but women? That were strange!
  Lor. *Misogynos*, hold vp thy hand.
  Swash. His name is *Swetnam*, not *Misogynos*.
That's but a borrowed name.
  Mis. Peace, you Rogue,
Will you discouer me?
  Aur. Swetnam is his name.
  Swash. I, *Ioseph Swetnam*, that's his name, forsooth,
Ioseph the Iew was a better Gentile farre.
  Lor. Then *Ioseph Swetnam, alias Misogynos,
Alias Molustonus, alias* the *Woman-hater*.
  Swash. How came he by all these names?
I haue heard many say, he was neu'r christen'd.
  Lor. Thou art here indicted by these names, that thou,
Contrary to nature, and the peace of this Land,
Hast wickedly and maliciously slandred,
Maligned, and opprobriously defamed the ciuill societie
Of the whole Sex of women: therefore speake,
Guiltie, or not guiltie?
  Mis. Not guiltie.
  Swash. Hum.
  Omnes. Not guiltie.
  Mis. No, not guiltie.
  Aur. Darest thou denie a truth so manifest?
Didst thou not lately both by word, and deed,
Publish a Pamphlet in disgrace of vs,
And of all women-kind?

Mis.

Arraigned by Women.

Mis. No, no, no, not I.
Swash. Hum.
Atl. Calling vs tyrannous, ambitious, cruell?
Aur. Comparing vs to Serpents, Crocodiles
For Diſſimulation, *Hiena's* for Subtilties,
Such like?
Lor. And farre worſe:
That we are all the Deuils agents,
To ſeduce Man agen?
Scold. That all our ſtudies are but to delude
Our credulous Husbands?
Mis. I denie all this.
Swash. Hum.
Lor. Nay more,
Thou doſt affirme, without diſtinction,
All married Wiues are the Deuils Hackneyes,
To carrie their Husbands to Hell.
Aur. Inhumane Monſter, haſt thou neu r a Mother?
Swash. No, forſooth, he is a *Succubus*, begot
Betwixt a Deuill and a Witch.
Mis. If I did any ſuch, let it be produc'd.
Atl. Bring in the Books for a firme Euidence,
And bid the Iurie giue the Verdict vp.

Enter two Old Women.

Old W. Guiltie, guiltie, guiltie.
Guiltie of Woman-ſlander, and defamation.
Atl. Produce the Bookes, and reade the Title of vm.
Lor. The Arraignment of idle, froward,
And vnconſtant women.
Aur. What ſay you, Sir, to this?
Mis. Shew me my name, and then Ile yeeld vnto't.
Aur. No, that's your policie and cowardiſe,
You durſt not publiſh, what you dar'd to write,
Thy man is witneſſe to't: ſirrah, confeſſe,
Or you ſhall eu'n be ſeru'd of the ſame ſawce.

K   *Swash.*

SWETNAM,

Swash. No, no, no, no, Ile tell you all,
He is no Fencer, that's but for a shew,
For feare of being beaten: the best Clarke,
For cowardise that can be in the World,
To terrifie the Female Champions,
He was in England, a poore Scholer first,
And came to Medley, to eate Cakes and Creame,
At my old Mothers house, she trusted him:
At least some sixteene shillings o'the score,
And he perswaded her, he would make me (leeu'd:
A Scholer of the Niniuersitie, which she, kind Foole, be-
He neu'r taught me any Lesson, but to raile against wo-
That was my morning and my euening Lecture. (men,
And in one yeere he runne away from thence,
And then he tooke the habit of a Fencer:
And set vp Schoole at Bristow: there he liu'd
A yeere or two, till he had writ this Booke:
And then the women beat him out the Towne,
And then we came to London: there forsooth,
He put his Booke i'the Presse, and publisht it,
And made a thousand men and wiues fall out.
Till two or three good wenches, in meere spight,
Laid their heads together, and rail'd him out of th' Land,
Then we came hither: this is all forsooth.
  Aur. 'Tis eu'n enough.
  Mis. 'Tis all as false as women.
  Omnes. Stop his mouth.
  Atlan. Either be quiet, or y'are gag'd agen.
  Aur. Proceed in Iudgement.
  Atlan. Madame, thus it is.
First, he shall weare this Mouzell, to expresse
His barking humour against women-kind.
And he shall be led, and publike showne,
In euery Street i'the Citie, and be bound
In certaine places to a Post or Stake,
And bayted by all the honest women

Mis.

Arraigned by Women.

Mis. Is that the worst? there will not one be found
In all the Citie.
　Omnes. Out, you lying Rascall.
Forbeare a little.
　Atlan. Then he shal be whipt quite thorow the Land,
Till he come to the Sea-Coast, and then be shipt,
And sent to liue amongst the Infidels.
　Omnes. Oh, the Lord preserue your Grace.
　Lor. Oh, oh, oh.
　Aur. Call in his Bookes,
And let vm all be burn'd and cast away,
And his Arraignment now put i'the Presse,
That he may liue a shame vnto his Sex.
　Atlan. Sirrah, the charge be yours: which if you faile,
You shall be vs'd so too: it well perform'd,
You shall be well rewarded. Breake vp Court.
　Omnes. Away, you bawling Mastiffe.
　Clow. Pish, pish.　　　　　　　　　　*Exeunt.*

Enter Atticus, Sforza, Nicanor, *and one or
two Lords more.*

　King. Why doe you thus pursue me? Can no place
Shelter a King from being bayted thus
With Acclamations beyond sufferance
Of Maiestie, or mortall strength to beare?
We will indure't no longer. Where's our Guard?
Where is *Aurelia*? where's *Iago* gone?
To studie new Inuectiues? If agen
They dare but vtter the least syllable,
Or smallest title of inueteracie,
They shall not breathe a minute. Must a Prince
Be checkt, and schooled, pursued and scolded at,
For executing Iustice?
　Nic. Royall, Sir.
Be pleased, to cast away these Discontents.
Iago's sorrie for his bold offence.

K 2　　　　　　The

SWETNAM,

The Queene repents her too, and all the Court
Is clowded o'r with griefe: your sadnesse, Sir,
Fils euery Subiects heart with heauinesse.
Will't please your Highnesse to behold some pastime,
There is a Maske and other sports prepar'd:
Prepared to solace you,
To steale away your sorrowes.
   King. Who's that spoke?
Nicanor, is't hee? I thought as much:
I knew no other would be halfe so kind,
Nor carefull of our health: doe what thou wilt,
We will deny nothing that thou demandest,
My dearest Comforter, stay to my age,
The hope of Sicilie lyes now in thee.
Come sit by vs, weele see what new deuice
Thy diligence---- *Nic.* My dutie.
   King No, thy loue
Hath studied to delight thy Soueraigne.
Come sit, *Nicanor.*
   Nic. Pardon, Sir, awhile,
Ile giue command to see it straight perform'd,
And instantly returne.
   King. Make no delay:
We haue no ioy but in thy companie.
   Nic. Nor I no Hell, but thy continuance.
Ile present that will shorten it, I hope.
   King. Sforza, thou louest me too: come neerer vs:
But old *Iago* is a froward Lord,
Honest, but lenatiue, ore-swaid too much.
With pitt'e against Iustice, that's not good:
Indeed it is not in a Counseller.
And he has too much of woman, otherwise
He might be Ruler of a Monarchie,
For policie and wisdome. *Sforza* sit,
Take you your places to behold this Maske.

Arraigned by Women.

Enter Nicanor.

Nic. Now they are readie.
King. Let vm enter then.
Come sit by vs, *Nicanor*, and describe
The meaning, as they enter.

Enter Iago, *and the Queene.*

Iag. Heere your Grace
May vndiscouered sit, and view the Maske,
And see how 'tis affected by the King:
I know, 'twill nip him to the verie soule.
The Maskers.　　　　　*Enter Musike, dance.*
Nic. He that leads the Dance,
Is called wilfull Ignorance.
King. The next that pryes on euery side,
As if feare his feet did guide,
Is held a wretch of base condition,
He is titled false Suspition.
Nic. The third is of a bolder Faction,
But more deadly, 'tis Detraction.
The last is Crueltie, a King that long,
In seeming good, did sacred Iustice wrong.
King. This Moral's meant by me: by heauen it is,
By Heauen, indeed: for nothing else had power
To make me see my Follies. I confesse,
'Twas wilfull Ignorance, and Selfe-conceit,
Sooth'd with Hypocrisie, that drew me first
Into suspition of my Daughters loue,
And call'd it Disobedience: false Suspect,
'Twas thou possest me, that *Leonida*
Was spotted and vnchaste.
Nic. So, now it workes.
King. And then Detraction prou'd a deadly Foe.
Iag. I knew 'twould take effect.
Aur. Most happily.

SWETNAM,

King. I am that King did sacred Iustice wrong,
Vnder a shew of Iustice, now 'tis plaine,
It was my crueltie, not her desert,
That sacrific'd my Child to pallid Death.
Lisandro slew himselfe, but I, not he
Must answere for that guiltlesse bloud was spilt.
For I was Authour on't, my Crueltie,
Diuorcing two such Louers, was the cause
That drew him to despayre. How they all gaze,
Whisper together, and then point at me,
As if they here had being! yes they haue;
But it shall proue a restlesse bed for them.
Why doe they not begin?

Enter Repentance.

Nic. Belike they want some of their companie.
King. But stay, who's that descends so prosperously,
With such sweet sounding Musike? All obserue.

Musike, dance.

Nic. See how the splendor of that Maiestie,
That came from Heauen, hath disperst away
Suspition, Ignorance, and Crueltie,
And instantly o'rcome Detraction too,
Those enemies to vertue, foes to man,
Are vanisht from my sight, and from my heart.
But let Repentance stay. Ha, shallow Foole,
Doe I so slightly bid her? On my knees,
She must be followed, call'd and su'd vnto,
And by continuall Prayers, woo'd, and wonne,
Which I will neuer cease, if not too late.
I doe repent me, let this Sacrifice
Make satisfaction for those fore-past Crimes
My ignorant soule committed.

Repen. 'Tis accepted.
Imbrace me freely, rise: neuer too late
To call vpon Repentance.

Nic.

Nic. I am trapt.
Oh, the great Deuill! whose deuice was this?
Now all will be reueal'd, I neuer dream't
Vpon Repentance, I : but now I see,
Truth will discouer all mens Trecherie.
  King. Liue euer in my bosome. What meanes this?

Enter Lorenzo, Lisandro, Leonida, *a Siluan Nymph.*

  Lor. If a Siluan's rude behauiour
May not heere despaire of fauour :
Then to thee this newes I bring,
Thou art call'd the righteous King,
And as Fame do's make report,
Heere liues Iustice in thy Court:
Know, that all the Happinesse
I did in this World possesse,
Was my onely Daughter, who
Pan did on my age bestow,
She was named *Claribell,*
Whom *Palemon* loued well:
And she lou'd him as well againe;
So that nothing did remaine,
But the tying *Hymens* Knot.
But it chanced so, God wot,
That an old decrepit man
Most prepostroufly began,
With flatt'ring words to woo my Daughter,
But being still deny'd, he after
Turn'd his loue to mortall hate
Claribell to ruinate,
Striuing to o'rpresse her fame,
With Lust, Contempt, Reproch, and Shame.
  Kin. What wouldst thou haue Vs doe?
Good Father, speake.
  Lor. This fellow hath subborn'd a rout

SWETNAM,

Of some base Villaines here-about,
To take away my daughters life,
Or else to rauish her. To end this strife
Be pleas'd to ioyne these Louers hands
Into sacred nuptiall bands.
  Sfor. Nothing but put vm both together, Sir.
The good old Shepheard would faine ha't a match.
  Kin. We are content. Come giue Vs both your hands.
  Lor. You are a King; yet they are loth
To take your word without an othe.
  Kin. As We are King of Sicil, 'tis confirm'd
Firme, to be reuoked neuer,
Vntill death their liues disseuer.
  Lor. Princes, discouer: Here are witnesses
Inow to testifie this royall match.
  Kin. My daughter, and *Lisandro*, liuing?
  Lor. Nay, wonder not, my Liege, your oath is past.
  Kin. Which thus, and thus, and thus I ratifie:
There is but one step more, and farewell all.
  Aur. Oh, I am made immortall with this sight:
My daughter, and *Lisandro*, both aliue?
  Iag. This is no newes to mee: yet teares of ioy
Ore-flowes mine eyes to see this vnitie.
  Kin. Oh daughter, I haue done thee too much wrong:
And, noble Prince, We now confesse Our errour:
But heauen be prais'd that you haue both escap'd
The tyrannie of Our vniust decree.
  Aur. What happie accident preseru'd your liues?
Whose was the proiect? Was it thine, old man?
  Lor. Madam, 'twas mine: Those that I could not saue't
By eloquence, by policie I haue.
  Kin. Worthie *Atlanta*, thou hast merited
Beyond all imitation. We are made
Too poore to gratifie thy high deserts.
  Lor. Dread Soueraigne,
All my deserts, my selfe, and what I haue,

Thus

Arraigned by Women.

Thus I throw downe before your Highnesse feet.

Att. My Sonne *Lorenzo!* Oh, assist, my Lords.
The current of my ioy's so violent,
It does o'r-come my spirits. Worthy Sonne,
Welcome from death, from bands, captiuitie.

Aur. Welcome into my bosome as my soule.

Prince. My princely Brother, could I adde a loue
Vnto that dutie that I owe for life,
I am ingag'd vnto't, you are my lifes Protector,
And my Brother.

Lis. And for a life I stand indebted too,
Which Ile detayne, onely to honour you.

Omnes. And on our knees we must this dutie tender,
To you our Patron, and our Fames Defender.

Rep. Behold the ioyes Repentance brings with her,
Thy blessings are made full in Heauen and Earth.

Att. Was euer Father happier in a Sonne,
Or euer Kingdome had more hopefull Prince?
But in a loyall Subiect, neuer King
More blest then wo are: and the grace we owe,
Though farre too poore to quittance, shall make known;
Thy loue and merit. Now we can discerne
Our friends from flatt'rers. *Nicanor,* as for you,
But that this houre is sacred vnto ioy,
Thy life should pay the ransome of thy guilt.

Nic. Your Graces pardon. 'Twas not pride of state,
But her disdaine, that first inspir'd in me
This hope of Soueraigntie.

Att. Well, we forgiue.
Learne to liue honest now. Come, beautyous Queene,
We hope that all are pleas'd: and now you see,
In vaine we striue to crosse, what Heauens decree.

FINIS.

L

EPILOGVE.

Enter Swetnam muzzled, hal'd in by Women.

Swet. WHy doe you hale me thus? Is't not enough,
I haue withstood a tryall? beene arraign'd?
Indured the torture of sharp-pointed Needles?
The Whip? and old Wiues Nayles? but I must stand,
To haue another Iurie passe on me?
    Loret. It was a generall wrong; therefore must haue
A generall tryall, and a Iudgement too.
    Leon. The greatest wrong was mine; he sought my life,
Which fact I freely pardon, to approoue
Women are neither tyrannous, nor cruell,
Though you report vs so.
    Swet. I now repent,
And thus to you (kind Iudges) I appeale.
Me thinkes, I see no anger in your eyes:
Mercie and Beautie best doe sympathize:
And here for-euer I put off this shape,
And with it all my spleene and malice too,
And vow to let no time or att escape,
In which my seruice may be shewne to you.
And this my hand, which did my shame commence,
Shall with my Sword be vs'd in your defence.

FINIS.

Also Available from Thoemmes Press

For Her Own Good – A Series of Conduct Books

Cœlebs in Search of a Wife
Hannah More
With a new introduction by Mary Waldron
ISBN 1 85506 383 2 : 288pp : 1808–9 edition : £14.75

Female Replies to Swetnam the Woman-Hater
Various
With a new introduction by Charles Butler
ISBN 1 85506 379 4 : 336pp : 1615–20 edition : £15.75

A Complete Collection of Genteel and Ingenious Conversation
Jonathan Swift
With a new introduction by the Rt Hon. Michael Foot
ISBN 1 85506 380 8 : 224pp : 1755 edition : £13.75

Thoughts on the Education of Daughters
Mary Wollstonecraft
With a new introduction by Janet Todd
ISBN 1 85506 381 6 : 192pp : 1787 edition : £13.75

The Young Lady's Pocket Library, or Parental Monitor
Various
With a new introduction by Vivien Jones
ISBN 1 85506 382 4 : 352pp : 1790 edition : £15.75

Also available as a 5 volume set : ISBN 1 85506 378 6
Special Set Price: £65.00

Her Write His Name

Old Kensington *and* The Story of Elizabeth
Anne Isabella Thackeray
With a new introduction by Esther Schwartz-McKinzie
ISBN 1 85506 388 3 : 496pp : 1873 & 1876 editions : £17.75

Shells from the Sands of Time
Rosina Bulwer Lytton
With a new introduction by Marie Mulvey Roberts
ISBN 1 85506 386 7 : 272pp : 1876 edition : £14.75

Platonics
Ethel Arnold
With a new introduction by Phyllis Wachter
ISBN 1 85506 389 1 : 160pp : 1894 edition : £13.75

The Continental Journals 1798-1820
Dorothy Wordsworth
With a new introduction by Helen Boden
ISBN 1 85506 385 9 : 472pp : New edition : £17.75

Her Life in Letters
Alice James
Edited with a new introduction by Linda Anderson
ISBN 1 85506 387 5 : 320pp : New : £15.75

Also available as a 5 volume set : ISBN 1 8556 384 0
Special set price : £70.00

Subversive Women

The Art of Ingeniously Tormenting
Jane Collier
With a new introduction by Judith Hawley
ISBN 1 8556 246 1 : 292pp : 1757 edition : £14.75

Appeal of One Half the Human Race, Women, Against the Pretensions of the Other Half, Men, to Retain them in Political, and thence in Civil and Domestic, Slavery
William Thompson and Anna Wheeler
With a new introduction by the Rt Hon. Michael Foot and Marie Mulvey Roberts
ISBN 1 85506 247 X : 256pp : 1825 edition : £14.75

A Blighted Life: A True Story
Rosina Bulwer Lytton
With a new introduction by Marie Mulvey Roberts
ISBN 1 85506 248 8 : 178pp : 1880 edition : £10.75

The Beth Book
Sarah Grand
With a new introduction by Sally Mitchell
ISBN 1 85506 249 6 : 560pp : 1897 edition : £18.75

The Journal of a Feminist
Elsie Clews Parsons
With a new introduction and notes by Margaret C. Jones
ISBN 1 85506 250 X : 142pp : New edition : £12.75

Also available as a 5 volume set : ISBN 1 85506 261 5
Special set price : £65.00

CHARLES BUTLER
is a Senior Lecturer in literary studies at the University of the West of England, Bristol. Having completed his doctoral thesis on Edmund Spenser at the University of York he went on to study computing, and worked for some time as a technical author before returning to academia, where he now specializes in Renaissance literature and the history of science. His current research is centred around the seventeenth-century scientist and language philosopher, John Wilkins.

Marie Mulvey Roberts is a Senior Lecturer in literary studies at the University of the West of England and is the author of *British Poets and Secret Societies* (1986), and *Gothic Immortals* (1990). From 1994 she has been the co-editor of a Journal: 'Women's Writing; the Elizabethan to the Victorian Period', and the General Editor for three series: *Subversive Women*, *For Her Own Good*, and *Her Write His Name*. The volumes she has co-edited include: *Sources of British Feminism* (1993), *Perspectives on the History of British Feminism* (1994), *Controversies in the History of British Feminism* (1995) and *Literature and Medicine during the Eighteenth Century* (1993). Among her single edited books are, *Out of the Night: Writings from Death Row* (1994), and editions of Rosina Bulwer Lytton's *A Blighted Life* (1994) and *Shells from the Sands of Time* (1995).

COVER ILLUSTRATION
Cry of the Oppressed *from Moses Pitt*
Cover designed by Dan Broughton